A Monkey Could Do It
How Wall Street Robs Main Street

The Value of Work and
The Values of Class Warfare

©2012 Lance Moore
All Rights Reserved

Available in softcover and ebook from:
Sky-Fy Publishing and Third Coast Media
www.Sky-Fy.com
and at www.Amazon.com

ISBN: 9781470151867

For Melissa and Amanda
With Love and Admiration

Acknowledgements:
Thanks to Eddie Moore, Mitzi Werline, Dan Michal, Gaynor Robinson, Pat Siano, Carey Moore and James Wright for encouragement, proofreading, and editorial suggestions.

"There are those who hate the one who upholds justice… and detest the one who tells the truth." ~Amos 5:10

~~~

Table of Contents

Preface: A Must-Read

Chapter 1: The New Aristocracy
   Are the rich better than us?

Chapter 2: Crayons and Class Warfare
   An overview of my case... and a broken crayon

Chapter 3: Socialism=Communism...& Other Myths
   The underlying mythologies of Capitalism

Chapter 4: The Lucky Monkey
   The Lie of Meritocracy and the real worth of CEOs

Chapter 5: Is God a Socialist?
   A: What Jesus really said B: What other religions teach

Chapter 6: The Gap
   The growing, gaping abyss separating rich and poor

Chapter 7: The Fourth Reich of the Rich
   Politics and fear-mongering: best friends of dynasties

Chapter 8: Greed is Heroin
   Why Greed is the world's most dangerous addiction

Chapter 9: Money for Nothing, or Bubbles of Trouble
   Bankers, usury, bubbles and derivatives

Chapter 10: Welfare for the Rich, Taxes for the Poor
   Corporate subsidies and taxation myths

Chapter 11: Getting There First—a Game of Monopoly
   eBay, Facebook, Microsoft and the New Frontier

Chapter 12: The New Pharaohs and Their Pyramids
   The geometry of wealth; The American Way not Amway

Chapter 13: Oil and Energy—A Case Study on Greed

Chapter 14: Hope and Solutions
   Individual, government and private-sector solutions

Epilogue

Preface: *A Must-Read!*

I am a firm believer in the people. If given the truth, they can be depended upon to meet any national crisis. The great point is to bring them the real facts. ~Abraham Lincoln

Just because you do not take an interest in politics doesn't mean politics won't take an interest in you." ~Pericles

Fact: you have been burgled. No one called the police because the bandits came and went unseen. At first. For years, the amounts taken were small, gradual. But in 2008, half of your pension disappeared overnight. Then you knew you'd been ripped off. The officials came, but instead of arresting the perpetrators, they *rewarded* them. Most infuriating, they used *your* money to bail out the corporate burglars, even while plotting to cut your Social Security. Republicans call this "responsible government." And Democrats, once the people's party, now give trillions to Wall Street and other monied special-interests. In the budget debates of 2011, the TEA Party—that we had hoped was on our side—refused to remove tax loopholes for the rich, such as deductions for corporate jets and oil company subsidies.

So you lost faith in government. The authorities were in league with the bank robbers, or more correctly, robber-banks. And robber-stock manipulators. And robber-insurance companies. And robber-politicians. You have been fleeced, shaken down by monopolistic corporations that used Third World slave wages to suppress your salary. Some of you may feel economically secure, but what about the future for your children and grandchildren? The Robber Barons have already spent their inheritance!

Or perhaps you don't miss what you never had. Few people realize how much wealth has been created in the last thirty years—created by people like you and me but hoarded by the Top 5%. Here's why: computerized technologies made production *much* more efficient. Women entered the work force in vast numbers. Work-hours *and* production soared. But where are the fruits of those labors from the last three decades? Fairness would have meant that working folks thrived, too. Instead, our wages stagnated and personal debt exploded. Soaring profits never "trickled down" as promised; all the profits flowed up the pyramid, a reversed funnel, into the hoarding hands of a tiny elite. Are you angry yet?

It gets worse. Together, those über-rich comprise an incidental, even accidental, political conspiracy, a corrupt *Fourth Reich*. Unlike the Third Reich of the Nazis, the Fourth Reich rules not by military strength, nor by a uniting political ideology or philosophical creed. They rule by and for the power of money, and lots of it. If you don't know the difference between such a *plutocracy* vs. a *meritocracy*, you owe it to your children to read this book. An *oligarchy* once referred to a mere handful of rich rulers, like the "noble" families of British, French and German royalty. The patriots rebelled against the oligarchy to establish a *meritocracy*: wealth and success would be a reward, not an entitlement. Nowadays, we have lost their vision, we are enslaved by a *plutocracy*. These plutocrats number in thousands and are found in nearly every nation, of every creed. The mega-rich power brokers are Democrats and they are Republicans and they are Communists and some are even Islamic theocrats. Only two things unite them: an addiction to excessive wealth, and a failure to understand how harmful their addiction is to the entire human race. We have an ethical duty to limit their greed, not only for economic reasons, but also to prevent the death of democracy.

Conservative values that once shaped the American Dream have now been warped to serve the few rather than the many. Freedom, opportunity, self-determination, free enterprise—these founding values have been twisted and exploited by the 1% to cheat the 99%. We have to "un-warp" our ethics, reclaim our true values. We must revisit the populism of Jefferson and Lincoln and the best virtues of our religious heritage, which teach us to love our neighbor as an equal to ourselves, and to put people before profits and human labor above capital. A *populist capitalism*, if you will.

Our only hope to stop the plutocrats is education. Ethics and social values begin with education, whether in a church Sunday School class or by reading books like *Common Sense* or *Uncle Tom's Cabin*. My hope is that this book—with hundreds of supporting facts and references to other mainstream books and articles—will be part of that education. I cannot force anyone to read the facts, but if you are a citizen who cares about our republic, you will be brave and intellectually-honest enough to accept the challenge.

In re-claiming our American ethics, the next biggest challenge is to convince the upper middle class and hardworking small businesses that this book is not attacking you. Even "leftwing" proposals for tax increases exempt you if you are making less than $250,000 annually. If you have a million in assets and a six-figure salary, you still have more in common with the "rest of us" than you do with the 5% Fourth Reich, who are *beyond* "upper middle class." The Fourth Reich are those who have *more* than two homes (homes more costly than an entire village), have more than two cars but also own yachts and aircraft. Even while living like royalty, the Top 5% hoard a thousand times more income and assets than they can ever use. They travel extensively, using jets and airports subsidized by taxpayers. They consume more electricity and fuel in their mansions/cars/yachts/jets in a week than most of us use in a year.

The "lifestyles of the rich and famous" weigh heavy on the global environment as well as the economy. Their hoarded resources sit idle instead of circulating through the wider economy; their stash could have instead funded energy-efficiency research, created jobs in better housing and transportation industries, lifted thousands of people out of poverty, or helped millions of students excel in college instead of dropping out for lack of funds. Yet, as billionaire Warren Buffet pointed out, many of his class pay lower taxes than you or I.

This book doesn't throw the baby out with the dirty bathwater: productive elements of capitalism should be embraced, such as the value of family businesses, home ownership, and rewards/incentives for hard work. Superior Effort not only *deserves* a Superior Reward, but financial reward *encourages* superior innovation and production. Herein lies the irony: the modern Robber Barons claim allegiance to the merits of capitalism, yet they produce little of value. Many reap vastly-superior paychecks for inferior work. They lie and call it *meritocracy*. Failed CEO's get golden parachutes. Wall Street brokers make money on every transaction even when their client/investor loses. Failed corporations declare bankruptcy and get Federal bailouts. Those who complain the most about "Big Government" made their fortunes with its *help*: subsidies, TARP, defense contracts, government resources/ infrastructure.

A surprising number of the Top 5% Wealthiest are not involved in productive or creative industries, but tend to accumulate great wealth by using other people's money, or by exploiting the inequities of world commerce, or by trading on notoriety more than substance, or by developing cartels and monopolies. There is nothing fair or even "capitalistic" about this system. Wall Street is more akin to the world of illegal gambling, where clients pay a percentage to the "bookie" whether they win or lose. We ask: *Who is currently being rewarded, and why?* The true geniuses who attain success by a combination of brilliance and hard-work, who bring real value to society through innovation, often find themselves making a fraction of what the later exploiters reap. Did Bill Gates invent the computer, or the mouse, or even the idea of clickable "windows" on a computer screen? No. Did Meg Whitman, while raking in millions as eBay CEO, invent auctions, the internet, or even internet-auctions? No.

So it is time to *re-invigorate* capitalism, not to reject it. One principle of capitalism is indisputable: money motivates. But we have not been rewarding the innovators, the engineers and scientists, the manual laborers, the teachers—the workhorses of our economic engine. In the name of de-regulated "free markets," reward and hard work have been de-coupled. Profit and productivity should not require a "Girls Gone Wild" capitalism. A trained and reined

Kentucky Derby winner runs faster than unbridled wild horses. It's time to re-examine the *laissez-faire* proposition that the "invisible hand" of the market is an intelligent way to run our world. It's time for a new ethic, time to put people before profits, time to save the American Dream. We must address the topic of greed.

If that word angers you, please ask yourself: *Why?* When I have discussions with folks about other topics, such as their opinion of the best movie ever made, or if UFO's are real, tempers don't rise. But some people get snippy and defensive about the word *greed*, about the ethics of economics. *We work hard, and we don't want a guilt-trip imposed upon us*. Yet deep down all of us feel a bit guilty when we enjoy relative luxury while children are starving. Guilt or shame are unpleasant emotions that cause us to lash out defensively; no one likes to be called "greedy." Imagine, however, if greed were a purely-physiological disease, a viral epidemic destroying our planet. If you could remove guilt and shame from the equation for a moment, and just see greed as an infectious agent, perhaps your attitude toward someone offering a diagnosis and cure might be less defensive. Greed *is* a disease, and in particular, it affects the eyeball: it blinds people to seeing themselves in the mirror as they truly are. The cure is to find the courage to rip the scales from one's eyes, to calmly examine one's own heart. To the über-rich: I do not wish you ill. I just beg you to change sides. Become an ally of justice and love. We *need* the rich to help us end the class war, to help save the world.

To move us from abstract philosophy to real-life practice, here's the question: "When a corporate CEO makes dumb choices, forcing a major budget cut, why does the CEO continue to be paid $30 million while a thousand low-wage employees are laid-off or their benefits cut?" This book is the answer.[1]

~~~

Chapter 1: The New Aristocracy
Are the 1% better than us?

The most certain test by which we judge whether a country is really free is the amount of security enjoyed by minorities. ~Lord Acton

A long habit of not thinking a thing wrong gives it a superficial appearance of being right. ~Thomas Paine

Children see it. Adults go blind. They can't see through **the false myth that wealth or power anoints an elite with a higher personal value than the rest of us—a "Divine Right."** The wrong-thinking has been with us for ages. Few dared ask aloud if kings, beneath their crowns and robes, were just ordinary men.

The Emperor's Nakedness

One of the first to peel back the veneer of "divine right" was Hans Christian Anderson. As a small child standing in a crowd with his mother, Hans strained to get a glimpse of King Frederick VI. As the king passed by, little Hans peered at the rather ordinary-but-crowned chap and cried out in disappointment, "Oh, he's nothing more than a human being!" His horrified mother chided him, but years later he wrote the famous fairy tale, "The Emperor's New Clothes," in which the illusion of royal splendor was shattered when a child blurted out that the Emperor wore no clothes![1]

One thesis of this book is that people in power have a blindness, a psychological delusion about wealth and class fairness that is driven by self-interest, tribalism, greed, and class-identity. In their distorted mirror, they see themselves dressed in fine arguments, royally wrapped in the "social good" of free markets and incentive-based economies, even as they support a form of Capitalism that has no basis in true productivity.

I am a child who sees that their garments are an illusion.

Hans Anderson saw the king was just a man. But Hans was not alone. Five centuries ago, a minor bishop named John Ponet boldly challenged the so-called "Divine Right of Kings," the false doctrine that God blessed, supported and endowed a royal class. Bishop Ponet realized that royals were nothing more than commoners lifted high on gilded thrones. And he understood the source of their wealth: the royals **controlled the minting and loaning of money.** In 1556, he warned of "princes...who rob the people...by altering the coin from gold to copper...."[2] President John Adams credited Ponet as the true father of the American Revolution, crediting Ponet's *Short Treatise on Political Power* as the seminal volume which inspired political philosophers such as John Locke, Jefferson, Adams and more, and bore fruit in 1776.

Ya Say You Want a Revolution?

The American Revolution owes a debt to Bishop Ponet's thoughts as much as to the words of the Thomases: Jefferson and Paine. Jefferson's famous "all men are created equal" echoes Ponet's understanding that royals are just ordinary people. Anti-royalist Thomas Paine stood on Ponet's shoulders as he warned of **"human inventions, set up to terrify and enslave mankind, and monopolize power and profit."**[3] Paine saw through the "superficial appearance" of royalty. The myth that kings were entitled to their rank and wealth, born to be elite... this myth had been "habitually repeated," Thomas Paine said, it requires more than just "common sense" to debunk. So he wrote the booklet ironically entitled *Common Sense*, to warn against the rich barons who fail to "pay those poor men their wages, whom they force to labor and toil in their works."[4]

And now it is necessary for me to stand on the shoulders of Ponet and Paine to write a book challenging the false assumptions of our age: **the lie that merely because someone can "earn" a billion dollars, they therefore deserve, or are "worth," a billion dollars.** To the contrary, we have a system of unfair, arbitrary "rewards" in which Leona Helmsley's dogs inherit estates and monkeys can make millions on the stock market (as we shall see in Chapter 4).

Through monopolies and bubbles, by manipulating markets and mortgages, Wall Street brokers, corporate CEOs, bankers, politicians and lawyers made trillions. You got nothing, lost half your pension,[5] and now are expected to pay higher taxes to support their bailout. At least the monkey got a banana.

The emperor has no clothes!

Caterpillar Progress

Human progress crawls along at caterpillar-speed until a eureka "butterfly" moment, when suddenly it leaps or lurches to a new level of civilized behavior. After thousands of years, civilization lurched into the realization that slavery was wrong, and soon after that, lurched into women's suffrage. In the first half of the 20th Century, humanity fell backward with terrible wars, but leapt forward in technology. In the last portion of that century, you and I observed a leap forward in civil rights and greater equality among the races.

But now a new chasm has opened up before us, and I fear we are not leaping; we are stumbling into an abyss as dark as... well, as the Dark Ages. The chasm is **the gargantuan and growing gap between rich and poor**.

If *all* humans are created equal, not only in terms of race and creed, are they not also equal regardless of their salaries? At the root of the growing gap between rich and poor is an elitism, an attitude of class entitlement. This goes beyond the "supply and demand" that would explain why skilled workers make slightly more than unskilled. The vast difference, the *exponential* difference between those at the top and those at the bottom, stems from **the illusion that a CEO is intrinsically worth a thousand times the value of factory worker.** As an antebellum plantation owner tried to justify slavery by viewing Africans as sub-human, similarly today we find Wall Street bankers fully convinced they are super-human "masters of the universe, doing God's work." The ultra-rich believe they should earn, and *deserve*, more money for a day's work than most of us make in a lifetime of labor. This is a grotesque failure in ethics for them... and a failure of creative thinking for the rest of us. Too many people accept the *status quo* uncritically, never envisioning that life could or should be different. I understand that kind of thinking, having watched something similar: the tragedy, and metamorphosis, of racial ethics in the South.

Sub-humans: Drink Here!

As I finished 5th grade elementary school, my dad was re-assigned as pastor to a Methodist church in a small Southern town in the middle of the civil rights movement—literally. We were an hour away from Selma, Alabama, site of Martin Luther King's famous march over the Edmund Pettus bridge. (Years later, I would become a classmate of his daughter, Bernice King, but that's another story.) While accompanying my mother to the courthouse as she updated her car tag, I stopped in the hall to get a drink. Above the water fountain was a bold sign proclaiming, "White." Near it was a second water fountain, with the sign, "Colored." *Puzzling*. Both fountains were white porcelain, and the clear water in both came from the same pipe. While I pondered which fountain to drink from, an African-American woman walked past and drank from the fountain labeled "Colored." A Caucasian man next came and drank from the "White" fountain. Then I understood. Sort of.

That evening, I asked my dad about the water fountains. He explained that some people believed blacks carried disease. He was quick to add that this was not true—a stupid, despicable, evil myth. Soon I would learn that the racist subjugation went further: when public school resumed session, I saw that the white politicians in power made sure my school was newer, nicer and better equipped than the school the "colored children" attended. I did not know the word *apartheid* then, but what I did know was that the slogan "Separate but equal" was a bald-faced lie. I observed it with my own eyes in visits to the other campus of our school system. Some people were like my dad, viewing the arrangement as grossly unfair, as a violation of America's founding principles. But most folk, on both sides of the equation, were like the lady of color who blithely walked up to the "Colored" water fountain. Most people are too preoccupied to challenge old customs. They just do what they are told.

Peasants and Kings

For centuries, we've been told that some people are kings, and some people are peasants. We've been told that the man who wears a suit is worth millions, and the man who cleans his toilet is worth pennies. We're told that the stock broker is worth more because his work is special—even though the *Chicago Sun-Times* proved a chimpanzee could do better at picking stocks.

The point here, by way of introduction to this book, is a bold one: **I want to change the world**. The change begins with first shifting our view of wealth and aristocracy. Picture yourself standing before the segregated water fountains over forty years ago. Would you be willing to question the morality of the system? Would you be willing to listen to the facts and philosophies contrary to the bias of that day (that whites deserved preferential treatment)? And now, I hope you are willing to read, with an open mind, a book that challenges the last remaining false-bias of civilization: that the rich are superior people who deserve preferential treatment, and that some blind market force should be entrusted with guarding economic justice.

My Grandfather... and Numbers

In recent years, trillions of dollars have been stolen from us by Wall Street banks and brokers and other robber barons. Our eyes begin to glaze over when we try to comprehend the numbers involved in the greatest bank heist of history. Therein lies one of the biggest problems in trying to build a just society: few can envision the sheer size of the theft and mistreatment inflicted upon the "lesser" classes (economically-speaking) by the uppermost class. Even millionaires don't have an easy understanding of just how much money a million dollars is, much less a trillion. In the end, the story is not about numbers but about people.

My grandfather understood numbers. A dirt-poor farmer, Robbie Moore had eight children during the Great Depression (he obviously understood math better than he understood the science of birth control!). I am dependent on a pocket calculator; numbers are abstract to me. But he knew exactly how heavy a 50-pound sack of potatoes felt in the hot Southern sun, how many seeds to plant to guarantee a profitable crop, and how many hands he needed to pick the harvest. He knew exactly how many of those sacks he would need to sell to save a few dollars for the upcoming winter. Like Jed Clampett, he "barely kept his family fed."

And yet he survived the Great Depression, and finished his 70-plus years of hard, honest work, without ever borrowing more than a few hundred dollars. He died without owing anyone a penny. He understood numbers because the numbers were limited and straight-forward; there was no credit card to feed his family in winter.

Years later, I took my turn at farm labor. I worked for a millionaire named Alton for $1.60 per hour. No, I'm not some bitter underclass guy who resents the rich because Alton paid so little for sweaty labor. I genuinely liked Alton. I was thrilled to get the job at 16. And he worked hard himself. He had a million dollars because he worked diligently and smartly, invested wisely, and pinched his pennies. Yes, he benefitted from cheap labor, but he also accumulated wealth by living a relatively-frugal lifestyle. He drove an old pickup truck and lived in a house that would be modest by New England standards. I don't envy his success; I respect it. But if he were alive today, his company would not stand a chance against corporate farmers.

That is not the point. This is: one day, Alton said to me, "I knew your grandfather. He was a good man. Years ago, I ran a potato shed where he sold me his potatoes. One day he came to me with one of my checks I'd paid him with five years before. Ya know, after so many years go by, a check becomes legally worthless. He had stuck it in a sock drawer for safe-keeping and forgotten about it. He finally found it, but the bank wouldn't cash it... out-dated. So he brought it to me for redemption." Alton smiled proudly as he concluded, "I didn't have to do it, but I paid him cash for that old check!"

I was too young to say or do anything but reply, "That's nice. I'm glad you knew my grandfather. I barely knew him myself, he died when I was six." What I wanted to say was, *I'm not sure I'd brag about resisting the urge to NOT pay someone the money you honestly owed them... regardless of some banking technicality.*

Alton was a decent man, and I suspect he gave generously to his church even if he was miserly in what he paid his workers. But his problem is one that is crippling America: he had a legalistic ethic rather than a heart ethic. From an ethical standpoint, his boast was the same as bragging, "I could have taken a gun and robbed First National Bank, but I didn't." My grandfather had sold him the potatoes, which enabled Alton, as a potato-brokering middle-man, to make a good profit. My grandfather did not begrudge Alton that profit, he freely agreed to the exchange. But for Alton to even consider that it would be legal and reasonable to deny Robbie his hard-earned paycheck betrays a mindset that is all too common... and deeply flawed.

What is legally earned is not always ethically earned. We need a higher "economic ethic."

Legal and Ethical are not Synonyms

Most wealthy people believe that if some law empowers them to take advantage of the working class, then their wealth is ethical and good. They swear by the word *meritocracy* and live by the creed, *Caveat emptor*. They cannot envision themselves as evil or greedy, because they are not "breaking the law." We must admit that lawmaking is an imperfect, corrupt process, and this book does not have a political answer to how to fix that. This book is first of all concerned with **ethics, values, and attitudes.** *Ethics* is a higher law. This book is appealing to your sense of justice and fairness.

Government alone is not the solution to our problems. Laws don't change hearts (although law *is* an essential safeguard until the heart is changed). Hearts must be softened and enlarged if we hope to improve society. Like the Grinch whose "heart grew three sizes."

I am Not a Communist!

Let's open our hearts... and open our eyes to a vision of economic fairness: the *dolce vita*, the sweet life, should be available for everyone — not just for a few fortunate winners of a rigged lottery that is our financial system. And I say "rigged," because if a monkey can get rich while a hard-working farm hand can't feed his family, the system certainly is broken. More than merely broken, post-modern capitalism has become rigged to the point of being cruel. Immoral. Evil. With that said, I beg of you to read on, trusting that:

- I am not a communist or socialist. Monetary reward, private-property ownership, and the other principles of capitalistic incentive do make for a more productive society.
- I do **not** believe that government can create a utopia. Government has all the flaws of a large, cumbersome corporation. Big government is terribly inefficient. Trillions spent annually; billions wasted.
- Yet government *is* needed. It benefits people in ways that private, for-profit companies never will. Our government is dysfunctional and corrupt, but it needs broad reform, not obliteration.
- I will try to keep the topic entertaining, but we must endure eye-glazing numbers in order to understand our dire predicament. If you

will enter this covenant with me, and pass the book on to others, the reward will be a better society. The final chapter will offer pragmatic solutions to our crisis. But the first solution comes in a *change of mindset*, and that in turn only comes by reading my entire argument — including the numbers.

The Future at Stake

Will your grandchildren live in a two-class society, where hope and opportunity extend only to those born into wealth and privilege? Without reform, that is where this world is headed. The middle class is an endangered species.

We grew up with a romanticized view of benevolent kings and queens, palaces and peasants who lived a happy life in a pastoral setting, with occasional feasts and festivals. That two-class society of royalty and commoners was never as idyllic as the picture-books and movies portrayed it. Read Charles Dickens for a more accurate portrayal. Our gilded view of the past is not a helpful mythology. Even if there were some Golden Age of virtue and prosperity, the way things worked in yesteryear is no longer an indicator of how they will work in the future. **Things have changed.** And in our age, we were told that the American Dream meant that even peasants had a chance to marry, or become, Prince Charming. But the brave new world upon us is more nightmare than fairy tale. Upward mobility is rarely a possibility for millions stuck in Third World poverty.

We are moving to a world-wide police state. Not a gestapo working for a lone dictator, but a hodge-podge of state and private security teams tasked with protecting the wealth of the upper class. Michael Dell gives himself — from Dell Computers profits — a million dollars for personal security.[6] In India, the upper class builds private gated enclaves instead of public infrastructure, investing millions in securitization and self-luxury while the poor have no running water, no indoor toilets.

As I wrote these words, a revolution was underway in the Middle East and governments teeter. In January, 2011, the media mostly reported on the Egyptian revolution as a combination of Islamic unrest and a political longing for freedom. Only later did the media begin to admit that the riots were driven by **economic hardship** — as finally reported on February 17 by Paul Mason on the BBC. Winter wheat prices made bread too costly for the masses (prices were inflated mostly due to commodity speculators). According to the February 2011 *Atlantic Monthly* a fifth of Egyptians live on less than $2 a day, while President Mubarak was worth between $40 billion and $75 billion and lived in a gilded palace with a fleet of luxury cars.[7]

The Two-Tier Society

Riots broke out in adjoining countries, including oil-rich lands that, despite their mineral wealth, have widespread poverty. Libya, awash in petroleum and one of the the richest-in-GNP in Africa, suffers from 24% unemployment among young people because millions were hoarded by dictator Qaddafi.

The protest riots give cover to looters, which in turn is prompting upper class residents to form small vigilante armies to guard their homes and businesses. If the looters had modest middle class homes of their own, they'd be home protecting those rather than out looting and pillaging. But in the Middle East, as in most lands, a two-tier society is doomed to insecurity.

In the most prosperous periods in successful democracies, leaders saw the value of a multi-tiered society and a strong middle class. Herbert Hoover did. He was the only *Republican* President ever accused of being a socialist.[8] When he campaigned on "A chicken in every pot and a car in every garage," it was from **a genuine concern for the middle class**. But the plutocrats sabotaged and smeared him, blaming Hoover for causing the Great Depression that their own greed had actually created. It is rarely reported that in 1925, then-Secretary of Commerce Hoover had warned President Coolidge that stock market speculation was a ticking time-bomb, or that Hoover did many things to lessen the severity of the collapse.[9] While Roosevelt echoed some of Hoover's rhetoric and started Social Security, FDR seemed more concerned with using the middle class as a sociological buffer between the poor and the ultra-wealthy. Here's the scary thing: the ultra-wealthy plutocrats nowadays don't even give a damn about having a "buffer" from the poor—they have bodyguards.

The Dream, the Gap, and the Great Divorce

President Hoover was criticized for taxing the rich and implementing an activist government, but his seminal actions helped father the prosperous middle class that bloomed in the period 1946-1980. In the post-war years, the hopes of the American Dream were aglow in the burgeoning middle class... the dream was coming true (even if poverty was widespread elsewhere on the globe). After 1980, the dream began to turn into a nightmare. The family fractured. Decline and dysfunction took over. Another, less-caring, Republican had been chosen to become Papa Capitalism, and he divorced the Dream to chase a mistress, Money, leaving the middle class orphaned. (How's that for an extended metaphor!)

The American Dream had been a wedding partner to Capitalism, and they made an attractive couple. They worked well together and gave birth to a strong middle class. Average folks had a piece of the

Dream instilled in them and believed that if they, too, worked hard and smart, success would be theirs, prosperity would blossom. It seemed fair, and it seemed to be good for society by providing incentives that boosted everyone's standard of living.

Changes in the post-modern world demand we re-evaluate the ethical framework of capitalism:

•**First**, the surge in productivity and technology over the last thirty years should have brought prosperity to the middle class, but instead, it brought massive personal debt. From 1980 to 2010, women entering the workforce and the development of computers *dramatically* increased production worldwide. But this did not translate into higher wages... a major, nefarious event we will examine in detail.

•**Second**, so-called "de-regulation" ushered in an era of legal fleecing. The playing field is no longer level but is slanted in favor of *bigness*: big corporations and big money score, while lone entrepreneurs and small businesses must run uphill.

•**Third**, the gap between rich and poor has grown so immense, so proportionately-larger than ever before, we can no longer say "hands-off." Capitalism is failing. And wealth has warped our democracy.

•**Fourth**, over-population (pushing 7 billion) and industrialization's burden upon earth's resources/environment force us to abandon the American-frontier notion of unlimited expansion and growth.

That is the new reality. Everything you learned in elementary school about America, democracy, and capitalism has changed.

New Frontiers

I cannot embrace the doomsday, sky-is-falling pessimism found on the extremes of both Left and Right. Technology is making transportation more efficient and cleaner, computer efficiencies build more with less and stretch commodities/resources in ways that give me hope. We do not have to live a life in fear of scarcity.

We do, however, need to **abandon the myth of the unlimited frontier**. You may disagree, citing the internet as an example of an infinite horizon of opportunity. The "Internets," as Stephen Colbert jokingly calls it, is a new frontier, for sure. But you can't build houses on the internet. We can't feed people with bytes (forgive the pun). Humans will always need living space, physical shelter, transportation and food—things which demand resources and which create pollution/garbage—and no matter how efficient computers may make us, seven billion people strain our planet's resources. (If anything, technology *raises* material expectations.) And even the internet has fallen prey to the monopolists: Google, Amazon, Microsoft, Apple and eBay are taking over the net in much the same way that a handful of moguls monopolized the frontier railroads.

The Limits of Supply and Demand

Look at the contradictions in these false arguments: "We have unlimited frontiers and resources, so *anyone* can lift themselves up by their bootstraps and be an entrepreneur or rich CEO." "Because of tight supply, because talent is *rare*, only elite gifted ones can be CEOs, thus we must pay outlandish salaries."

The inconsistency and hypocrisy also applies to commodities. In one context, they boast of "unlimited frontiers," in another, the rich claim "scarcity" to justify high commodity prices. Despite the scare tactics used in the "energy crisis" of the Seventies to inflate gas prices, we actually had an over-abundance of oil (not that I'm recommending a continued reliance on fossil fuel). The plutocrats want us to believe in scarcity when it serves their purposes, but when we begin to say, "Wait a second: we can't justify gluttonous consumption of fuel by an elite class in their fuel-sucking yachts and jets," suddenly they see no limits. Using petroleum as our example here: the BP oil spill reminds us of the increasing cost and ecological damage of mining oil and minerals. Oil and coal *extraction* damages our environment as does fuel *burning*. Natural resources **do have a limit**. They are finite.

Modern bubble-driven capitalism depends upon the notion of unlimited resources and unlimited growth—a premise that flies in the face of fact. We must change our paradigm to value conservation, efficiency and smart distribution. If society is structured to only value *profit*, we are indeed dooming a future generation to a life of pollution and poverty.

Economist Peter Victor states, "I think we live in very abnormal times. And the signs are showing up everywhere that the burden we're placing on the natural environment can't be borne."[10] Other economists, some of the most conservative and venerated, have seen the fallacy in unlimited growth. John Stuart Mill felt it best that society reach limits of a comfortable standard of living and then shift into a "stationary state" rather than "trampling, crushing, elbowing, and treading on" each other. John Keynes predicted a time when a healthier society would devote time to arts, education and leisure instead of constantly-expanding industrialization. Even the conservative's patron saint, Adam Smith, foresaw limits to natural resources and limits to growth. But they all placed too much trust in the invisible hand of "supply and demand."

The early proponents of capitalism could not imagine the mountains of wealth amassed by billionaires, the excess of luxury, consumption and waste of the modern elite classes, or the great pain and damage wrought upon the lower classes. Adam Smith failed to acknowledge that the "invisible hand" cannot restrain human expansionism, and his later disciple, Alan Greenspan, failed to foresee the power of unbridled greed. After the crash of 2008, Greenspan finally admitted that the laws of supply and demand can be circumvented by the greedy and the unscrupulous. In testimony to Congress on October 23, 2008, Greenspan conceded, according to *The New York Times*, "that he had put too much faith in the self-correcting power of free markets and had failed to anticipate the self-destructive power of wanton mortgage lending." He, like most classical economists, had underestimated *greed*.

No Pie for the Poor

In the U.S., when gas goes above $4 a gallon, the world of opportunity for the working class dramatically shrinks. Even something as basic as job mobility disappears when energy prices rob a fourth of one's paycheck.

In the emerging world, high commodity costs have more severe consequences: widespread famine and violence. When commodities shrink in supply and rise in price, the rich keep buying them—even buying more of the commodity to drive the price higher—because they don't see the connection between their actions and the poor. When a rich person builds his or her fourth house, it is a choice to leave children living in cardboard boxes elsewhere on the globe.

Historians doubt that Queen Marie Antoinette actually said of the starving masses short of bread, "Let them eat cake," but the sentiment still persists among the privileged classes: *I have plenty. Work hard, and you'll have plenty too*. The affluent can't imagine a world of limited resources. But if speculators in the First Estate drive up the price of wheat, it results in children dying in the Third World.

When we learned that Imelda Marcos owned a thousand pairs of shoes, most of us cringed, because in her small island country, many of the children were fortunate if they owned *one* pair of shoes. **We are all on the same island.**

As John Donne put it, "No man is an island entire of itself; every man is... a part of the main; if a clod be washed away by the sea, Europe is the less...," concluding: "I am involved in mankind." You are a part of the giant island called Earth, you are involved with humanity whether you wish to be or not. That irrevocable connectedness gives us the right to limit what you do on our island. You may not wish to hear that. No one likes to be restrained in their freedom. I love freedom. But **individual freedom without social responsibility is evil.** It is the thing of dictators and megalomaniacs.

Some Perspective on a Billion

When someone hoards a billion dollars, it becomes like the astronomical-phenomenon, a Black Hole, warping and controlling everything around it. We cannot have "freedom and the pursuit of happiness" with a Black Hole in the neighborhood. This book is a challenge to the mega-wealthy to become more generous, and to the rest of us, a challenge to re-examine what constitutes true virtue. And in the context of economics, that begins with a necessary quoting of numbers-and-statistics.

But how can we fully grasp the size of a billion dollars? Can the human brain even envision it? How do you explain Mount Everest to a child raised on the plains of Kansas? Do we count the dollars relative to human lives, to how many people had to give lifetimes of work to accumulate a billion?

We'll revisit that question again and again, but to start gaining perspective, consider this: according to *Forbes* magazine, there were **over 1,000 individual billionaires** worldwide in 2008. That one small class of people—the billionaire club, a group you could fit into a single civic center or large church building—controls the equivalent of the entire economic output 35 of our states put together! The tiny billionaire club controls $4.5 trillion—a year of the strained and sweated livelihoods of every man, woman and machine in 35 of our wealthy states.[11] And the real number may be higher. Many of the ultra-wealthy hide or under-report their assets for tax avoidance purposes. One example: Michael Dell claimed his giant mansion was worth less than $7 million, though it was appraised for $22 million.[12] No one has any notion how much cash is hidden in off-shore bank accounts or in gold bullion in private safes. So when we try to envision the vast wealth of the Fourth Reich, we are only seeing the tip of the iceberg... and our minds can't even imagine the size of the tip!

The absurdity of trillions being hoarded by a handful of elite becomes even more striking when we compare their wealth to the poorest countries—rather than to the wealthy U.S. The *nation* of Pakistan, for example, with a population of about 170 million, has an annual Gross Domestic Product (GDP) comparable to our *state* of Arkansas (less than three million residents). So consider entire national economies compared to the individual wealth of billionaires. **50 countries have a GDP of less than one billion dollars.** Gross Domestic Product is a measure of the size of a nation's entire production; Annual GDP is the sum of all goods and services produced, grown, mined, and manufactured, by humans and their machines, within a country in a year. So a single individual like Mexican billionaire Carlos Slim could buy *all* of that—the entire output of several nations!

And the problem is not just the 1,000+ billionaires hogging the planet's resources. Millionaires and multimillionaires add to the burden placed on the "worker drones." How do the ultra-rich justify this atrocious injustice? The secret lies in the pyramid.

Pharaohs and Pyramids

When I first read stories of how the pyramids were constructed, it boggled my mind. Not as an engineering feat: even unskilled laborers, with ropes and levers, can build a mountain of stone blocks, broad at the bottom and getting smaller at the top. What strained my brain was this: How could one man, a Pharaoh, rob the lifetime labors of thousands and thousands of slaves merely to build himself a receptacle for his carcass... and why would the people under him agree to the project? The answer is they viewed him as **a god, as superior to the rest... elite.**

A similar rationale is needed to justify why we allow a single person to own a pyramid of billions, built by the efforts of millions beneath him. Is the billionaire special, godlike... a unique species of elite human equipped to enjoy the finer things in ways the rest of us "commoners" cannot? This question begs for a story, a story from nature's pyramid—a *mountain* story.

Poverty and Elitism

My friend, Dr. Carol Txipama, is a missionary and professor at Africa University, and in the early eighties, served as a missionary in the beautiful but poverty-stricken mountains of Appalachia. She offers this glimpse of life in one of the poorest areas of the U.S.:

"We headed up the mountain in a 'bookmobile' of sorts, to offer books and general Christian goodwill to the elderly and impoverished mountaineers that had no transportion. The winding roads were challenging to maneuver in good weather, and this particular winter day, the dirt roads were still covered with snow, so it was a battle to get the van through the snow pack without sliding in the ditch. We finally reached a remote log cabin home of a 90-year-old woman named Flossie. Smoke poured out of the chimney, but no other sign of Flossie. We called out to her and heard a response near the mountain top. Shortly she appeared, wearing a heavy worn-out coat and black rubber work boots, with an ax in one hand and a bucket of water in the other. Flossie was overjoyed to see us and explained that she had been up on the mountain breaking ice on the spring to get her some fresh water for the day. Then showing true mountain hospitality, she invited us in for a cup of hot coffee, and we settled into the sparsely furnished living room, warming our feet by the stove. As she served up the coffee, we were surprised to see her set out three lovely tea cups with intricate designs of pink roses. Somehow the fine China cups seemed out of place in the rough log cabin setting, the beautiful porcelain juxtaposed in the hands of an old mountain woman—calloused hands a bit dirty and black in the creases from handling the coal for the stove. Flossie must have seen our surprise. My associate said, 'Why Flossie, these tea cups are beautiful! Where ever did you get them?' She chuckled at our reaction, answering, 'My daughter in Ohio sent them to me many years ago for Christmas.' Then Flossie became more serious as she ran her fingers over the beautiful design, and added: 'You know girls, even poor people like to have beautiful things.'"

Even poor people want, and value, beautiful things. Flossie died and rose to a "higher mountain" some years ago, but her legacy humbly reminds us that the poor can of course appreciate art, beauty, and luxury. Some in the upper class imagine themselves to be pharaohs, godlike, or at least superior **aristocrats**, fitted by God with a special taste for finery, calling themselves "Epicureans," connoisseurs of the arts and the "refined" sensual pleasures of fashion and gourmet foods.

Ironically, the Greek philosopher, Epicurus, taught that the highest pleasure comes via knowledge, friendship, and living a simple, modest, virtuous lifestyle—verging on deprivation. Turns out that Flossie was more of an Epicurean, in the original sense, than Rockefeller.

Eye-Glazing Numbers We Must Understand

A 2006 study shows that worldwide, the top 10% wealthiest people control about 85% of all non-governmental wealth.[13] That data is old, but all signs indicate things have worsened since. The gap between rich and poor has grown; salaries of CEO's soared again in the post-crash years of 2009-2011. As we weigh the data and gauge the gap between the have-lots and have-nots, we must also remember that huge sums are unreported, hidden in Swiss and off-shore bank accounts or squirreled away in secret locations (Russian mafia, Latin American drug lords, etc.), *Forbes* list of billionaires probably overlooks half; there are many more who hide their wealth. Thus, it is likely that **today 10% of the population controls 90% of all worldwide personal wealth, and 1% of the population controls 99% of all governmental resources and power.** We still worship the pharaohs and their pyramids.

Is this Class Warfare?

Am I calling for a class war? Is class warfare already underway? It's more like genocide. Warfare implies *two* sides with weapons firing at each other. The poor can't afford weapons. The middle class have kept their weapons holstered, while the rich have just beaten the stew out of everyone for the last 30 years... maybe 30 centuries. Class war? More like a one-sided invasion and occupation. We are Poland. They are the Fourth Reich of the Rich.

The poor are already defeated. Now the middle class is under attack. The hoarding of vast wealth and misuse of resources by the mega-rich is the single-greatest threat to our future. Why does acknowledging that fact get a person labeled as *radical*? When activist Robin G. Hoode started the website **www.FireTheRich.org** he first considered calling it "ShootTheRich," for dramatic but humorous effect, but he knew he would be (falsely) accused of trying to foment a violent class war. The invasion began centuries ago. I would like to free us—not by "shooting the rich," but rather by appealing to the conscience of "the rich and powerful" and urging voluntary change.

In the next chapter, as a continued introduction to the whole book, we consider the ramifications of this phrase, "Class Warfare," and hear a story of a child's broken crayon that could change the world.

~~~

Postscript to Chapter 1: Definitions:

This book is not just about money, greed, poverty and wealth. Money controls **political power**, and political power feeds wealth. We all may need a quick refresher on the Greek words used to define various ruling classes:

•**Plutocracy** is *rule by the wealthy*. **Plutocrats** working in concert have been called "**The Fourth Reich of the Rich**," because the last time someone almost conquered the world, it was Hitler's *Third Reich*. Currently there is no military-based reich or rule that threatens to dominate global power; the world is now ruled by a plutocracy—the "fourth rule," or reign, of the rich (see Chapter 7). The Fourth Reich is apolitical. Republicans, as a group, almost universally defend the Fourth Reich system, but do not be fooled: many Democrats are also plutocrats.

•**Oligarchy** is a broad term for rule by an elite few: an enclave of military leaders, or a royal family, or plutocrats, or aristocrats. An oligarchy is the opposite of a **democracy:** rule by all the people.

•**Meritocracy** traditionally referred to a form of government in which the most talented and hardest-working are chosen and promoted to higher positions of leadership and responsibility. More recently it has come to describe an ideal economic and class system based on individual achievement and productivity; Republicans assert that the current U.S. economy is a meritocracy, despite the many examples of failure being rewarded, of lazy rich getting richer. Nor do politicians explain how they can claim to favor a meritocracy when they vote to abolish the inheritance tax—a contradictory notion.

•**Aristocracy** means rule by an upper class. Aristocrats believe their class consists of superior humans marked by higher intelligence, greater wealth, and more social refinement than the rest of us. Alexander Hamilton believed the aristocracy should rule because they are more "fit" to rule. Other founding fathers saw the arrogance in class politics—the danger of silver-spoon rule— and argued for democracy, a rule by the people: populism.

•**Populism** is rule by the people. Not to be confused with the word "popular," as populism respects minority views rather than blindly following a "51% poll" of momentary whims. True grassroots populism believes in the value of everyday citizens' common sense, but is not anti-intellectual. Populism demands a *check and balance* on the disproportionate power of the rich. Populism is often connected with **Progressivism**, the idea that government must be reform-minded, constantly vigilant, adaptive to change. It is not by nature "leftwing" or opposed to conservative values that respect the wisdom of the past, but willing to embrace technology and culture through education. Our two greatest Presidents, Lincoln and Theodore Roosevelt, embodied populism, even though the former was a Republican and the latter was born an aristocrat. Teddy Roosevelt led the **Progressive Populist** Party, in his words, "to destroy this invisible Government, to dissolve the unholy alliance between corrupt business and corrupt politics...."

For the purposes of discussion, I define the **"middle class"** as those who don't qualify for significant government aid, but who work 40 or more hours per week out of necessity. Households who make over $250,000 annually, or with over two million in assets, may be considered "Upper Class." This varies with geography and family size and other commitments and liabilities. We do well to remember that there is another "class," the uppercrust of mega-rich, also known as the Fourth Reich or Rule.

Labels can be misleading, but so that you may know my bias: I believe in democracy and true meritocracy, and I'm a Christian Progressive Populist, skeptical of big government yet quite sure that human nature needs the restraint a democratic government can provide.

~~~

Chapter 2: Crayons and Class Warfare
An overview of my case... and a broken crayon

There's class warfare, all right, but it's my class, the rich class, that's making war—and we're winning.   ~Warren Buffett, Billionaire

Buffet and I agree on one thing: **if a class war has begun, the rich started it**. I'm a peaceful man, not prone to violence, never picked a fight, but neither will I run from a bully or a fight—okay, when I was five years old, I *did* run from a fight... but only after being hit with a big stick! We'll return to that story in a moment. But first: "Why are you writing that book?" a stranger asked me when he learned of my work. My reply, "I'm tired of Wall Street beating up on the little guy, and nobody fighting back." I don't compare myself to the brave patriots of the Revolutionary War, but they do provide inspiration. Patrick Henry in his famous, *Give me liberty or give me death!* speech, said: "There is a just God who presides over the destinies of nations; and who will raise up friends to fight our battles for us. The battle, sir, is not to the strong alone; it is to the vigilant, the active, the brave.... Gentlemen may cry, peace, peace—but there is **no peace. The war is actually begun!"**

I'll say repeatedly here that I reject violence and warlike metaphors. But if you wish to call this a class war, be honest: we of the "lesser classes" didn't start it. Whatever we call this struggle, you cannot just be a spectator: if you are not the aggressor (those who exploit others for wealth), you will either fight non-violently for justice, or you will be a passive victim. You must choose. Are you brave enough to critically question your core belief system? Will you re-examine beliefs and values that have been inculcated in you from grammar school? Emotions are involved. Allow me to share some of my personal beliefs —passionately—even as I plead with you to *calmly* consider the matters at hand. And at the end of this chapter, I'll share "the story of the broken crayon" and how it moved me, through tears, to try to change the very foundation of our ethics and economics. But first there is a wall we must scale and a moat to cross before entering the castle of honest debate on these issues. The wall is the cry of "Class Warfare and Class Envy!" and the moat is the fear of those dreaded words, "Liberal Socialist."

Beating Up Five-Year-Olds

If I had a nickel for every time a television pundit has complained of "class warfare," I'd be rich enough to wage war upon myself! This nonsensical but inflammatory phrase is used in response to calls for more progressive taxation or justice for the underprivileged. In April of 2011, President Obama gave a speech defending the need for budgetary reform, with a call for modest tax increases on those making over $250,000. Obama even praised the upper class for their "success" and fulfillment of the American dream. It was a speech that George Bush could have delivered. Yet Representative Jeb Hensarling, (R-Texas), said the president's tax proposal set "a new standard for class warfare."[14] There was nothing in the speech that even remotely agitated class differences. But the knee-jerk catch phrase was used because they had no other way to defend the rich. Again in late September 2011, Obama's mild proposal called "The Buffet Rule" to close some tax loopholes for the richest was met with howling by Republicans such as Paul Ryan and Lindsay Graham, who used the phrase again: "This is class warfare."[15]

They must love the phrase, as they invoke it repeatedly—even though I've never once heard the middle or lower economic classes call for such a thing. It is a ridiculously-exaggerated metaphor, an *ad hominem* insult by the ultra-wealthy and their media-mouthpieces, the last refuge of scoundrels who lack any real argument—a rant, not a defense from any actual warlike threat. Wealthy folk have nothing to lose in a class war, because they own or control most of the weapons, security guards, fences and gates. But if you have the audacity to suggest that society may not be fair, they equate you with someone driving a Panzer tank down Wall Street. Absurd.

Five Year Old Beating Up ME

This absurdity reminds me of the first physical fight I was involved in. The scene was the woodsy city park located behind my childhood home. A neighbor friend and I, both five years old, got mad about some now-forgotten disagreement and he began swinging fists at me. I fought back, and having the advantage of experience in previous wrestling matches with my older brothers, I began to be victorious. (Okay, this was *not* my first fight... but the first one outside our home.) The neighbor boy, seeing the war about to be lost, wisely picked up a fallen tree branch and began hitting me with it. I surrendered and ran back home, crying in pain, cradling my bruised arm where he'd struck me with the stick, whilst cradling a life-lesson: *Some people don't fight fair*. And my five-year-old buddy went to his home to finish reading Sun Tzu's *Art of War*.

Whenever I see pundits and politicians and moguls—all with six-figure paychecks and limousines—whining about "class warfare," I see losing five-year-olds picking up sticks because they can't fight fair. And let me clarify: they are only losing rhetorically. Like my friend with the tree limb, the rich are winning in every other way. And they are, literally, beating up five-year-olds—their greed *is* physically hurting, even killing, children around the globe.

The Art of War

One reason the rich get richer and stay richer is they are better at the art of war than the rest of us. Not long after military strategists discovered the value of a big stick, they soon realized the importance of propaganda in war, beginning with the claim, "We're the peaceful nation merely responding to an evil aggressor!" That claim is as childish as boys tussling on the kindergarten playground who whine to the teacher, "*He* started it!" I find it odd that when the middle class are excessively taxed and cheated at the hands of the wealthy and powerful, they aren't the ones who yell, "Class warfare!" The oligarchs started the war, and continue to wage it, and yet paint themselves as the victims.

The class "war" began eons ago, when kings used peasants as cannon fodder to protect the king's wealth and power. With the advent of democracy, having swords was not enough; the winning warrior also employed propaganda. Since we know, historically, that the rich and powerful are the ones who have instigated most (though not all) wars, and we know that the rich are quicker to employ guns to protect their largesse, and that the rich usually win because they can afford bigger guns, we therefore know how hypocritical and disingenuous their cry is.

Pearl Harbor

I do not advocate violence. Had I been one of the key leaders at the eve of the Revolutionary War, we'd probably be drinking tea and crumpets today and toasting the Queen. I still believe the pen is mightier than the sword, and the only "war" I wish to wage is metaphorical. (And let me state clearly to any psycho-nuts reading this: Do not start shooting rich people!) Since the pundits insist upon using the term "war" (at a great disservice to veterans who know the horrible costs of a *real* war), I'll not shrink from the battle. We *are* in a battle, because millions do die every year because of the greed of the mega-wealthy. With apologies to soldiers who endured the real Pearl Harbor, I'll join the rhetorical fracas and say that the bombs have already fallen on the peaceful Pearl-Harbor-of-the-poor, and if they need a Roosevelt to stir the sleeping giant to arms, I'll do so. Rhetorically. (Though what we need today is not *Franklin* Roosevelt, but the monopoly-busting *Teddy*.)

The long-running war upon the lower classes has changed. The greed of the upper class is no longer limited to beating down the poor. Now the middle class is also under attack. And why not? The rich learned it is not enough to exploit cheap blue-collar labor. They now simultaneously rob the fatter wallets of the white-collar and professional classes. Moreover, the size of the thievery dwarfs all previous generations combined. Without firing a shot, but just as stealthily as the Japanese Zeroes upon Pearl Harbor, the corporate tycoons and Wall Street kings flew in quietly and looted more cash and property in the last thirty years than the spoils pillaged by all the armies of history. Economically-speaking, today's middle class has more grounds for revolution than our founding patriots in 1776.

War of the Words

The rich and the powerful (do you ever hear the phrase, "the *poor* and the powerful?") have been waging war against the rest of us for millennia. Until the Declaration of Independence, the rich always won. Why? Because they pick the battleground (they define the terms of the debate), they have more guns (power), and the referees are on their side (the lawyers/judges). The rich determine the battlefield, and they do so in part by defining the language.

The current favorite semantic "battlefield" is drawn up by re-defining the word **"socialism."** They define socialism, or even progressive taxation, as synonymous with *communism*. An outright lie, but it works for them—because most Americans were deeply indoctrinated in elementary school to fear communism.

Communism has been widely discredited by historical experience as an unworkable system. Communism is dying, yet *fear* of it is rising, thanks to exploitative media, to fearmongers like Glen Beck, Michael Savage and Rush Limbaugh. And so, the plutocrats create a false linkage between communism and socialism, to frame the "war" in terms of a Cold War between holy patriots versus godless evil communists—people such as *me*, despite the fact that I'm a minister opposed to communism.

Not only do I reject communism, I also reject socialism—in the classic, European style—as inefficient and impractical. We must transcend classic socialism and move to an intelligent hybrid of a limited free market linked with an activist-but-people-first government—a populist capitalism. But if I am forced to defend the charge of being a socialist, exaggerated as it is, I will do so.

What Really is Socialism?

Socialism can be defined as an economic and political system that sees the **social connectedness of modern life**... a style of government that seeks what is best for society as a whole. A limited-socialistic government, if it also protects the freedoms of the individual, is nothing to be feared. Majority rule does not mean we give in to every whim of the masses at the expense of the minority. That's un-American. Any socialism that attempts an artificial "leveling" of society or disregards the facts of human nature and motivation is no better than Fascism.

We are social people living cooperatively and lovingly; we are not individual animals in brutal competition. If this makes me a socialist, so be it. Most citizens support progressive taxation, public education, social security retirement and other helpful social programs. Conservative politicians receive millions of votes from Social Security recipients and treat Social Security as a sacred cow—never admitting that this does, in fact, make them Socialists.

The vast majority of populists are not seeking to implement radical socialism or nationalization of industry. **All we really ask is for our economic system to be fair and honest.** If unbridled capitalism had achieved the things it has claimed for itself—job and wage growth, equal opportunity, self-policing markets—communism would never have been a threat. The appeal of freedom is so attractive, an honest and fair "free market" capitalism would have consigned Karl Marx's ideas to an academic footnote. But Reagan's trickle-down capitalism proved to be a hoax, so the quirky socioeconomic theory called communism still lingers. Capitalism's failures fertilized Marxism.

The ideas offered in this book are not radical ideas exclusive to the domain of Liberals. Most people, whether they admit it or not, enjoy a plethora of "socialist programs" (like highways, libraries, social security, police). So, what is wrong with admitting we are a *society*, an interrelated, intra-dependent community, rather than just individual unconnected islands? Why do we allow the rich Right-Wing to act as if there is some great flaw in caring about society as a whole? I will argue herein that *greed* is the biggest immorality we face. Socialism can be evil. It can also be good. Greed, however, is *always* evil.

That premise is backed up by every major religion on our planet. No sooner than I express these truths, the plutocrats scream that I am guilty of "class envy." Even if it were true, greed is far more harmful to others than envy. Envy and greed are two of the Seven Deadly Sins, but most of those "deadly vices" are personal, private. Envy only harms the individual. Greed, however, has social consequences—the worst of the Seven Sins. Thus I dedicate an entire chapter to the topic of "Greed" (Chapter 8). But what about the accusation that when the lower classes complain, we are merely being envious?

Penal Envy

Consider someone locked in a penal institution or concentration camp, confined for years in solitary confinement with bread and water rations. Through the barred window, the prisoner sees people come and go at will— people with plenty of food, comfort and personal freedom. The prisoner naturally yearns for their freedom. Is it a sin of *envy* the prisoner experiences? No. It stems from a healthy human emotion to say: *I want to be free, and I don't want to be cold or hungry, I want a meaningful life of choices and opportunities.* A prisoner of war longs to be free. His yearning is not envy, it is a natural, morally-neutral desire.

Poverty is like a prison. It limits freedom in a hundred ways. The poor have little choice of where they live, what they can do for a living, their hobbies, what they can experience in life, even what kind of education they can offer their children. Money doesn't buy happiness. But a lack of money creates a condition of captivity, fear, anxiety, and discomfort.

If a poor person longs for a better life, the rich pile on the moral baggage: "You are filled with envy." True envy or *schadenfreude* is a sin wherein one person delights in seeing a successful person suffer, or wants to take another person's possessions. I am not guilty of that. **I want everyone to prosper** and I have no desire to take from you what you legitimately earned through hard work, smarts and talent. But there are **limits to the amount of goods that any one person can legitimately "earn"** by his own solitary efforts. The rich ignore the interconnectedness of life, blind to how success is a team effort. Other than Robinson Crusoe, no one gets wealthy alone on a desert island. Government-built infrastructure, low-paid workers in their factories/stores, consumers who buy the products... all help the rich get richer.

Speaking of Islands...

As Leon Russell sings, *I'd like to go back to the island.* Imagine again an island as our metaphor. Picture a hundred of us stranded on a "Survivor Island" where the only food is coconuts. We all work hard to bring in the seasonal harvest to store for winter. We collectively gather 1,000 coconuts, but ten people say, "We are special elites. We get to keep 90%. So those ten fellows walk off to their side of the island (the side with the nice huts) with 900 coconuts... they can each eat 10 coconuts a day for 30 days and still have a mountain of coconuts left (600). They have so much coconut meat, they're throwing it around in food fights just for fun! The rest of us are left with just 10 coconuts to feed **ninety** mouths for a month... one spoonful per week per person!

That is a simplistic, reductionistic view of how the world operates economically. If you were on that island, and your child was starving, what would you do? Would you vote to force the rich folks to share their mountain of rotting coconuts with the starving men, women and children? Then you, my friend, are a socialist! Or would you let your child die of malnutrition? We *are* on an island—Planet Earth floating in space—and children *are* starving.

The Mythical Justification for Greed

It is easy to determine, in small group settings, who is greedy and who is not. So the ultra-rich respond to my island story with a story of their own... *story* as in a false fable. The **myth of unlimited resources** is told and re-told by those lucky enough to have overabundance. Rather than share, it is easier to simply claim that there's plenty of money laying around: "Anyone can be rich." Rather than understanding the finite limits of the pie (the economy and its resources), they envision some magical pie-making machine that can infinitely bake more pies.

In a book entitled *The War on Success*, (discussed further in my Chapter 3), Tommy Newberry presents the myth this way:

"Socialism relies on spreading the perception of scarcity.... Imagine there are only 300 million potatoes in America, and we have to feed everyone out of the 300 million. If... the founder of Starbucks has too many potatoes, then, to the socialist that means someone else won't get any potatoes at all. Because of this fear-induced blind spot, the only option in socialism is to grab someone else's potato, chop it up, and hand it to the potato-less individuals. It never occurs to them to plant and harvest bigger crops of potatoes. It's simply unfair [to the socialist mind] that some have planned, nurtured, and produced excessive potatoes."[16]

The number of holes in that Swiss-cheese logic are so many, I hardly know where to begin. Newberry presents a typical reductionistic analogy favored by conservatives. It doesn't begin to explain the complexities of economics and the way resources are owned and distributed. I could quickly rebut saying, "How can I plant potatoes if I don't own farmland—when my paycheck at Starbucks doesn't even cover my living expenses?" That, too, is reductionistic, so allow me to peer through the swiss cheese holes for a more detailed answer:

•First of all, I am not arguing for socialism, but for a smarter, fairer capitalism. But I'll take the bait and even defend "socialism." Newberry misrepresents socialism as a system that only wants to re-distribute, not produce. But most socialist governments are always looking for ways to boost productivity and jobs. Re-distributing the potatoes is not the only option socialists consider... though I'd have to admit, if you had 1,000 potatoes and I had none and my child was starving, I'd want you to share.

•Second, I do agree that resources on this planet *are* expansive. The problem is, **most of those resources are not available to the average person**; they are owned or controlled by tycoons, corporations or corrupt governments. Newberry is stuck in the "frontier pioneer" mentality of Ronald Reagan, propagating the myth of free "land spreadin' out so far and wide." If there is a speck of habitable, temperate, unclaimed land left, I'm unaware of it. A rural African has no money, property or even infrastructure on which to build prosperity—you can't pull yourself up by your bootstraps, Reaganites, if you don't own boots!

• Third, look how reductionistic Newberry's illustration is: "The only option in socialism is to grab someone else's potato, chop it up, and hand it to the potato-less individuals."

This is not a case of *the rich guy has one potato, three poor guys have none... cut the potato in three and let the rich guy starve*, as the analogy implies. We evil "socialists" are not plotting to deprive anyone—that's the capitalist's job. The truth is, the rich guy has a *lot* of potatoes. The rich guy has a kitchen cabinet full of potatoes, potatoes filling his garage, a barn full of potatoes, a second home at Miami Beach full, a third winter home in Aspen full of potatoes. And millions of children have, literally, no potato at all.

So the bitter irony of Newberry's metaphor is that there are indeed huge amounts of resources on our planet, but **because of the greedy hoarding by the rich,** children are truly dying for a lack of a potato or bowl of rice. It is not that the founder of Starbucks "has too many potatoes," he has too many houses and cars and spends too much on jet travel and luxury while paying his employees a wage that one cannot possibly afford to raise a family on. Starbucks' CEO rakes in about $3 million a year, and the Board Chair took in even more—while they pay employees less than $10 per hour.

The answer the fat-cats offer is that if I don't like the starting pay at Starbucks, I should just go and be an entrepreneur and open my own Starbucks. Problem is, Starbucks doesn't offer a franchise, but a similar coffee shop franchise costs about $100,000. The average American can't even afford a $4 latte without using a credit card!

For most of us, resources are very, very tight. Not even looking to the Third World, but right here in America millions of people are scraping the bottom of their coin dish to buy a bag of potatoes at the end of the month. This is not an exaggeration. The ultra-rich do not want their myth of plenty destroyed because it soothes their greedy consciences, their belief that if bread is scarce, we can "let them eat cake." In the homes of the rich, there's plenty of cake. And potatoes.

How Much is a Billion? I Don't Know, I Failed Geometry

The CEO of Starbucks is a filthy rich fellow who could afford to buy every child in America a potato and still have money left for a Porsche. But he alone is not the problem. We not only have scads of multi-millionaires hoarding resources, we also have over a thousand **billionaires**!

A billion is not a thousand million. Well, it is in math, but not in real life. A billion is so big, it doesn't actually exist in "real life" tangible form; the U.S. Treasury Department doesn't *print* million-dollar bills, and in fact, the *entire* output of the Treasury's printing machines for an entire year is less than one billion dollars cash! If you gave me a billion dollars in one dollar bills, and told me to count it by hand, I would die before I could finish. So the pile of money involved is beyond human comprehension.[17]

But secondly, a billion dollars doesn't function in a linear fashion. It requires geometry and other higher math (as in, pyramids and algorithms) to understand its functional proportionality. If you make $100,000, you can live a comfortable, lavish lifestyle. And you can understand what your money can buy. You can count it. And you could easily, even after taxes and Cadillacs, save 10% annually so that with compound interest, you'd die a millionaire.

But a billionaire could *spend* a million dollars every year for a lifetime and still be a billionaire... again, because he would have investments that become leveraged by his wealth to grow exponentially. He can afford the best lawyers, accountants and brokers to insure that his billion performs in ways that defy simple arithmetic. But simple math can tell us there is a limit to how many houses and jewels and cars one person can enjoy. So if you can't spend a billion in a lifetime, why does anyone need a billion dollars?

Why It is Okay to Criticize the Upper Class

In our lifetimes, systems and technologies have changed in such a way that outlandish, excessive resources pool in tiny spots on the globe while other expanses lie barren. There is no longer a single line sloping gently upward to indicate the gradual increase of wealth from lower class to middle class to upper class. The gap between billionaires in palaces and workers in hovels is **so large it can't be charted linearly on graph paper.** A billion dollars does not have a linear relation to the average paycheck—it is a *geometric* ratio. And when one compares the "disposable income" of the rich to the struggling middle-class, it is *exponentially* larger. The gap can't be conveyed with pen and paper.

So, one reason the ultra-wealthy get away with robbing from the poor is that most of us simply can't grasp the size of the burglary. The huge inequity between someone who makes a billion dollars in a *year* versus a working class person who might make a million dollars in a *lifetime* is beyond the number-counting vision of the human mind! The inequity can only be hinted at with metaphors. Imagine if Bill Gates' income for a day was compared to what a person makes at one of his Asian manufacturing plants, using stacks of silver dollars. Their stack would be measured in inches; Bill's stack would be several *miles* high. Most of his workers will not earn in a lifetime what he *spends* in a day. Compounding—the snowball effect of wealth building more wealth—exacerbates the gap. In a lifetime, the average Asian worker will be lucky to have saved a handful of silver dollars because he cannot get ahead; Bill Gate's compounded stack of lifetime silver dollars will stretch from Detroit to Salt Lake City... 50 times![18]

How much is a billion? It's impossible to comprehend. A billion minutes ago Jesus was alive. A billion days ago no-one walked on the earth. It is impossible to grasp a number that big, but we try.

Two Billion Could Transform An Entire Country:

Take the nation of Costa Rica. Neither the smallest nor the largest country: not in square miles, not in GDP, not in population. Yet, it is one of the wealthier nations in Central and South America. According to our State Department, Costa Rica has approximately four million citizens and their average income is about $10,000 annually. Imagine in such a culture if you could give every household (approximately 4 people average per household) a 20% pay increase! For many families, it would remove the burden of debt, for others it would ease the pressure of worrying about being behind on bills, and for others, it would offer the opportunity for college education for their children. So, $2,000 x one million households equals 2 billion dollars. Distributed evenly and directly to the citizenry (not sucked up into some government-bureaucrat's pet project), two billion dollars could change the history of an entire country for the better.

So, how much is a trillion? Enough to transform the lives of the entire populace of 500 nations like Costa Rica!!

But "just" a billion dollars could make an astonishing transformation of our planet if distributed wisely. A billion dollars, divided among the poorest, would be a momentous historical event, with the potential to change the lives of millions of earth's citizens.

Instead, we spend it on a single aircraft. Or we allow a single individual to control that billion and squander it on extra yachts, cars, mansions and other frivolous things that they could not even possibly enjoy. How do you make use of all one hundred rooms in your mansion, or sail three yachts at once?

Poor Circulation

And perhaps even worse than millions squandered on mansions and yachts are the billions hoarded and sequestered, sitting idle in off-shore banks, no longer in circulation. Hardened and blocked arteries in the human body cause poor circulation that can ultimately be fatal. The Great Depression was the equivalent of failed circulation: money could not get to every member of the society, so the economy died. Rather than hoarding, it is far healthier to keep money flowing, and the rich would themselves benefit by putting more of their money back into society; much of the money the rich put into circulation by investment in philanthropy and entrepreneurial growth comes back to them. Money socked away in a Cayman Island bank helps no one, but money spent, invested and given away becomes lifeblood to the broader economy, enlivening consumer spending, boosting employment, and ultimately fostering a healthy economy in which *everyone* benefits, rich and poor.

According to *Forbes* magazine, the Mexican telephone magnate, Carlos Slim Helu, has over 50 billion dollars.[19] Carlos, I have personally driven through the garbage dump of one of your smaller cities and seen scores of people homesteading in the garbage dump, living off the trash, and seen with my own eyes children digging through the refuse to find scraps of something to live on. Just the interest on that 50 billion would provide healthy meals, and build news schools, for every poverty-stricken child in Mexico. The average monthly income of employed, educated professionals in Mexico is less than $1,000 dollars a month. 50 billion could pay the paychecks of the entire professional class for their entire careers. In Mexico, less than 2% control 90% of the wealth... and we are not sure how much more money is hoarded in the closets of drug lords while their people go hungry. This one man, Carlos Slim, alone owns more than the entire bottom half of his country. Who can defend the morality of this situation to a little child eating rotten garbage from the town landfill?[20] Give away a billion, Carlos, for the poorest of the poor, and a lot of it will come back to you!

The Time is Now

It would be a cop-out to sit idly by and wait on billionaires to fix society's problems. The purpose of this book is not to get people enraged, but to get you en*gaged*—in social and political change. We must start a (peaceful) revolution. Now. It's almost too late. As money takes over politics, the window of opportunity is closing on our chance to restore democracy and hope. **The gap between rich and poor is wider than ever in human history.**

Famed political writer David Cay Johnston wrote an analysis for the *New York Times* of a 2004 IRS report on income. Although overall income had grown by 27% in the span of 1979 to 2004, **33% of those gains went to the top 1%.** The bottom 60% saw a *decrease* in real wages: about 95 cents for each dollar they made in 1979. The next 20% had a two cents per dollar increase. But the very top 5% made significant gains ($1.53 for each 1979 dollar). The report also showed that the top 0.1%—a tiny elite of one-tenth of one percent—had more combined income than the poorest 120 million U.S. citizens put together. The gap is even worse internationally, and even worse now than it was in 2004.

There was a saying I heard as a child: "The rich get richer and the poor get poorer." It is no longer exactly true. The rich now get *obscenely* richer, and even faster! Vast mountains of wealth are in the hands of people who did not work any harder than the rest of us. Money does not make people evil, but evil people *are* drawn to money. Honest people are at a disadvantage. Most of the smart, talented, hard-working people are found within the middle class — the very class that shrank over the last three decades (even as GNP and productivity soared). This is an extraordinarily-dangerous Brave New World, where concentrations of wealth are so disproportionate that democracy is in jeopardy. We face Goliath, a giant tyranny, what some have called a "Fourth Reich of the Rich." The Nazis were defeated. This new Reich is at once stronger and more subtle.

It's About the Children, Stupid!

I fear this book could fail in two ways:

1. If readers become overwhelmed by the sheer size/scope of this topic, it is tempting to put it at arm's length, to intellectualize poverty and inequality as merely academic abstracts. Economic injustice is real and personal. Human hardship, which includes starvation and infant mortality, cannot be reduced to a topic for Ivy-league debate teams. This is why I've written in an informal, personal style.

2. And yet, as I bring my own "first-person" passion to the debate, even though it is chock full of facts and references and statistics proving the case, I fear people will dismiss me as an angry poor person, just ranting, driven by bitter envy of the rich.

I have all the material things a man could want, and live comfortably, if modestly. This is not about me. If anything, it is about **little children**. So I share a true story about my own child, and a broken crayon, that hopefully gives you insight into my motivation — and justifies my anger.

The Broken Crayon

My parents struggled financially, but we lived comfortably and my mother sacrificed to ensure her three sons had the things we needed. When I began first grade, she bought for me all the items the teacher recommended: notebooks, pencils, a wooden ruler and a large box of Crayola crayons. During "art class," I noticed that some of the poorer children could not afford the big box and had to make do with a few basic colors. For variety, they would sometimes borrow a crayon from those of us fortunate enough to have the large boxes with so many different, gorgeous shades of color-crayons to choose from. I was happy to loan mine; it made me feel rich. Sharing comes naturally for children.

I've never met a child who didn't enjoy coloring, and the joy I felt in opening that large beautiful set of crayons was no small thing.

Not long ago, my own daughter went on a mission trip to Honduras with other college students her age, each member of the mission team packing toys and crayons in their luggage, as much as space would allow, to share with the poverty-stricken mountain children. In that remote region of the Honduras mountains, most of the children had never even seen a crayon. They had neither stores nor money.

The mission team devoted some of their time to putting a tin roof on the crude "schoolhouse" in the village, with mornings reserved for hosting a "Vacation Bible School," a time for children to experience arts and crafts and Bible stories. The little ones enjoyed interaction with the college students from North America. My daughter thrilled at seeing their faces light up as she handed out blank paper and crayons for art time, but it quickly became apparent that they had more children than they had crayon boxes. By the second day, word of mouth had spread the news of the free opportunity for fun and learning. Eager children came from everywhere. The mission team rationed the crayons for yet another art class. More children poured in. One child, one crayon. More wide-eyed kids. Out of Crayola's. My daughter had no choice but to ask all the children to hand back their crayons, whereupon she broke each crayon in half. Having "created" two shorter crayons out of one, every child was thus able to have one half-crayon and all could participate in art-time. It reminded me of Jesus breaking the loaves and fishes in half to feed the hungry crowd.

The mission team had seen poverty before. But now they had a heartbreaking revelation about a shortage of resources. And about sharing. None of the children complained. They were accustomed to deprivation, and half of a crayon was better than no crayon. Their art might have been restricted to monochrome... but they instinctively knew the joy of sharing and they learned that all the colors of the rainbow were present in that schoolroom by exchanging half-crayons with others. Strangely, the more possessions people accumulate, the more they develop amnesia about the childhood impulse, and joy, of sharing.

I wept when my daughter told me this story. I cried not only for sadness, but also with happiness that not a single child was denied the joy of owning a color crayon. I still cannot re-tell it to others without tears. A broken crayon! It is not some invented anecdote designed to pull on heartstrings. It was a real day in her life, a real encounter with real people and real poverty. She was changed by it, and so was I. Will you be?

Summary

This planet is a gift. The ground we tread was never our own, we did not build it from thin air, nor did the oceans pour forth from the sweat of our brow. We have *joint* ownership of Planet Earth, if any ownership at all. We are long overdue for a discussion about the origins of wealth, about what social classes owe each other, about what constitutes smart and honest government, about wise stewardship of shared natural resources. It is past time to open our eyes, our hearts, our wallets, to the starving children at our door. We are past due to evaluate the fairness and efficiency of our systems. To consider these issues is not class warfare. It is merely a fair democratic debate, and such debate is guaranteed in our Constitution and Declaration of Independence. But we are already, like it or not, forced into a class struggle.

We should not shrink from seeking justice in the face of name-calling like "Class Warfare! Class Envy!" We have as much right to be in a war today as did the the colonists who battled King George in 1776. Like the first patriots vs. a tyrant, we have fewer numbers and inadequate arms as we face the entrenched power of wealth and elitist royalty. But take heart: the underdog won the Revolutionary War. And we do not need guns or violence or even violent metaphors. We do need the urgency, unity, and strategy of warriors — joined with higher virtue and higher learning. The pen is mightier than the sword, and right can defeat might.

Fifty years ago, I ran from the boy with the big stick. But I am not a little boy anymore. I will not run from the Fourth Reich of the Rich, no matter how big their sticks and stones. If they think that puts me at odds with the masters of the universe... then so be it.

~~~

Chapter 3: Socialism = Communism, and Other Myths
The underlying mythologies of Capitalism

These capitalists generally act harmoniously and in concert, to fleece the people. [But] labor is prior to, and independent of, capital. Capital is only the fruit of labor, and could never have existed if labor had not first existed. ~Abraham Lincoln

An Overview of My "Case"

I am not a socialist. At least, not in the sense of a mythological vampire sucking the freedom out of God-fearing citizens, then infecting them with Marxist atheism. But I *am* a socialist if the definition is *a belief that everyone in society is connected and deserves a fair chance at a decent life*. **You are a socialist**, too, if you plan to accept Social Security and Medicare, or if you call the taxpayer-funded police department when a thief breaks in.

I am also a capitalist. I accept the core premise of capitalism: incentive. **People work harder when they are rewarded for it.**

However, when the rewards become completely arbitrary, with no correlation to how hard or smart a person works, incentive becomes a mirage. Our economic system has been gamed, like a jiggered roulette wheel in a crooked casino, where some people hardly work and hit jackpots and others work hard and go bust. The benefits of capitalism—competition and incentive—disappear in the shadows of towering corporate monopolies that leave no room in the forest for seedling small businesses and sapling entrepreneurs.

Moreover, modern capitalism has enshrined money as more valuable than people, cash as more important than actual products and productivity; our system rewards financial manipulation more than manufacturing, exploitation more than innovation.

Abraham Lincoln believed that *people* should be more important than *profits*, and labor more valuable than numbers and decimals in bank accounts. Nowadays the monied class spurns Lincoln's wisdom, valuing "capital" (the hoarding and manipulation of money) above labor and talent. They want rewards that are a thousand times what is reasonable and proportionate—and they don't want you or me complaining when we work for minimum wage. Worldwide, the capitalists have so de-valued labor that a human life can be purchased for a dollar a day... Lincoln freed the slaves of his day, but economic slavery continues.

This system survives because of "capitalist propaganda": the underlying myths of capitalism once served a purpose in saving us from the real threat of communism. But communism is dying, and now these vestigial myths only serve to keep the poor poor and make the rich richer.

Before we bog down in statistics to prove this, let's take a big-picture look at my arguments and their myths, and excavate the pro-wealth propaganda buried in our heads since childhood.

Tiger Blood and Biting the Hand that Feeds

Did our founding fathers and mothers shed their blood to establish the system we have today? No. They did embrace capitalism and free markets, but they would be horrified at the way those terms have been re-defined, repulsed at how our modern oligarchy more resembles King George's monarchy than Adam Smith's original vision of a free, incentive-driven economy. The patriots died to defeat an enemy who believed he had royal blood and a divine right to power and wealth; today we have celebrities who boast of "tiger blood" and think they have a class-entitlement to excessive riches.

What if our beloved capitalism has a flaw so big and dangerous that we are like the man who made a pet of a cute baby tiger, but when the tiger grew to full-size, it bit off the man's arm? Capitalism does indeed bite the hand that feeds it. You and I feed the system with our own blood, sweat and tears. A wild and out-of-control capitalism has both an *ethical* **flaw** and a *systemic* **flaw**. Modern unrestrained capitalism has become a monster in our midst.

Bank Robbing: The Systemic Flaw

You might think I'd use a bank robber as an example of the *ethical* flaw. Yes... but it also illustrates the *systemic* flaw in capitalism: Bank Robber Zack Smith had problems. His failure to find meaningful work had much to do with where he was born and to whom he was born; his failure to pay his bills had more to do with his vice: he diverted bill-paying-money to his drug habit—a full-blown addiction. Zack's only success in life had been as a salesman: peddling dope on the street. Unfortunately for him, he snorted his inventory and had no money to re-stock. So he surprised no one, other than the bank teller, when he donned a mask and robbed the local bank of just under five thousand dollars. He also surprised no one by getting caught: he had scribbled his hold-up note on the back of a deposit slip—his own, with his name printed on it. In short order, he was arrested and convicted and sent to prison. He was an idiot. But other, smarter bank robbers do escape with riches and get to keep it. In a purely-capitalistic view, they are "successful."

One myth of modern capitalism is that anyone who has money must deserve the money because they *earned* the money. They use circular reasoning to say a CEO is worth a million because he is paid a million and because he is paid a million he must be worth it... by the same reasoning, the bank robber earned, and is deserving, of his money. We foolishly use money as the measure of worth.

Society looks down upon Zack with palpable disgust, and rightly so: in order to get a "high," he didn't care who he hurt as he stole a few thousand bucks. But when the bank robbers wear suits....

Bank Robbers

Jaime Dimon enjoyed another kind of "high." He circulated in the high-society enclaves of New England, enjoying the best of everything and viewed by most as an upstanding citizen. He socialized with Presidents. But Jaime Dimon walked into J.P. Morgan "bank" and came out with $53 million dollars. Not by a bank hold-up. It required two years of "work." 2007-2008 were not even the most profitable years for Dimon—two "bad" years during which, while Dimon reaped that windfall, my friends and yours lost half their retirement savings because of the shenanigans on Wall Street. It would have taken Zack Smith over 10,500 trips to the bank with a gun and a ski mask to amass that kind of jackpot. One trip per day would have taken Zack 42 years of daily bank robbing to accomplish what Jaime Dimon did in two years![21]

Dimon made off with millions, without a gun, without straining a muscle. Whether or not he broke the law is subject to dispute. You may argue: "The bank robber, Zack, broke the law, so he didn't earn the money!" But what if Zack had managed, in advance, to change the law to read, "People named Zack are allowed to rob banks legally"? Then, by economist Thomas Sowell's definition (see Chapter 4), Zack *earned* and *deserved* the money he robbed.

Many of those involved in the derivatives debacle who walked away with millions probably did break the law, even though they had already rigged the laws in their favor. And Dimon and his ilk of Wall Street-based bank "robbers" and stock pillagers have done far, far more damage to you and me than a petty thief and drug addict like Zack. Dimon seems to be addicted to a more dangerous drug: greed. Greed is the most overlooked curse on humanity, an addictive and dangerous vice (we explore *greed as an addiction* in Chapter 8).

A Rabbit-Trail of Vice

As we move forward on a path to describe the better society, let us detour down a rabbit-trail about "vice" for a moment. Most vices are *personal*, their consequences inflicted on the individual and his/her family. Greed is a *social* sin in its consequential damage... so much so we shall devote an entire chapter to it. I remain puzzled by the failure of philosophers, preachers and pundits to fight greed and the flawed economic-ethics of our times.

Late in his years, my father (a pastor) became convinced that the greatest sins are those that hurt other people. Greed is chief among such sin, yet few in politics or religion acknowledge this. Two ideas divide the political rightwing: *Libertarians* don't want government tending to their personal sins and ethics, while *Conservative Christians* long for a crusading government to rule over sexual orientation, marijuana, pornography and other "behind closed doors" vices. But *neither* conservative vision seems to care for the needy or give a darn about greed and the hoarding of resources. They both ignore the more important "sin," or to paraphrase Jesus, they are tending to splinters in the eye when there is a giant wooden stake in the heart of our Republic.

The TEA Party is flirting with Libertarianism, because it is a pleasant fantasy. Everyone loves the notion of liberty; no one likes bureaucracy. But the TEA Party can't resolve the paradox between their anti-government passion and their desire to impose "righteousness" through activist legislation. TEA Partiers idolize the Founding Fathers, even though Washington, Jefferson, et. al. rejected Libertarianism in the end, for the simple fact *it will not work*. But we digress. The core concern here is not politics, but the ethics and philosophy that underly our economic system.

Simple Philosophy

At the impressionable age of 18, I took my first philosophy course, Ethics 101, taught by a zealous advocate for the Libertarian Party. In the first week of class, the professor wanted to reduce life down to simple maxims. And this is the chief flaw of libertarianism: it is overly-simplistic, a reductionism driven by laziness. It would be so easy and lazily wonderful to say, "Hands off!" of society, hands off of my personal responsibility to other humans. To say, "Let people do whatever they wish, beyond a few basic laws like don't murder and don't steal. We don't owe anybody anything." It's hard to argue with simplistic logic. Simplicity is appealing.

So this professor, rigid in his full navy suit and tie, meticulous in how he groomed his hair and pencil-thin mustache, wanted to do away with most of the messy Federal government. A student argued, "But what about programs for the poor?" The prof was hoping for such a question to pounce upon. He boldly asked the class: "What do we owe the poor?" And a few idealistic students gave pat answers of Liberalism: we owe them health care, or food for their children, or shelter and clothing. To which he said, with an unfeeling logic rivaling Vulcan's Mr. Spock, "No, we owe them nothing. Now, you may make an argument that your faith, your religion, causes you to care for the poor. Which is fine. Give to the poor if you wish. But religion is not the business of government. Outside of charity, give me one logical reason why we owe the poor anything?"

I had the impression that this professor had always won his

argument, that aside from a few Christian students quoting Jesus, no one had rebutted Professor Libertarian and his "Spock logic." He repeated: "Sentimentality aside, we owe the poor nothing. Give me one reason that proves otherwise."

Meek as I was at that age, I still rose to the challenge. Not literally. I remained seated and just meekly raised my hand. It was the only hand, so he called on me. "Professor, there is at least one reason we owe the poor something. Wealthy people can't exist without the rest of us. Without someone to work in their factories, without someone to buy their products, without someone to fight in their armies, they would not have their wealth. So they owe something back."

The professor paused. It would be the longest span I'd ever observe him without words. The pause, the mulling I could see in his eyes, told me that for all his brilliance, he had never thought of society in those terms! Next, he considered his rebuttal. Trained and skilled in classic rhetoric and debate, he fingered his mustache and sought a hole in my logic. And to his credit, when he found none, he confessed aloud to the class: "That is a valid point. That may be the only valid point I've ever heard of why we owe the poor anything. I'll have to think about that." And then he changed the topic.

I respected him greatly for not offering some knee-jerk defense. He honored the rules of debate. Most people are not willing to be open-minded or logical about this issue; they get emotional when their long-held precepts are challenged. They stomp and call names. They dredge up anecdotes of the lazy good-for-nothing poor person who bought beer with foodstamps. They yell about communism. And I understand: the hard-working middle class has a visceral dislike for freeloaders and a respect for those who "succeed" at amassing wealth. But those are emotional responses. As IBM once mottoed: *Think*. Or as God said in the Psalms: "Come, let us reason together."

The Second Reason

Having won the debate with Mr. Spock, I found later that people with emotions are not so easily persuaded. They have been indoctrinated in school with a great fear of anything resembling communism, and in church or synagogue with a work ethic, and by media with an individualism that enshrines wealth as the just reward for hard work. I take no issue with that: hard work is virtuous.

But the matter doesn't end there; society doesn't run like a Vulcan computer. We have hearts as well as minds. We do, 90% of us on this planet, believe in some sort of God. Most of us are not Darwinian, we do not live like animals, where only the strong thrive. We have *ethics*. The question is not, "What do we owe the poor?" The question is, "Shall we live by ethics and love, or shall we live as savage beasts?" If you choose the former, then why are you not living by your ethics?

Some people view the academic field of ethics and philosophy as too abstract... forgetting that philosophy is **about our daily living, about what kind of ethics shape our inner selves and our real relationships to other humans.**

The most common root of all ethics is The Golden Rule, "Treat others as you would like them to treat you." It is the perfect rule for human society. It is both pure logic and fairness, but it also hints at the emotional value of loving neighbor and even gives a self-interested rationale for living that way: I should love my neighbor because I'd like to be loved myself!

The Gold Exemption to the Golden Rule

But people become self-deceptive and falsely rationalize away the Golden Rule when it comes to their pocketbooks. "Oh, if I was poor, I wouldn't want a hand-out from the rich!" Or with the emerald glasses of romanticized memory, they forget how miserable it was to work in the hot sun as a youth for slave wages, "Hard work was good for me! I worked hard, they should too!" And suddenly, they have exempted themselves from "do unto others."

They have over-simplified the matter. Working hard as a young person before moving up the ladder to corporate comfort is not the same experience as a person stuck in a working class job for a *lifetime*, with no hope for a better future, with too small a wage to offer a quality life for their children. And we've not even begun to talk about an entire separate reality in the Third World, where starvation and deprivation creates a living hell for most of humanity.

From those Hippie Radicals: *Citigroup*

Our world is in grave danger as unrestrained capitalism moves us to a two-tier economic system of "haves" and "have nots." To those who think that statement is the exaggerated rant of some hippie-radical-commie, consider this: **I'm not the only one saying this—Citigroup is!**

That's right, the same assessment—that the world is run by a plutocracy aimed at destroying the middle class—comes from the world's largest financial services company. Citigroup, that bastion of capitalism which makes millions on stocks and insurance and government bail-out bucks, issued a paper entitled "Revisiting Plutonomy: The Rich Getting Richer," which confirms this chapter's premise. The Citigroup paper was not intended to expose to the world the frightening trend; it offered advice on how the rich can further exploit the trend to make even more money! They admit that "the World is dividing into two blocs—the Plutonomy and the rest."[22] Their words! Their purpose: to "exploit" these "global imbalances" in order to make the growing gap between rich and poor—you guessed it—even bigger! Here are more excerpts from Citigroup:

• "In plutonomies the rich absorb a disproportionate chunk of the economy and have a massive impact on... consumption levels, etc."

• "This imbalance in inequality... [means that] the top 1% of households in the U.S. accounted for about 20% of overall U.S. income in [year] 2000, slightly smaller than the share of income of the bottom 60% of households put together. That's about 1 million households compared with 60 million households, both with similar slices of the income pie!"

• "The top 1% of households also account for 33% of net worth, greater than the bottom 90% of households put together. It gets better (or worse, depending on your political stripe): the top 1% of households account for 40% of financial net worth, more than the bottom 95% of households put together." Citigroup's words!

I'm not making this up. Again, those are direct quotes from the Citigroup paper. Did you catch it? They are not writing the paper to call for political reform or to urge egalitarian responses from their (upper)classmates. They see this as *good news* (quote, "it gets better"), and the purpose of the paper is to show how to use the news of the "plutonomy" to make the rich even richer! One section heading is: "Riding the Gravy Train."[23]

J.P. Morgan Chase also admitted, in the summer of 2011: "Profits are up because wages are down." The same article reporting this added, "The money produced by everyone's hard work gets funneled to the guys at the top."[24] Real income has soared $528 billion since the Crash of '08, but only 1 percent of that growth has gone to workers.[25]

Plutocracy and Plutonomy: The Worm Ouroboros

More ominous are the *political* goals spelled out in the Citigroup report. It encourages government policies that keep the vicious spiral of "rich getting richer." The paper warns that a threat to the rich is "left-leaning government" and suggests: "Society and governments need to be amenable to disproportionately allow/encourage the few to retain that fatter profit share. The Managerial Aristocracy, like in the Gilded Age, the Roaring Twenties, and the thriving nineties, needs to commandeer a vast chunk of that rising profit share..." by using favorable "taxation" and reducing "regulation."

Plutocracy (rule by the rich) uses money to gain power; *plutonomy*, Citigroup says, means using political power to protect their wealth. It is the Serpent Ouroboros. Self-feeding.

The only thing refreshing about this paper is its candid confession, admitting that one of the few threats to itself is its own success... if the Elite become too rich, the paper warns, there could be a "social backlash." Damn right.

Doing God's Work

Most other fat-cats are in great denial about their greed and selfishness, even to the point of viewing their disproportionate wealth as *success* not as *excess*. Lloyd Blankfein, the former chief executive of Goldman-Sachs, famously proclaimed, even after the Wall Street crash, "I'm doing God's Work."[26] The upper classes rarely reject ethics or religion outright; the wealthier they are, the more they bend backwards to prove their largesse is "righteous" or even sanctioned by God. As we shall see in Chapter 5, the greediest and wealthiest have clung tightly to their spiritual mythologies, publicly given lip service to religion or ethics, when the truth is, they have abandoned the teachings of every major religion.

The Mythology of Success

For example, the worn argument, "Wealth is the reward for hard work," is used widely to make wealth seem virtuous. We earlier used Tommy Newberry, author of a defense of capitalism called *The War on Success*, as our foil. He sees material *success* as synonymous with *virtue*. Old adages like "money legally earned belongs to the one who earned it," "wealth comes from hard work," and "those who take the risks deserve the rewards," are rarely questioned. Throughout this book, we will explore several fallacies in this success mythology and the **lie** the that America is still a meritocracy. Here's an opening list:

1. MYTH: *I got my wealth legally, so I'm entitled to it.*
TRUTH: Legal is not always ethical. Slavery was once "legal," as were profits "earned" by the plantation/master. We now know better. When something legal is unethical and detrimental to society, we must change the law—legal exploitation of child labor, for example.

2. MYTH: *I earned my billions by hard work.*
TRUTH: Our definition of "earned" is obsolete. Simply because money flows to a tycoon's Swiss bank account does not mean he "earned it." Seventh Generation CEO Jeffrey Hollender was born wealthy yet has the honesty and integrity to admit, "A lot of it is luck, and we're standing on the backs of those who came before us."

3. MYTH: *I'm rich because I took more risks.*
TRUTH: When it comes to risk versus reward, the coal miner who risks life and lung beats the investors who bought the coal

mine. Many folk still accept the notion that investors deserve windfall profits just because they risked money. By that measure, police should be billionaires! Life and work always involves risk. In terms of human health, blue-collar workers take far greater risks than stock brokers. And now we live in an age where golden parachutes, loss insurance, government aid and bailouts mitigate risk for the rich.

    4. MYTH: *This property belongs to my family forever.*
TRUTH: This land is my land, this land is your land. God made it, not you. Ironically, the greatest advocates for private property—white Americans—live on land stolen from Native Americans. The notion of "belongs to" must be re-examined in our modern age of world population boom and interconnectedness. Who owns the air we breathe? Who does the ocean belong to? As resources shrink, how we use energy and property will become contentious. Do you have a "right" to pollute my air, to burn 50 times more fossil fuels than I use? Just because your grandfather owned half the state, does that give your family exclusive claim to a vast expanse of planet earth for all time future? Thomas Paine wrote: "Men did not make the earth... It is the value of the improvements only, and not the earth itself, that is individual property... Every proprietor owes to the community a ground rent for the land which he holds."[27]

    5. MYTH: *CEO salary correlates to intelligence, hard work, talent and efficacy. We have a meritocracy.*
TRUTH: The track record of CEOs shows that salaries do NOT match performance. Failure is now rewarded handsomely. Salary levels are arbitrary, not based on merit. We will examine (in Chapter 4) whether CEOs, investment bankers, and others who make huge paychecks are worth even a fraction of what they "earn," versus the monkey who could have made a killing in the stock market.

    6. MYTH: *Royalty and other elites are rich by the will of God.*
TRUTH: The "divine right of kings" is not a principle found in Holy Scripture. There is no logical or ethical defense for family dynasties. The sheer stupidity of tax money supporting "royal families" simply because of bloodlines flies in the face of science—and violates the very tenets of capitalism. The proponents of "earned wealth" self-contradict when they defend dynasties, whether they be British royals or Walmart Waltons benefitting from estate-tax exemptions and trusts. We are all tied together genetically and geographically in a shrinking world.

    7. MYTH: *The poor should not complain, because Capitalism provides equal and unlimited opportunity. Be self-reliant: pull yourself up by your bootstraps.*
TRUTH: Frontiers and opportunities still exist, but for a variety of reasons, not everyone has an equal shot at them. Those who

already have capital have a distinct advantage. And natural resources, like land and energy, are not unlimited.

One of the creeds of capitalism is that there are unlimited opportunities and resources, thus any poor person should just become an entrepreneur. Successful rags-to-riches folks forget the luck that came to them across the years, and assert: "Well, the poor can work hard like I did and climb up the ladder." Indeed, many do. But just because John and Jane succeeded, doesn't mean that Tom and Tina can. John and Jane may have been born with a high IQ or with gobs of creative talent or in neighborhoods with ample jobs and opportunities. Their parents may have given them a vision for self-improvement. Tom and Tina, on the other hand, may have come from broken homes without a mentor, or with moderate to low intelligence and not an inkling of how to get a good job. Born in an area of vast poverty, some of the poor had children at an early age and cannot save money for a business start-up. Others may have a physical handicap or illness. Some simply have bad luck.

There you have, in random order, seven myths of modern Capitalism, which we will examine further as the book unfolds. Winding up this chapter, allow me to expand on that last myth.

Opportunity for All?

In justifying cuts to welfare, President Reagan famously said, in the midst of a recession and high unemployment, that the newspaper had pages and pages full of job openings in the classifieds. He truly believed the myth of unlimited opportunity. Wealthy folks, even those with a modest upbringing, tend to forget how hard it can be to find a job, or how poverty and family commitments limit mobility and choice.

I have a doctoral degree, yet in looking through the "hundreds of jobs" in the classifieds, I usually find only one or two jobs that I have the experience and specific education for—and a hundred applicants are competing for each of those few jobs.

National unemployment figures also don't reveal the geographic nature of high unemployment. If you had purchased a now-unsellable home in Detroit—just as the boosters of the American Dream encouraged—it is nearly impossible, economically or emotionally, to uproot your enmeshed family in search of a job elsewhere. But the Reagans of the world can simply write a check for plane tickets, pay professional movers to swoop in, and be whisked away to a new home overnight. Executives are paid for their relocation expenses, so they do not understand this lack of mobility in others.

Not only is this unfair to people who value their ties to extended family and friends, it also ignores the practical limits of working class pocketbooks. If the wife has a meaningful job in Detroit, but the husband's employer moves his factory to the South (as happened in the auto industry), it would be a major expense, sacrifice and gamble to uproot the family and the employed spouse. *Reader's Digest* gave examples of just such broken-family scenarios, where one spouse stayed with the children while the other spouse worked out of state.[28] The heartbreaking stories of splintered families don't show up on any unemployment statistics; both spouses had jobs!

The Reagan-Pioneer-Bootstrap Myth

Ronald Reagan was a loud proponent of the bootstrap theory. He believed opportunity was abundant for all—but he never lived in the inner-city or in an area like Appalachia, where the rich stripped the land of value and left the poor behind.

Libertarians, capitalists and free market enthusiasts spin a myth that America's success stems from the rugged individualism and entrepreneurship of "great men." Tall, rugged pioneers. Reagan fit into that myth, modelled himself after it, and perpetuated that pioneer fable with photos of himself chopping wood in blue jeans. Associated with the bootstrap myth is the lie that the pioneer success was rugged individualism, not government. Never mind that the pioneers were assisted by government "welfare," from the government-paid calvary that helped them steal land from the "Indians," to the government-sponsored transcontinental railway, to the Homestead Act, etc.

The full truth is that America is wealthy not just because of genius and hard work or our special virtues. Whatever I have, I owe in part to blessings of inheritance, not just my individual effort. Abe Lincoln realized this when he said, "We find ourselves in the peaceful possession of the fairest portion of the earth as regards extent of territory, fertility of soil, and salubrity of climate. We find ourselves under the government of a system [more conducive to] civil and religious liberty than any [in] history.... [We are] the legal inheritors of these fundamental blessings. We toiled not in the acquirement or establishment of them; they are a legacy bequeathed us...."

Yes, Abe, we inherited the most fertile, resource-laden expanse on the planet, in a temperate region. We had an active government offering such economic incubators as nationwide communication (phone, internet, TV), cheap and reliable electricity, the best highway system in the world, seaports and airports, the transcontinental railway, public education, the space program and other technological marvels—all of which provide tremendous economic blessings. The way the free marketers tell it, "whatever is good in America's economy has always evolved with no guidance," or from entrepreneurial innovation, while "whatever is bad has been designed by government," said J. Bradford Delong.[29] "This claim is, of course, ludicrous," he adds.

Expansion and The Gap
Wealth *has* been expanding... but only for a select few. Computer-driven technology has boosted productivity immensely, but the fruit has been plucked by those at the top of the food chain, not shared with the working class. The poison fruit of the Seven Myths is a tragedy I call *The Gap*: a chasm between what average people earn and own versus the upper classes (see Chapter 6).

The Gap has always been with us, but its maw began to yawn wider in the early eighties due to the wealth-friendly policies of Ronald Reagan. Reagan is enshrined as a hero in our culture. However, the image of his "trickle-down economics" is not unlike the biblical rich man, whose bread crumbs "trickled down" from his banquet table to the poor man crawling under the table. Reagan's supply-side policies, his union-busting and de-regulation of banks and industry began a huge expansion of The Gap. He is not alone. The Gap continued to grow under the Bushes and Clinton and even with that "socialist," Barack Obama. President Obama bragged on Wall Street tycoon Jaime Dimon (a campaign contributor) as he continued Bush's TARP handout-to-the-rich. We are seeing an unprecedented bipartisan fleecing of America

"In 2009, the richest 10% of Americans accounted for about half the nation's wealth," reports CNN in 2011.[30] The "pigs at the trough," as Arianna Huffington calls them, are indistinguishable by party: Democrats and Republicans both have their snouts in the suey. They all stood by while de-regulation led to the Crash of 2008.

The Moral Problem with Capitalism
After the crash, Fed Chair Alan Greenspan had to admit his naiveté in trusting the morality of corporations—having believed that banks and investment firms would be self-regulating. In testimony to Congress, Greenspan confessed: "I made a mistake in presuming that the self-interests of organizations, specifically banks and others, were such that they were best capable of protecting their own shareholders." In other words, **self-regulation failed**. The reason it failed is it depended on honesty and ethics. But capitalism is amoral. It has no "conscience" or ethical guide.

A system in which the market is king is thus very susceptible to being controlled by marketeers: by monied people who manipulate markets for profit. Michael Lewis, contributing editor of *Vanity Fair*, expressed his dismay about the "outrageous" criminality of

Wall Street, that the very ones who scream against socialism got their "losses socialized, but their profits privatized." Lewis is aware that the average person is "angry" about the "injustice" of tycoons being rewarded for failure.[31] (Yet it took years before the protest movement, "Occupy Wall Street," emerged.)

Capitalism rewards those who already possess power and wealth; it is biased in favor of that small elite of society that controls capital; it allows, even encourages, through systems of monopolization and control, the exploitation of the average worker.

Please bear with me: I know that phrase is one used by Marxists. This book is **not** trying to convert you to communism. The truth is, communism doesn't really exist anymore. There are now 115 billionaires in China, and 101 in Russia! So it is time we see through the fear-mongering. When the wealthy warn us about communism, they are like an older brother scaring his sibling with warnings of the boogaman under the bed. When you actually look under the bed, there's not much left of the boogaman but dust-bunnies.

What if Our Holy Capitalism is Unholy?

We were indoctrinated from an early age to revere God, Mom, Apple Pie and Capitalism. So I ask you to set aside fear and preconceptions, I beg you to look with a discerning eye and an open mind, past the brainwashing and propaganda that you have heard all of your life from those in power, and consider this truth: **Free market capitalism, without limits, is evil.** It is not just mildly flawed, or a clunky system. It is evil. It brings great harm to billions of people, it is evil in the eyes of God, and if you dare to read this book in full, you will see that I don't make these claims lightly or without documentation.

My argument is also not allied with either political party or ideology. Some of my ideas herein are shared by extreme conservatives and some by extreme liberals. For example, Paul Craig Roberts has been an establishment conservative: assistant secretary of the Treasury under President Reagan, an associate editor of *The Wall Street Journal*, and a respected academic on the payrolls of Georgetown University, the Hoover Institution, Stanford University and more. Yet Roberts warns about the following topics in his book, *How the Economy Was Lost: The War of the Worlds*:
•The outsourcing of manufacturing and higher-paying, once-middle-class jobs, and the impending destruction of the American middle class. •The soaring income disparity. •Resources and wealth are not "inexhaustible" or unlimited. •How current governmental policies and trends (in both parties) will "destroy the prospects and living standards of... working people." •How a college education no longer guarantees good wages.

These are all themes I developed in my earliest manuscript before discovering his book. He writes from a more-conservative perspective, but we both arrive at the same frightening conclusions. What does that tell us about the coming decimation of the American middle class?

Summary

My opponents offer a false choice between a bad Capitalism and a bad Socialism. I'm arguing for a *reformed* Capitalism. Capitalism may be the best system on earth, but being the best is not a reason to shut down discussions about how we can make things better. Capitalism is right in its understanding of fallen human nature, but not smart in its cure. Humans are motivated by money, and we tend to be better stewards of privately-owned property than of shared property. And yes, government bureaucracies are not as efficient as the free market. Those problems must be addressed: Communism failed because it ignored the presence of the disease, Capitalism failed by offering only a blind surgeon to fix it. But we should not dismiss every aspect of capitalism *or* socialism simply out of fear. The "invisible hand" slaps the poor and the middle class. The unseen "free market" force has no attached brain or eyes, so it is neither smart nor moral, and creates as many problems as it solves. Adam Smith's market mechanism is ignorant and uncaring.

We can calmly look for a healthy balance in ethics and economics. And while we complain about government, one cure may be worse than the disease: the TEA Party and Libertarianism could destroy the best of our institutions. We seem to forget the wonderful things that government offers us, from highways to space research to public schools and far more.

Returning to our metaphor of bank robbers: if you owned a bank, and a robber took $50,000 at gunpoint, you would be incensed. But suppose a nice clean-shaven man in a suit burrowed under your vault and quietly took $50 million, and then showed you an obscure state law that reads, "It shall be legal to steal from the bank so long as guns aren't used and suits are worn." Would you be enraged at a ratio of $5,000 to $50 million? Would you not want that law changed immediately?

Americans are being "legally" robbed. They have every right to be enraged. They have every right to want the laws changed.

But most are still reluctant to take action. Our society still functions like a primitive tribe, unsure if it is right to argue with the tribal leadership, still paying excessive tribute to the chief… chief executive officer, that is. The CEO.

~~~

Chapter 4: The Lucky Monkey
The Lie of Meritocracy and the real worth of CEOs

We pretend that success is exclusively a matter of individual merit. But there's nothing in... the histories... to suggest things are that simple. ~Malcolm Gladwell in *Outliers*

The Monkey Who Could Do It

I've called *meritocracy* a lie. Here are the facts: a monkey can pick stocks better than those overpaid human primates on Wall Street! *The Chicago Sun-Times* used a Brazilian cebus monkey named Mr. Adam Monk to pick stocks. Okay, I know zoologists will fault me for using a chimpanzee on the book cover with the title "monkey," but in popular jargon, *chimp* and *monkey* are interchangeable. In this case, a real monkey—pet-named Adam Monk—made a monkey out of those who claim Wall Street mavens are worth their seven digit salaries.

For several years running, the *Sun-Times* had their rented monkey annually pick 5 stocks (we assume at random, unless he has learned to read). At the end of each year, they compared the monkey's results versus the experts and the indexes. He's been pretty successful: "In the four years since Mr. Monk has chaired and inspired this contest, his stocks have posted annual returns of 37 percent, 36 percent, 3 percent and, in 2006, 36 percent, beating the major indexes [and high-paid human stock pickers] every time," David Roeder writes.

Roeder then compared his "expertise" to another "expert," Jim Cramer. Adam Monk, our super-chimp, made a monkey out of Cramer, the loudmouth TV stock guru who never saw the market crash coming. Here's a three year comparison of the monkey's picks versus Cramer's:

Adam Monk 2006 picks = 36% gain; Jim Cramer 2006 picks = 7.67% gain
2006 winner: the monkey

Adam Monk 2007 picks = +1.6% gain; Jim Cramer 2007 picks = 3.81% gain
2007 winner : Jim Cramer, slightly

2008: (stock market crash)
Adam Monk 2008 picks = -14.4 % loss; Jim Cramer 2008 picks = -29.8%
2008 winner: the monkey... Cramer lost twice as much in the crash!

Results: the monkey won 2 out of 3 years against the human expert, and won all 4 against the wisdom of the market index![32] That's right: for four years, the monkey beat the major stock indexes *every* time, and overall, had a better return than the informed, intelligent, well-researched experts. (The monkey is now retired... he's recumbent in the Bahamas, drinking banana daiquiris and living large off his investments.) Roeder concluded that the experiment shows that you don't have to be an insider CEO, hedge-fund manager or a loudmouth on CNBC to make money in the market.

I understand their jobs are more complex than just picking stocks... but my argument is not entirely reductionistic. In the end, stock-brokers, Wall Street analysts, hedge fund managers, they all are making *projections* about what markets will do, moving digits around in cyberspace based on what they believe the future will be. Unless they have a crystal ball, they are, actually, guessing!

And in so doing, they do not produce any product, they do not increase the quality of life on this planet. They are, like the monkey, *guessing and then reaping profits based on what other companies do*. Amazingly, most brokers make money whether their guesses are correct or not! They do something the monkey would not do: they cheat. They have the market rigged. The market collapsed in 2007-2008, most hard-working Americans lost money, but the market manipulators continued to rake in millions. So they are not monkeys at all... they are **leeches**, drawing blood out of another organism.

A Wall Street broker may counter, "But I made my client a million dollars!" No, you did not. You did not personally *create* anything of value, you merely were fortunate that your guess worked out before a calamity hit. Even when the market rises, are the wizards worth what we pay them? Are they bringing a good to society that provides value worthy of their multi-million dollar paychecks? If they were inventing cold fusion, providing free pollution-less energy to the entire planet, maybe. If they were curing cancers with a single pill, maybe. I am not saying there is no value to having a place to invest our retirement funds, or having a system for funneling funds into worthy industries and enterprises. But the service they provide is neither profound nor trustworthy... nor worth the price!

Masters of the Universe or Masters of Sausage?

Nor am I suggesting that stock analysts, brokers and investment bankers just sit around all day and throw darts at an NYSE bulletin board to pick stocks or that they have the IQ of a chimp. But I suspect the truth lies somewhere in the middle, between "monkeys" and their self-proclaimed titles of "Masters of the Universe" or "geniuses." They are masters at one thing: baiting unsuspecting investors with promises of easy money. (I'll skip the obvious but crude joke.) If these Wall Street moguls are such geniuses, why did they allow the worst market collapse since the Great Depression to sneak up on them? Please understand: while most of them are still making tons of dough, and thus think of themselves as success stories, if it had not been for massive bail-outs from taxpayers, AIG would have surely gone under, starting a domino effect that would have toppled hundreds more financial firms and thrown America into another Great Depression. Geniuses?

Many of these traders and consultants were once average students, in a field that doesn't require the educational rigor of a doctor, college professor, research scientist, or even a minister like myself. Indeed, in our upside-down economic system, we pay inversely for hard work. This is true not only in physical work (think farm laborers in 100 degree heat vs. NY martini lunches) but also in mental work.

These "geniuses" come from one of the easiest academic fields: the business school. Business majors spend less time preparing for class than students in any other field, according to the most recent *National Survey of Student Engagement*. In a poll from late 2010, about half of seniors majoring in business spent fewer than 11 hours a week studying outside class… lower than every other major. In their new book, *Academically Adrift: Limited Learning on College Campuses*, the sociologists Richard Arum and Josipa Roksa report that on a national test of writing and reasoning, business majors had the weakest gains during the first two years of college. *The Chronicle of Higher Education* reported that when business students take the GMAT, the entry examination for M.B.A. programs, they score lower than do students in every other major.[33]

While a tiny percentage of the players on Wall Street might be mathematical wizards, most are not. One former senior money-man at Lehman Brothers confessed, "I'm no genius. Certainly, many of the top guys [of Wall Street] were only just of average intelligence."[34] Again, I'm not seriously suggesting that monkeys could do their job. And anyone who has a college degree and works hard, plus chooses to be in a sector that pays well, **deserves above average wages**. But a million dollars for juggling numbers on a computer screen is not just ridiculously-overpaid, it is *evil*… unless they are giving away half their profits to starving children in the Third World.

The Sausage-grinders

Yes, some of the cast of the Wall Street Greek tragedy were smart mathematicians. A few might even score "genius" level on an I.Q. test. But even the math wizards wouldn't pass the test for common sense or integrity. These "geniuses" and their "brilliant" algorithms helped the investment banks pour billions into sub-prime mortgage derivatives, with the lame-brained notion that if you take bad loans, slice and dice 'em, stir 'em up, then slice 'em again, you can leverage them for more than what even good loans were once valued. This is like taking botulism-tainted meat from five different diseased hogs, putting them into a meat grinder together, and selling the combined sausage as clean. The metaphor only works if you then used the poison sausage as collateral for more loans! Ironically, if it had been food they were selling, no one would have bought it; if you were in the supermarket and saw "Jimmy Dean Sausage" on one shelf, and "Derivative Sausage" on the other shelf, which would you reach for? So when critics attack me for belittling investment brokers, for calling them sausage-makers or monkeys, let me just say the real monkey never sold worthless derivatives, never ripped off Grandma's retirement savings. Adam Monk never took government bail-outs, and asked for a golden banana, not a golden parachute.

Arguing with the Professor

But I digress. This chapter is not about the crooks on Wall Street (see Chapter 9). Here I answer the question implied by my book's sub-title: *Are the rich worth what we pay them?* The well-respected college professor, economist, and columnist, **Thomas Sowell**, thinks so. He says *the rich earn their pay*. So Sowell will be my adversary in this debate. He has long defended no-holds-barred capitalism and over-paid executives, marshaling all the arguments I've heard across the years. Debunking them will be more fun for me than, yes, a barrel of monkeys! In his newspaper columns and particularly in his book, *Economic Facts and Fallacies*, he gives **four defenses of the multi-million dollar salaries**:[35]

1. Sowell: The free market sets salaries, and its "invisible hand" should be trusted because capitalism works better than any other system. Or put another way: their salaries are a product of supply and demand… companies have to pay millions because that's the only way to attract quality executives.[36]

2. Sowell: CEOs are worth their pay because of the huge profits their corporations make. Warren Buffet made his firm billions, so therefore he should be paid billions.[37]

3. Sowell: CEOs are worth their pay because they *earn* it. They are so smart, they are the elite cream that has risen to the top.[38]

4. Sowell: You and I are too stupid to argue with the way salaries are set, we are not *expert* enough to know whether a CEO is overpaid.[39] Sowell wrote: "No third parties can possibly know… who really deserves how much income." He claims it is "inconceivable that any given individual could be capable of assessing the relative value... of different people in different industries…."[40]

I will rebut Sowell's nonsense in no particular order—his arguments intertwine and overlap, and my rebuttals do the same. **He is wrong on all four points.**

Executives are paid a thousand times their workers. Why?

Sowell's core argument is this: *the rich are worth their pay because the free market determines their salary*. Pretend the monkey had inherited a million dollars, and had invested that money in his stock picks. We would then have a monkey making a fortune through luck, with no exertion of brain or brawn, while honest, hard-working humans make minimum wage. Is that "monkey system" defensible?

Sowell tries. In one of his newspaper op-eds he stated, "If... outstanding executives were a dime a dozen, nobody would pay 11 cents a dozen for them."[41] Hyperbole aside, Sowell asserts that corporations pay outlandish salaries for the simple reason that good executives cannot be had for a penny cheaper. But they *can* be, and the fact that Japanese CEOs do a better job for far less money proves it. And hundreds of smart, experienced vice-presidents at companies would eagerly accept the number-one spot even at their current (much-lower) salaries, for the status and power alone.

Maybe I'm Stupid

Sowell is right in one sense, in saying that I am too stupid to understand. Truly, I don't understand! I don't know why Home Depot was paying Robert Nardelli $200 million to run Home Depot's profits and stocks into serious decline. While Home Depot's stock fell, rival store Lowe's increased 173%.[42] Why isn't "supply and demand" used by corporations in a reverse way to *lower* executive pay for bad performance, or in the hiring process? When hiring, out of a hundred applicants for CEO, pick the top three, then notify them: "You are tied with applicants, so we will award the position to the one who will accept the lowest salary." Remembering that you've already pre-selected the "cream of the crop," the one who will work for less might just be more motivated, more eager to work hard!

Professor Sowell posits that executives earn their money through the laws of supply and demand, and that their salaries reflect their worth. He cherry-picks a successful investor, Warren Buffet, citing the billions he made as CEO at Berkshire-Hathaway, and concludes Buffet was "worth it." Sounds very logical at first glance. In some cases, it may even be correct. But it is not universally correct. Is a smart and competent CEO worth a healthy salary? Of course. But Sowell fails to factor in the many cases of **utterly-incompetent CEOs still making millions**. He never shows a direct correlation between CEO pay and company profit, because he never factors in the times when CEOs have been paid millions for sheer failure. This alone disproves Sowell's assertion. A system like ours, that rewards failure, exposes the lie that the free market will incentivize success.

Circular Reasoning

But his argument is flawed in other ways. Sowell's first point boils down to, "CEOs are worth millions because the market pays them millions." That's circular reasoning. In the rules of formal debate, this would be dismissed *a priori*. In classic debate, you cannot prove a premise by merely tautologically restating the premise as proof of itself. An example: "I know a black cat got into my garbage can last night because I saw a cat who had no coloration." Further inquiry might discover that it was a *brown* cat, but the moonlight was too dim to reveal its color. My argument was circular: I assert the cat to be black because I believe that I saw a dark cat. We need some other evidence brought forward, not just a re-statement of the first premise.

For What It's Worth

Let's dig deeper than Sowell. What of the word *worth*? If we use it as a synonym for *price*, *cost* or *dollars*, then a CEO, even a poor excuse for one, may be "worth" a million bucks because someone is foolish enough to pay him that. But shouldn't *worth*, in a more intelligent and helpful definition, be about **intrinsic value to society**?

By that definition, what someone is *paid* may not be at all related to what they are truly *worth*. Think of it in terms of the reverse: let's say that Brad Pitt is paid a million dollars for a celebrity endorsement ad. But he next agrees to do a *pro bono* ad for the Red Cross as an act of charity and is paid nothing. Does that mean that Brad Pitt is now *worthless*? According to Sowell's logic, the answer would have to be "Yes," because Sowell says we are *worth* what we are *paid*.

Anyone who ever hired ten laborers knows that some are worth more than the others, and one of them is close to worthless. Just because a company makes ten million profit under a quality leader, is the CEO thus "worth" ten million? This is an elitist argument that denigrates the contributions of all other workers at a firm.

Why do organizations give the lion's share of profits to the CEO? Partly because the structure of most organizations is pyramid-shaped, creating an "upside down pyramid funnel," in which money flows to the top. And partly because power comes with being chief executive. And partly because of a group mentality that is psychologically rooted in barbaric tribalism. The primitive emotional need for a "tribal chief" in our very language: CEO stands for: "CHIEF Executive Officer."

This is Only a Test

I propose a real-world test to Sowell's argument. Take ten

multinational corporations. "Lay off" the 500 lowest-paid employees at each company for a period of six months (with pay). Then, the following year, "lay off" the CEO (whose pay was roughly the same as the collective pay of 500 bottom-level employees) for six months. We know that in very large corporations, neither would cause the instant collapse of the company (CEOs die or get fired and in the interim period, the companies rarely fail; likewise, corporations lay off hundreds of employees without going under). For example, if you "fired" 500 employees in the Customer Service Department, profits would actually rise for the first year... it would take a year or more for rumors of poor customer service to drive away customers. But over time, we would clearly see that the 500 low-level employees are more valuable than the CEO. Vice-Presidents could step up and fill the shoes of the missing CEO with little to no harm to the company; conversely, the absence of 500 workers in the manufacturing end could seriously cripple operations and profits. (In most companies, the CEO's Executive Secretary knows more than the boss! Put her in charge for fraction of the boss' pay.) What I propose here is a real-world test that would be a far better assessment of a CEO's worth than Sowell's circular argument of: "He's worth it, because that's what we pay him."

Good Leadership is Vital

But my test is over-reaching. I'm not actually claiming that a CEO is *worthless*. Far from it: I think good leadership is vital. My point is merely that *overpaid* does not equal *good*. We need a better test of value than traditional assumptions.

What if we devised a test to see if we could have profitable companies run by a CEO who would accept, oh, 60% of the current salary and still be as profitable? Surprise! Such a test has *already* been undertaken. For years. In a place called Japan. And my hypothesis has been proven correct: Japan has one of the lowest CEO-to-employee pay ratios in the world, with most chief executives earning just 10 times more than the average worker. (vs. **364** times more for U.S. execs). Yet, over the last thirty years, has any other country consistently produced such high-quality goods as Japan?[43]

Low Paid, High Quality, Execs

Sowell and others who put so much stock in the assessment of the "market" love to ignore the facts. The result of this lower pay for Japanese executives has been quality products, healthy profits, no huge housing or market crashes, innovation—in sum, *success*. And what is the track record for a comparable industry in the U.S., paying outlandish salaries? The nearly-bankrupt U.S. auto industry proves the absurdity of Sowell's case. In the period leading up to the economic meltdown of 2008, Japanese automakers' Top Ten executives earned less money *combined* than GM's one CEO. That's right, GM's Rick Wagoner single-handedly made more money than all of Japan's auto execs combined. And what did this high salary bring GM? Bankruptcy. Wagoner was even paid more than his American competitors in 2008: Ford's CEO Alan Mulally, Chrysler's CEO Bob Nardelli, who had slightly more success than he had. Even Mulally and Nardelli did a lousy job compared to the Japanese automakers.[44] There simply is **no** consistent correlation between high pay and high corporate performance in the longterm... and even in rare instances where such a correlation may exist, it still begs the question, "Could they have hired a CEO equally qualified for less?"

It bears repeating: **Japanese firms outperform most U.S. companies, yet pay their CEOs 70-90% less!** This fact alone completely destroys Sowell's myth that such ridiculous salaries are a necessary cost of doing business, or that "they are worth what the market pays them." Sowell endorses the *global* marketplace, but then ignores facts like this: ten times *less* pay for Japan equals success; ten times *greater* pay for U.S. automakers equals failure. If Sowell still wants to claim the free market intelligently pays people what they are worth, the universities that pay *him* need to reconsider just why they hired him to teach our children nonsense.

Paying Millions for Failure:

Because the market is blind and stupid, we should not be surprised that the market continues to pay huge sums for complete and utter incompetence. It is easy to find countless examples of **the market paying millions to failures**, like Charlie Weis of Notre Dame, who made $17 million for disastrous coaching at a championship football program; Ken Lay of Enron ('nuff said, but see Chapter 13); Dick Fuld and Angelo Mozilo who helped reduce their respective financial firms to bankruptcy while contributing to the world financial meltdown; Bernie Ebbers, who made millions while destroying WorldCom; millionaire John Akers, who managed to take the then-most prestigious, best-branded computer company and make it a footnote in the greatest computer growth era during his reign at IBM, 1985-1993; all of the CEOs at General Motors for the 20 years leading up to bankruptcy of the biggest car company in the world; Bob Nardelli, who piloted the ship as stock values sank at *two* major corporations—Home Depot and Chrysler; Tony Hayward at BP (another *'nuff said*); Dennis Kozlowski at Tyco (paid millions while losing billions)... and on and on. Washington Mutual protected its top executive's annual bonuses even while their profits slid to a $1.8 billion loss and as they canned 3,000 employees.[45] The list from Wall Street (a place where a monkey succeeds) would fill the page.

Consider Carly Fiorina at Hewlett-Packard, a poster child for failed CEOs who were still paid a fortune. Under her "leadership," a merger with Compaq was a "total flop," profits were down, stocks were down, and she laid off thousands of working class folks... but she still walked away with millions. According to the *New York Times* and *CNN*, when HP finally fired her, they offered "a severance package worth about $21.4 million, but [Fiorina] stands to reap another $21 million [in stock, pension and other benefits] after she was forced out by the computer maker's board...."[46] Yep, these CEOs are clearly genius masters-of-the-universe who *deserve* millions!

Cash for Being Famous

Another category of overpaid millionaires is Celebrity Endorsements. According to a University of California study, shareholders **lost** over $5 billion due to the PR damage caused to Tiger Wood's corporate sponsors in the wake of his scandal.[47] But even if he'd kept his nose clean, there was no evidence that his endorsement improved profits for AT&T or Buick equal to the largesse he had been paid. Remember, the key word here is *profits*, and in evaluating that, one has to factor out profitability trends (compared to other companies in the same field) that would have existed anyway, without the endorser's presence. AT&T's profits over the last five years have more to do with Apple's iPhone than Woods' ads. It is hard to imagine many people buying a cell phone, or a Buick, based on an endorsement by Tiger Woods. (If anything, little known brands have more to gain from celebrity endorsements, but big, well-known name-brand companies hire the big celebrities).

These are not just my observations. Ace Metrix studied every celebrity ad in 2010 and found that not only were most such ad campaigns of little value, one-fifth of the ads actually had a *negative* impact! When all factors are considered, even successful celebrity campaigns yield little net profit after paying for the celebrity and the campaign, and some of the more effective ads have used no-names.

Celebrity athletes almost never justify their wildly-excessive paychecks on the playing field, either. JaMarcus Russell was paid $36.4 million in his three years as an NFL quarterback at Oakland, during which time his field performance was so poor they fired him.[48] Another case of the "genius of the free market"—paying thirty-six million for failure. Giving a single person the equivalent of 100 school-teachers' salary to play a GAME is absurd; to pay that for someone to play *poorly* is beyond absurd.

Lance Says It's Dumb to Hire Lance

Are the executives who squander those mountains of cash on fame and celebrity truly benefitting their shareholders or customers, or just their own egos? Another egregious example is the U.S. Postal Service's hiring of cyclist Lance Armstrong for their ad campaign... another head-scratching example of execs making dumb choices, which then raises questions about their own fat paychecks. The USPS spent a fortune hiring Armstrong (who then had scandals of his own emerge, reminding us again that placing your corporate image in the hands, or face, of a flawed celebrity is akin to casino gambling). The head-scratcher is that not only did the USPS waste money on Lance (and my name *is* Lance, but I'm still opposed to this!), they also spent over a million dollars on media—television, magazine and radio advertising—when they could have advertised for *free*! How many companies would love to have the postal service's unique position, to be able to place a postcard into the hands of every single American at no cost!? Yet they are buying TV time!? Oh, some pencil-pusher came up with a survey that indicated an ad campaign could increase the use of express mail. But again, I challenge the USPS to show that increased *profits* (not gross sales) in those services justify the mountain of cash spent on Lance and his ubiquitous ads. By contrast, a free postcard campaign might have caused an even greater increase in sales without spending a penny (even the cost of printing the mail-outs could have been covered by selling commercial ad space on the flip side of the card.) WalMart thinks so. It regularly spends more on direct mail campaigns than on broadcast media or celebrity endorsers... even without free postage.

Monkey Business

The Postmaster General had his rationale—perhaps words like "image" and "improving customer attitudes." But most Americans would scream: "Ya wanna improve your image? Then have stamp machines that work and more than one line open at the local post office!" Once again, we see the **double-stupid-extravagance**: overpaid CEOs authorizing overpaid celebrity endorsements.

A monkey in charge would do less damage to the bottom line. And the monkey would work for less. *The Washington Times* reported that Postmaster General John Potter received a 40 percent in pay raise 2006-2009, plus a $135,000 bonus plus new perks.[49] Fox News reported: "As the U.S. Postal Service considers cutting delivery service in the face of dwindling mail volume and rising costs, the postmaster general received a big pay raise and a performance bonus... at the same time the Postal Service... is crumbling [and] when total mail volume had its largest single drop in history."[50]

ESPN reported that the U.S. Postal Service spent $31.9 million on Armstrong's ad campaign/Olympic sponsorship... yet during that same period, had the biggest postal-volume declines and financial losses in history. It is obvious that paying Postmaster Potter and Cyclist Armstrong millions for utter failure is doubly stupid.

I'm Too Stupid to Recognize Bloated Pay...

But Thomas Sowell, never afraid to expose his elitist stripes, asserts that only experts in a field can judge the smartness or fairness of salaries in that field. Such an elitist proposition: you and I can't understand clear facts about the low value of failed executives. Even a Fifth Grader could study the facts and make a fair judgement that GM's execs and the Postmaster General were not worth it!

While Sowell is happy to *teach* about topics in which he has no real world experience, he condemns you and me as too ignorant to make judgments about a CEO's worth—because we aren't experts in the field. But experts are routinely just as wrong as amateurs. With all due respect to experts: try telling 100,000 football fans, when a player catches a ball two feet out of bounds and the referee on the field declares him *in* bounds, that they cannot determine the fairness of the call just because they are not "experts on the field."

I'm not a medical "expert." I could not recommend a specific salary for a cardiologist or a proctologist (a fun argument: do we pay the cardiologist more because he saves lives, or the proctologist more because of where he has to put his fingers?). But certainly, I can tell you that a cardiologist deserves a healthy salary because of his high level of education and the hours and stresses of his job. He is literally saving lives, so I would rank him very, very high in his intrinsic worth to society. Yet many cardiologists earn about $100,000 per year, which is peanuts compared to Wall Street. Any reasonable person can see, by contrast, that **no one** who is *not* saving lives in their profession deserves $50 million a year. Yet, **Sowell's logic asserts that a Wall Street mouse-clicker is worth 100 times more than a cardiologist**... just 'cuz the market says so!

Wall Street's incompetence, failure, and accompanying excessive pay has become the poster child for economic reform. The 2007-2008 crash proves the utter failure of *laissez faire* capitalism. These multi-million-dollar salary recipients *failed*... and should have been rewarded with fines, prison, or at least firing. But a year after the dust settled from the collapse, the *Wall Street Journal* (November 2010) reported most of these same players received a record-setting $144 billion in bonuses!

The Value of Luck

A fair society would share serendipitous fortune. In ant colonies, when Little Timmy drops a Milk Dud onto the ant bed, 2% of the ants don't hoard the giant blob of sugar for themselves; the entire colony shares in the good fortune. (Yes, there is a queen in the colony, but she is not a *prima donna* lazily lounging on a throne. The ant queen is an imprisoned, highly-productive organic machine.)

Some capitalists do not even have the morals of an insect! They think if the Milk Dud landed in their proximity, they can lay claim to it at the exclusion of everyone else in the colony. Take petroleum as an example. Think of an oil field like a Milk Dud for ants: it came serendipitously to us, a big blob of "natural value" there for the taking. The ants would share it; the oil execs hog it.

For centuries since Balboa tried to claim the Pacific, no one has tried to lay claim to entire oceans. But now the petroleum industry lays claim to oceans of underground oil they did not create; they exploit it and have no qualms about huge mark-ups to the working poor who need gas to drive to work. (It is not just oil. In a later chapter, we will examine some of the business niches that afford unfair advantages to those people lucky enough to have landed in the right field at the right time. See Chapter 11.)

Unicorns, Jed Clampett, Free Markets and Other Fictions

There are more problems with Sowell's logic. He and others use the term "free market," when there is no such thing. This, too, would be thrown out in a formal debate, just as if I had claimed, "A unicorn knocked over the garbage can." Since there is no such thing as unicorns, my claim to know who knocked over the can should, again, be thrown out *a priori*.

And so should Sowell's. The mythical "free market" is just as a rare as a unicorn, certainly so these days. Even the most "open" and business-friendly markets still impose various regulations, taxes and tariffs — often favoring those who gave the most campaign donations. The system is rigged. And inconsistent. In addition to governments tilting the playing field, markets develop their own anomalous bubbles, and those who happened to be sitting on the bubble at just the right moment are carried with it. Often sheer luck is behind vast wealth more than competency.

In partnership with luck is the category of "exploitation of serendipity." Hillbilly Millionaire Jed Clampett comes to mind, "...a man named Jed, Poor mountaineer barely kept his family fed, Then one day he was shooting for some food, And up through the ground come a bubbling crude...." If oil tycoons had been born fifty years before the internal combustion engine was invented, what would they be worth? If God had not put the petroleum underground, what would BP and Exxon be worth? If government laid full claim to the reserves under the Gulf of Mexico and Alaska, and charged oil companies the *true* value of the natural resource the oil execs are exploiting, what would the profit picture be?

Before his stray bullet hit black gold, society viewed hillbilly Jed Clampett (in cold Sowellian terms) as a bum, and his rocky remote land as intrinsically worthless. Serendipity led to the exploitation of a God-given natural resource and suddenly he's "worth" millions. ("The Beverly Hillbillies" TV show was quite subversive, because it not only lampooned oil tycoons, but portrayed banker Drysdale as a sniveling parasite whose wealth came not from any real work, but from leeching off of Clampett's millions!)

The Myth of CEO Productivity

Sowell tries to validate the lofty salaries by showing statistics of how much money CEO's "make their companies," versus craftsmen and factory workers. Make, or *take*? The monetary success of a corporation proves nothing about an individual CEO's actual "worth," because first of all, Sowell can show no consistent correlation between CEO pay and company performance, and second, corporate monetary success itself is not a measure of true value—it ignores my premise that the system is funneling too much money into non-producing sectors. Do we want the whole society working at paper-shuffling, at computer-screen-manipulations of dollars and decimals? That's where we are putting our money. If CEOs and brokers are the most valuable, and if everyone strived to reach such "talented" positions, who would be left to make our products, build our houses, grow our food and clean our offices?

Speaking of productivity, over the last 40 years, worker productivity has soared. In part due to computer efficiencies, in part due to more educated and harder-working employees, the wealth brought about by that productivity never went into worker's pockets. It flowed up the pyramid to the lucky monkeys at the top.

According to *The Washington Spectator*, the income ratio of CEOs to average workers in major U.S. corporations went from about **40 to 1** in the 1970's to **475 to 1** at the end of the Nineties. *The Progressive* magazine goes further to point out that in 2007, the Top 100 corporate executives exceed workers' pay at a rate of **1,723 to 1**. The 1999 salary of General Electric's CEO Jack Welch was more than the combined wages of 15,000 of GE's Mexican workers.[51] Could Jack Welch have accumulated his millions without those 15,000 workers? No. Would those workers have still had jobs if Welch retired? He did, and they do.

The Definition of Earned

So our definition of "earned" is obsolete. It now means that one can press a few keys on a computer keyboard and manipulate the economic system so that thousands of dollars are altered, leveraged or gambled in cyberspace, then profits moved to one's bank account, without any true labor transpiring. One brokerage house ironically adopted as their slogan, "We make money the old fashioned way: we earn it." If that were true, they would make a reasonable return for their job of research and accounting, about 5% of the money handled according to "old-fashioned" standards. Old state laws once said that charging anything greater than that was usurious—in a time when bankers actually had to touch the dirty green stuff and personally tabulate it by hand and pencil. They "earned it" because **they actually did real work**. Nowadays, thanks to computers, financial institutions enable brokers to acquire fortunes with very little risk and even less real work. The greatest accumulation of wealth in this world is going to people who are not inventing, growing, producing or manufacturing... just sitting on top of the pyramid-funnel.

In a two year span, political scion Mitt Romney "made" nearly $50 million from a *blind trust*... in other words, he never lifted a finger or raised an eyebrow of stress in figuring how to manage his money, it just happened automatically—so truly, he made $50 million simply because he was already rich. The rich do get richer, and they want you to believe they do it by "working hard" and that they pay high taxes... when neither statement is true. (Romney paid only 15% in taxes, less than many middle class folk.)[52]

When the size of "reward" has absolutely no correlation to "labor," and when hard, intelligent, honest, diligent work pays pennies compared to the millions "earned" by, say, stock day traders, inheritors, ball players, drug dealers, self-congratulating celebrities and glad-handing politicians, it is time to discard the notion that they are entitled to all they can "earn."

But the Experts Agree with Sowell?

Some experts do. Many don't. Some executives and politicians agree with the premise of this book. Representative Henry Waxman used charts and stats to show Congress the absurdity of high pay for lousy performance. Using the example of Lehman Brothers' CEO Dick Fuld, the Congressman showed how Fuld was raking in millions even while "steering Lehman Brothers and our economy towards a precipice." Some in the financial industry themselves admit that the system is unfair. Leon Cooperman, a former hedge fund executive with Goldman Sachs, confessed: "I say this as a citizen: I think what is going on [in Congressional attempts to cap pay] is fair. If business looks to government to moderate... risk, then the government has the right to control... reward."[53]

Those experts who justify outlandish salaries are notably biased. Three reasons we cannot trust the objectivity of pundits/scholars:
1. These "experts" —CEOs, media pundits, and Ivy League academics like Sowell—all make huge salaries themselves, so they have an emotional need to justify their own "worth." Emotion, self-view and greed all skew their reasoning.
2. The human brain cannot truly grasp the exponential difference between $100,000 and $100 million. It's abstract. Author Malcolm Gladwell shows how most people cannot accurately estimate exponential growth. He riddles us: if you could fold a thick piece of paper "over again, and then again, and again, until you have refolded the original paper 50 times, how tall do you think the final stack is going to be?" And the answer is, it would reach to the sun! This goes against all our "gut feelings" about math and sense of proportion, but my mathematician brother can tell you that 2 to the power of 50 (2^{50}) is about 1,125,899,907,000,000. Likewise, most tycoons don't understand the exponential size of their own wealth. *Alpha Magazine* reported that the income for the top earning hedge fund manager for the year before the crash began was $1.7 billion. BILLION!
3. Human emotions and memory have a **bias for the present**. "The work I'm doing *now* seems so stressful and hard." Even bosses who had once worked at menial jobs in their youth now romanticize it. They forget the pain and difficulty of low-pay manual-labor, much like a mother forgets the labor pains of childbirth. (Someone joked that without such amnesia, we'd be an "only-child" society!)

The Amnesia-of-Hard-Work Syndrome

The CBS television show, "Undercover Boss," proves that third point about a bias for the present. The reality series took chief executives of large corporations and placed them, incognito, at entry level jobs in their own firms. Most of the bosses selected for the show had started out in life at low-paying "grunt work" but confessed that now, as an executive, they had forgotten how difficult that earlier job had been. In most cases, the CEOs struggled mentally to learn so-called "unskilled labor" jobs, struggled physically at the unpleasant working conditions, not keeping pace, resulting in their "supervisor" questioning their competency, intelligence, speed or fitness for the job. Joe DePinto, chief executive of 7-Eleven Inc., said, "We have hardworking people out there. I realized that when I was standing up all day. I was beat.... Oh, man, my knees were sore." Similarly, Rich McClure of United Van Lines admitted being "very sore" after his undercover stint: "Moving is a physically demanding job, and until you actually do it yourself for an extended period of time, you don't realize how the movers make it look so easy." The experience inspired CEO McClure to have other office workers occasionally work the front lines with the movers so they have a better understanding of "what coworkers encounter day-to-day," the *St. Louis Business Journal* reported. Time and again, when bosses, late in their career, returned to the frontlines of tedious, entry-level work, they'd end the experiment saying, "Wow, I forgot how difficult/ boring/ tedious/ demeaning that work is!" Like Fernando Aguirre, Chairman of Chiquita, who was physically unable to perform a demanding job at their factory and had to be removed from the line. He confessed: "Going undercover inside Chiquita was an eye-opening experience. [It] helped me see how I can help others...." When his turn came for *Undercover Boss*, Rick Arquilla, President and COO of Roto-Rooter, worked for a week in blue-collar, putting his hands into sewage. After a few days, he admitted, "I found out this work is a lot harder than I thought it was." One more example: Norwegian Cruise Line boss Kevin Sheehan labored aboard a ship at jobs he described as "back-breaking." The low-pay jobs "were all incredibly hard... every single task that I did...I kind of failed miserably," he told *The Miami Herald*.

Similar comments came from all executives courageous enough to take the *Undercover Boss* challenge. Again and again, this touching television show demonstrated that a company president is not some kind of "superman," as Sowell claims. Stripped of their suits and titles, the CEOs looked and performed like run-of-the-mill workers.

So two things are evident from this experiment: 1. CEOs themselves admit that low-pay jobs are harder—physically, mentally, emotionally—than they knew or remembered... harder than their own million-dollar positions. 2. CEOs may have forgotten, but when reminded, they showed their humanity and began to truly care for their employees. This gives us hope that shows like that, and books like mine, can make a difference in attitudes.

Do You Believe?

"All men are created equal." Do you believe those words? Do you believe in the intrinsic worth, the transcendent value, of every human? The deep, sad truth behind the huge inequality of pay in this world is that some people believe they are better than others. Worth more. They believe that the people who scrub toilets, run garbage trucks, and pick fruit are sub-human—significantly less valuable because they aren't as smart or don't work as hard or aren't as talented or don't have God's favor. I've known low-paid college professors who are much smarter than investment bankers; I've worked in the fields with below-minimum wage workers who toil much harder than my hard-working bank president friends; and some of the most talented folks I know are starving artists. So the pay differential cannot be explained or justified in that manner. No, the arrogant, wealthy man truly believes he is a singularity, a special case, an Übermensch. Is a doctor more valuable than a garbage-man? Not in the eyes of God. And not in the highest order of logic: if everyone on earth except one garbage-man were doctors, the garbage-man would prove extremely value. As many lives can be saved by proper sanitation than can be saved by a plastic surgeon.

"Wait!" you may protest, "Garbage-men are common. There are fewer doctors, so supply and demand makes them more valuable." Test that theory: open your telephone book and count how many doctors are listed under, "Physicians." Doctors' listings outnumber the garbage-men 10 to 1. You continue to argue: "But the doctor is saving lives." More people die at the hands of doctors than at the hands of sanitation workers! Seriously, what if the garbage-man and his wife give birth to a child who who grows up to find the cure for cancer?

A Poor Man Who Saved the World

Ever hear the story of a mild-mannered boy, raised by a midwestern farming couple, who then became a super-hero and saved the world? No, not the story of Clark Kent alias Superman, but the real-life story of Dr. Norman Borlaug, who saved the world from famine by developing and distributing agricultural breakthroughs to the Third World. Here is a Nobel Prize Winner, called the "Father of the Green Revolution," who eschewed wealth in order to make the world a better place. He was born to poor Iowan farmers, could only afford college thanks to a Depression-era government scholarship, then later turned down an offer from the DuPont chemical company to double his salary and instead took a low-paying research position in Mexico because of his passion to feed the hungry. He is widely credited with saving the lives of a billion people. Who is of greatest worth in the eyes of God: Norman Borlaug or Donald Trump? Who has been the most valuable to society?

Judging who is most worthy, or who will be most helpful to society, is risky business. It usually flies in the face of the founding principles of our country (and how ironic that many of the defenders of capitalism worship the founding fathers but never follow their example!) If you are a patriot, committed to the heritage and creeds of America, you should read the words of a document that is rivaled only by the Bible in the way it is venerated by both conservative and liberal admirers—a document written by a most-gifted man who found himself selected by Fate or Providence to change the world by helping birth a great nation. The man is Thomas Jefferson, the document is the Declaration of Independence: "We hold these truths to be self-evident... that all men are created equal." Jefferson was a singularity in one sense, and yet in another, he was just like us all: deeply flawed. No need to rehash his many foibles, except to say that he was not a feminist, and he had no notion of gender-inclusive language. When he wrote those words about equality he used the word "men" as it was commonly used in his day: a genderless, universal term for humanity. He truly meant, in that moment, that all humans are created equal. That lone sentence, that proud portion of transcendent prose, sits as the firm foundation for everything good and noble the United States of America has ever achieved. Those words empowered the band of refugees who had once clawed their way onto American soil—ennobling and enabling that peasant rabble to rise up against a tyrant. England's King George believed he was of a superior race, the race of royalty ordained by God. Jefferson's words—freighted with a force higher than kings, a force higher even than ordination—contain the very heart of God, a God who created "male and female in the image of God," a God who came to "draw ALL people to myself."

All Created Equal
"All men are created equal." These "self-evident truths" are what buttressed Lincoln in his bloody fight to free the slaves. These words of equality energized the Allies at Normandy to storm against Hilter's Stormtroopers, who followed the false gospel of a super-race. Jefferson's holy writ emboldened Rosa Parks to take a stand, by sitting, against American apartheid, just as Mandela and Tutu would later stand against the South African version—all echoing the words of a slave-owning white American, Thomas Jefferson. Because these were not words just from a white man, these are words from the Creator. Once the New World Moses came down from Virginia with that Declaration—words later carved in stone but at the outset reflecting the very fire of God—this self-evident phrase of human worth and equality has changed the world for the better.

I challenge you to let those same words burn in your heart, like the refiner's fire, to peel away your prejudices, that you might see with searing seer's vision through the fog of selfishness and self-deluded elitism. Open your eyes, your heart, to this simple but elusive truth: you are not intrinsically better than a steelworker in Birmingham or a basketweaver in Botswana. You do not deserve to make one thousand times the wage that another working human makes. You are not that good. You are not that clever or skilled. You are not that holy or perfect or divinely blessed. You are human. You are equal.

You may work five times harder than me... and thus deserve five times the pay. You may benefit society in ways that are worth ten times what I shall offer society. But the number of your greatness is not a thousand or ten thousand. Norman Borlaugh saved a billion people, but the only large "paycheck" he ever got was the Nobel Prize money, part of which he donated to charity. If Alexander Fleming—underpaid as he was—had failed to discover penicillin, some other wise researcher would have eventually done so. If Thomas Edison had not tamed electricity, Nikola Tesla would. If Einstein had died as a child, Enrico Fermi and his cohorts still would have fathomed the mysteries of the atom. And each of these amazing people who made tremendous advancements for society were, all put together, paid less in their entire collective lifetimes than one mediocre broker at Goldman-Sachs. And you wish to defend that system as ethical? As children starve, you want to come at me with some flimsy argument about free-markets and invisible hands? God laughs at you. You'd best hope the true Master of the Universe is in a jovial mood and finds your self-delusion humorous... rather than a revolting stench in the nostrils of an angry God.

This is Real Life: Thomas, meet Mona

Mona is a smart, kind, gorgeous young woman of the highest integrity and with an engaging personality. With a bit of better luck, it would not surprise me that later in life she might become one of those who moves up the economic ladder to, ironically, "prove" Sowell's point about economic mobility and opportunity. Will that retroactively soothe her and her family in their current hell? Here is her situation: she married young and her husband was a successful builder and master carpenter, so they chose to have children before Mona completed college. They worked day jobs, took care of their children, and spent nights and weekends building their own home. But then the husband was injured. Workman's Comp insurance paid only a fraction of his former paycheck. Then Mona's job at a bank was eliminated due to a corporate merger. The merger made some executives at the top of the firm very rich. But at the bottom, the displacement was the feather that broke the camel's back for Mona and her family. They could no longer make the mortgage payment on their home. During the recession of 2008-2009, the burst housing bubble meant they could not sell their home—despite its considerable equity as a result of the earlier work her carpenter-husband. With government bail-out cash going quickly to General

Motors and AIG and Lehman Brothers but slowly to homeowners, Mona's family found themselves homeless. They moved in with grandma and grandpa. Mona had to look for additional income. In the area they lived, jobs were scarce and low-paying. They had done many of the things that Mr. Sowell expects the lower classes should do to improve their lot in life: worked 60 hours a week, sought better opportunities *while* doing that work, built their own home, then later downscaled. What they were not willing to do, understandably, was uproot their children to move out-of-state, away from extended family, for a better-paying job. So, yes, perhaps the opportunity existed *somewhere* in America for Mona to better herself, but at the price of damaging their family, leaving grandma and grandpa behind, and, of course, taking the risk of borrowing money to facilitate such a move. Even if Mona had done so, she had two children starting college. A move to another state would have thus disqualified her children, for two years, for in-state tuition discounts. Mona made the only choice she could for the good of her family: she continued to toil away every waking hour of her life for minimum wage, including a second job at Walmart.

Mr. Sowell, quoting statistics does not bring one ounce of joy or relief to Mona. Neither your jiggered statistics nor any of your weak syllogisms will change the fact that the Sam Walton family makes billions and live in multiple mansions in large part because they pay honest, hardworking employees like Mona less than a living wage!

Sowell absurdly claims that the rich do not gain their wealth at the expense of the poor. But how could the facts be any plainer? If the Waltons did not hoard as much, they could pay their workers more. Where does Sowell think profit comes from? Martians? No, it comes from the low overhead made possible by Mona, combined with millions of Monas buying Walmart's profit-margin-added products.

Monas of the World

Indeed, consider the plight of other WalMart workers worldwide, those who build the products that the Waltons then pass to us at a profit. The Chinese *Zhifeng Hardware* factory makes kitchenware for WalMart. Employees (i.e. slaves) there work seven days a week, over 80 hours a week, leaving just enough off-time for eating and sleeping. They have no social or recreational life. The base wage is 54 cents an hour, which barely covers their food and rent, so there is no way to ever get ahead. Or consider the scores of young women at *Classic Fashion* in Sri Lanka, sewing clothing for WalMart and Hanes. Some suffered routine sexual abuse and repeated rapes, and in some cases even torture. A *Classic* factory in Jordan had standard shifts of 13 hours a day, six and seven days a week. According to witness testimonies, workers were paid 61 cents an hour, cursed at, hit and sexually abused. They lived in primitive dorms lacking heat or hot water, infested with bugs. The low wages, limited mobility and list of stern rules makes the employees *de facto* slaves. One Third World worker summed it up: "I have no life... only work."[54]

Humans, Not Statistics

Those real-life human stories render Sowell's statistics moot. The fact that some other Mona might have been lucky and found a great-paying job, the fact that one in a million Chinese do become entrepreneurial tycoons, is irrelevant to the greater truth that most humans on this earth toil miserably at unpleasant jobs and do not enjoy the freedom of choice and mobility that Sowell suggests. Sowell expends much time placing blame on the individual's choices, such as locale, but what if every "Mona" chose to leave Alabama and Montana and Kansas—to descend upon whatever state *du jour* was momentarily booming with higher paying jobs? We'd see massive social problems, not to mention the economic collapse of rural states. What if every parent chose to put economic ambition ahead of quality of life for their children? Evidently for Sowell and his ilk, it is more important to have "free markets" than **free humans** allowed to make free choices of geography and family life.

Summary

In his books and newspaper columns, Thomas Sowell's defense of the ultra-rich has reeked of arrogance and elitism. In response to critics who question paying chief executives a wage 400 times that of average workers, Sowell's argument is that the poor and middle class are too stupid to understand the value of high-paid executives. In his own words, we "don't have a clue."

Sowell misses the irony in this—he might as well opine, *Stay on the plantation, boy, and don't question the master's wisdom.* He expects us to believe that CEOs possess arcane knowledge beyond our ability to even discuss. I do understand this much: hard-working employees must work an entire year to earn what a boss makes in a day. Should we bow at the intelligence of Donald Trump, or the fired-but-overpaid CEOs listed above?

Surprise, Mr. Sowell, but there are people with an IQ like yours that have a completely different view of capitalism. The core tenet of capitalism is sound: *money motivates*. But why does it take $200 million to motivate a CEO... and only $30,000 to energize an assembly-line worker? Are "market forces" and supply/demand actually creating a bidding war for a tiny super-race of corporate geniuses? Or isn't it more likely that the wealthy have established political and corporate systems that reward themselves?

According to CNNMoney.com, chief executives at the largest companies earned an average of $11.4 million in total pay (in the year 2010). That's **343 times more**, year after year, than a typical American worker, according to the AFL-CIO President Richard Trumka, who added, "Despite the collapse of the financial market at the hands of executives less than three years ago, the disparity between CEO and workers' pay has continued to grow to levels that are simply stunning." The AFL-CIO examined executive salaries at 299 firms traded on the S&P 500. Their compensation was up 23% in 2010, compared to 2009—this during a time of high unemployment and most workers feeling lucky to even get a 3% cost-of-living raise. Yet high executive pay has in no way guaranteed corporate success.

The proof in the pudding is when we take executives and place them in entry-level or menial-labor positions in their own companies, as the TV series we mentioned did. Then the CEOs began to admit that they had forgotten how difficult life is for the average worker. Once the bosses became intimately involved in the lives of their underpaid, over-worked employees, almost all of them showed great compassion. Most executives are not bad people. They have a heart. But they do need their ethics challenged, they do need to walk in the shoes of the underclass.

A new law (Wall Street Reform Bill of 2010) requiring publicly traded companies to disclose the ratio of CEO pay to the median pay of all company employees has yet to be implemented—and Republicans like Nan Hayworth fought to repeal the disclosure rule, calling it "burdensome." Telling the truth seems burdensome for politicians and rich CEO's.

We will see change only when truth is spoken, and when the wealthy begin to understand the hardships wrought by their resource-hoarding. Some improvements to social justice certainly require governmental laws and guidelines. But radical social change comes about by changing hearts and minds.

Which brings up the topic of religion.

~~~

Chapter 5: Is God a Socialist?
Part A: What Jesus really said
Part B: What other religions teach

[S]trange that any men should dare to ask a just God's assistance in wringing their bread from the sweat of other men's faces.
~Abraham Lincoln

An Entertaining Wrestling Match

If you are not a spiritual person, you may be tempted to skip this chapter. Don't. Even atheists should find it entertaining as I attack the economic politics of right-wing Christianity—especially since I am a Bible-believing preacher from south Alabama! And this chapter is of value even to those with no faith background or who doubt a sovereign God exists because, like it or not, **religion is the root of all social ethics**. Across millennia, religious sages have spent lifetimes in deep thought about social mores, fairness, economic justice—how we might best treat one another. Belief in God is not a prerequisite for finding value in the ancient wisdom and tradition of Scripture.

The Christian rightwing believes **God loves capitalism and hates taxes**. But what if the Bible—their Bible—says the exact opposite of what Reagan-Bush-Bachman-Perry Christians claim? Despite venerating Scripture and Tradition, the self-proclaimed Bible literalists ignore the very verses they so trust. Hypocritically, they disregard what **every major religion teaches:**
1) **The importance of tending to the poor.**
2) **The evil of great wealth and the danger of greed.** Some will concede these two points, yet still deny that *government* should be involved—claiming that alms for the poor should be voluntarily offered, not governmentally-imposed. So I will show a third teaching from scripture and religious tradition:
3) **While God prefers that individuals make a free choice to be generous, when that fails, God clearly endorses governmental intervention to help the poor.** Most ancient religions expected their kings and leaders to enforce justice for all, to aid the poor, and to limit the powers of evil. The Bible even supports coerced redistribution, as we shall see.

Since my expertise is in Christianity, allow me to turn first to the teachings of Jesus Christ. Later in this chapter (Part B) we will examine teachings from Judaism, Islam, and Eastern religions.

Part A: What Did Jesus Say? (WDJS)

In his book, *The War On Success*, Tommy Newberry presents a typical conservative-Christian view: *Socialism is evil, free-market capitalism is good, and God says so!* Rightwing Christians are quick to assert "this I know because the Bible says it's so." Newberry and his allies fail to read their Bible with open minds. They live with a fantasy-Jesus made in their own image, ignoring his actual words and deeds. Setting aside the fact that Newberry glosses over the vast difference between democratic, free-market Socialism vs. Marxist Communism, he is dead wrong about what the Bible says and means. Like most fundamentalist Christians, he uses the Bible selectively to make blanket statements with god-like authority.

I am just as arrogant in believing I know Scripture and rightly interpret God's Word. So briefly, my credentials: yes, I was trained in the "liberal" but prestigious Emory University seminary. Before Newberry brands and dismisses me, let me add: I was also raised in the theologically-conservative South, and my own father was a minister educated at the *conservative* Asbury seminary in Kentucky. I have a deep respect for Scripture, and unlike some Liberals, I don't play loose with words or twist phrases out of context. I respect Scripture. You can judge my bias—but read the verses first.

Name-calling

Newberry is strikingly unChristian and judgmental in his attack against "Liberals," calling them *evil*. He doesn't just disagree with those who view Scripture differently, he calls them names. I can be just as childish and say, "He started it!" as I accuse him of greed! He has first accused me of petty jealousy with a chapter in his book entitled, "Envy: The Real Opiate of the Masses." Sorry, Newberry, of all the less-than-rich folks I know, few spend more than a moment envying your Porsche... they are too busy worrying about paying their bills.

In resorting to *ad hominem* attacks, Newberry weakens his Christian character—and the strength of his argument. Instead of reading the Bible rationally and open-mindedly, he employs hyperbole, unproved assertion, and emotional fear-mongering.

Is Socialism Stealing?

Ironically, Newberry-the-Christian cites very little actual Scripture. Even when he quotes it, he grossly misuses it. First, he misinterprets the Ten Commandments' "Thou Shalt Not Steal" as a prohibition of taxation. It is a false equivalency nowhere found in Scripture. He writes: "The Bible is about giving... there is no mention of stealing, expropriating, or redistributing of any sort."[55] Just what Bible are you reading, Mr. Newberry? The Jewish religion imposed taxes! But more surprisingly, we will see how ancient Judaism even endorsed *plundering* (see Part B) and re-distributing when necessary to bring economic justice. As a Jew himself, Jesus knew this history.

Jesus and a Parable of Re-Distribution

In the New Testament, Jesus took a little boy's lunch and redistributed it among the crowd so that everyone could eat. Conservatives retort: "The boy *volunteered* his lunch and Jesus added a miraculous multiplying." True... though we might ask how "voluntary" it is to have a grown, burly fisherman standing over a small boy's lunch box, asking for it! Read the accounts in John 6:5-11 and Mark 6:35-44. Putting the accounts together, we see that the disciples had no food, but Jesus told them in Mark 6:38 to "go and see" how much bread they might find among the crowd. He was, in fact, asking his disciples to go into the crowd to look for food, which he then shared with those who had none (although he had to miraculously amplify the amount, as only one small boy had packed a lunch). The majority of the crowd were either too poor or too lazy or (most likely) too short-sighted to bring lunches. But none of that matters to Jesus. He simply had compassion for the hungry, viewed it as a communal problem, and his solution was not to call down manna from heaven, but to invite those who have plenty to share with those who have nothing.

Some may still protest, pointing out that Jesus miraculously created extra bread and fish. But that begs the question. If Jesus had the supernatural power to create baskets of food out of thin air (as the Bible asserts), why, then, did he even bother with confiscating the boy's lunch in the first place? Clearly, **Jesus used this as a "teachable moment,"** partly to show his ability to perform miracles, but also to show that humans (in this case, a little boy) can work synergistically with God to **meet the needs of a community.** By example, he was teaching the very principle of **re-distribution** that Newberry so abhors!

The Acts of the Communists

This is not an isolated event. Jesus and his disciples kept a single, common treasury. He was practicing a form of communism even amongst his own "commune" of followers. Never did Jesus say, "Okay, Peter and James worked extra hard this week, so pay them a bonus." (Instead, Jesus told a parable in which the workers were all paid the same regardless of the hours they worked.) Jesus said, "Give to anyone who asks of you...." There was no footnote adding, "...except the government."

The final proof that Jesus rejected capitalism is what happened after he left and his followers became leaders in the budding new church: they immediately established a commune-like system. In the Book of Acts (2:44-45), we find this striking account: "All the believers were together and had everything in common. They sold [their] property and possessions to give to anyone who had need."

The only rebuttal Newberry and defenders of Midas-like hoarding can fall back on is that these early churchmen were "voluntary socialists." And yet, in the very same book of Acts where the Christian church begins as a socialist enterprise, a wealthy couple was struck dead for lying about withholding money from the "socialist church." I suspect that didn't make other members think of generosity as an optional whim, after they witnessed the two dead bodies dragged from the room! While the Bible does teach that God *prefers* "a cheerful giver," it does *not* therefore follow that God is opposed to government helping the underprivileged. God allows us free will as individuals, but nowhere does the Bible teach that obeying government is optional or that government should not be less ethical or compassionate than the church; to the contrary, the Hebrew government *forced* people to tithe and to pay taxes. Yet Rightwing Christians seem intent on having government dictate ethics in every other category... except money/greed. Think about it: the Bible teaches that we should abstain from murder via the motivation of a loving heart. But the Bible does **not** then say, "If you *don't* have a loving heart, government shouldn't *force* you to abstain from murder." Absurd. No, just as in Bible times, today we have laws for the good of society that do indeed **force people to do what is morally right**. That's what law is. Christian teachings are clear in expecting government to be involved in economic justice, to enforce the ethic of protecting citizenry from gross abuses of economic exploitation.

Glen Beck Rejects Saint Luke

Speaking of "socialist" churches: FOX News host Glen Beck once held up pictures of a swastika and a hammer and sickle, warning that "liberal" churches who preach "social justice" are using code words for Nazism and communism![56] Apparently Beck never read the Gospels. Consider the passage in Luke 11:37-51. A group of fundamentalist, judgmental leaders known as "Glen Becks" ...oops, sorry, known as "the Pharisees"... attacked and harassed Jesus, criticizing him for breaking a tiny detail of the Mosaic Law. They railed against Jesus for eating with unwashed hands. Jesus answered the critics in a surprising way: "You Pharisees clean the outside of the cup and dish, but inside you are full of greed and wickedness.... But give... to the poor and everything will be clean for you...."

In all the gospel accounts, Jesus proclaimed that the highest priority for a Christian is to have compassion for "the least of these," which included the poor, the infirmed, the stranger, the foreigner, the child. This is consistent with the emphasis of the entire Bible. He also spoke in the broadest terms of corporate responsibility: sins are not merely individual, but collective as a society. Jesus concluded this section in Luke by saying, "I tell you, this generation [this whole society] will be held responsible for it all." A far cry from the way Beck and Newberry wish to make charity an individual whim rather than a societal responsibility.

Parables the Rich Never Read

Jesus taught using stories or parables—more than merely using pithy quotes—so let us examine one. *The Parable of the Rich Man and the Beggar* is one of the most powerful warnings found in literature. Yet many Christians ignore this parable's admonition. It deserves a closer look. From **Luke 16:19-28**:

"There was a rich man who was dressed in purple and fine linen and lived in luxury every day. At his gate was laid a beggar named Lazarus, covered with sores and longing to eat what fell from the rich man's table.... [W]hen the beggar died, the angels carried him to Abraham's side [in heaven]. The rich man also died and was buried. In hell, where he was in torment, he looked up and saw Abraham far away, with Lazarus by his side. So he called to him, 'Father Abraham, have pity on me and send Lazarus to dip the tip of his finger in water and cool my tongue, because I am in agony in this fire.' But Abraham replied, 'Son, remember that in your lifetime you received your good things, while Lazarus received bad things, but now he is comforted here and you are in agony....' [The rich man] answered, 'Then I beg you, father, send Lazarus to my... five brothers. Let him warn them, so that they will not also come to this place of torment.'"

What is the warning the rich man wishes to send to his brothers from beyond the grave? *Be more generous to the poor!* Jesus rarely spoke of hellfire, but when he did, the chief reason he cited for such punishment is greed, wealth and a failure to care for the poor and the needy. Funny, he never warned against socialism!

Jesus' Three-Point Sermon

The parable offers a strong, clear caution: Ignore the poor and risk losing heaven. Look closely at the story. Jesus describes three "classes" of people:

1. An Unfeeling Rich Class: A privileged class of ultra-wealthy, the rich man and his brothers are only concerned about themselves and their kind. They are unrepentant of mistreating the poor.

2. An Underclass of Poor and Unhealthy: The suffering poor whose main concern is survival in a harsh world, as represented by Lazarus, whose illness has him stuck in poverty.

3. The Caring and Generous of Both Classes: Jesus does not condemn all rich/successful people... Abraham, the wealthy patriarch, received God's heavenly blessing, along with Lazarus.

But Jesus clearly portrays the first class, Category 1, as the villains of his moral lesson. The rich man feigned piety and religious zeal, but ignored the sufferings of Lazarus. The respected conservative Bible commentator, William Barclay, says of this passage: "The [rich] man's whole attitude is the very reverse of Christianity."

The callous nature of some of the über-rich is astounding—then and now. "Christian" Newberry cannot see this parable for what it is, and becomes an apologist for Category 1 when he writes: "Success spills over to benefit many more people.... It is God's way of sharing abundance. No redistribution is required." Newberry has just described himself in exactly the same terms that Jesus described the evil rich man, whose crumbs "spill over" onto the floor for Lazarus to pick up. This is the Reagan trickle-down system, which even George Bush the Elder dismissed as "voodoo economics."

But Should Government Be Charitable?

Beck, Newberry and Rush Limbaugh would counter that this passage is only encouraging private philanthropy, that here Jesus only encourages the personal virtue of voluntary wealth sharing. Again: the threat of hellfire does not seem particularly voluntary! And there are clues in the parable that Jesus expects all of society to assume responsibility for the poor. Look again at the account: "At his gate was **laid** a beggar named Lazarus...." Lazarus could not walk: so he was carried to the rich man's gate by other people. The community did not have the resources to help him, so they entrusted him to the wealthiest among them.

Jesus' parable, told to a large crowd, is more than an individualistic appeal for private conversion. He chose his words carefully, each word laden with purpose: "At his gate was laid a beggar," makes this a story about communal responsibility. And indeed, when you consider the whole of Jesus' teaching and the context of the Old Testament, of which Jesus was an expert, we find a clear expectation that the greater society should take responsibility for the poor. Jesus did not chide those who laid the beggar at the gate; he only chided the rich man in the gated mansion. An uncomfortable truth that the comfortable ignore.

Is Taxation Stealing?

Tommy Newberry rants against progressive taxation and socialism, calling it "theft." If taxation were stealing, why did Jesus pay his taxes? He paid taxes to the Jewish (theocratic) government *and* the Roman (secular) government. Jesus paid the Jewish temple tax and famously said, when asked of Roman taxes, "Give unto

Caesar what is Caesar's." Note that when the Jews and Romans were trying to trump up charges against him, tax evasion was *not* one of the charges.

Taxes are not "taking" or "stealing," as Newberry claims; taxes are the price of living together on the planet, and we *all* benefit from taxation. The wealthier a person is, the more they benefit from things government provides: infrastructure, transportation and security (military/police). So it is a false argument when Newberry calls progressive taxation "stealing." If anything, if you don't pay your share of taxes, you are stealing when you get a state education or travel on the highway or airport that taxes purchased.

And to further refute Newberry's argument, in the section on Judaism we will point out verses where God even endorses stealing (plunder) for the sake of economic justice! But first, an aside.

The Boogaman: Karl Marx

Let me digress a moment: we cannot allow Newberry to set up a straw man: **communism**. I'm not arguing for communism. It doesn't work. Communism has not created a utopian society, does not provide economic justice, does not foster productivity. I support the concepts of profit incentive, pride in property ownership, healthy competition… and the Bible supports these elements of capitalism, too—when they aid production, innovation and the common good.

But there are limits. The Bible does not give capitalism *carte blanche*. Scripture does not endorse excessive profits, usury, hoarding nor unlimited claims to private land ownership. The Bible asserts that God owns the land. In Psalm 50:12, the Lord states, "… for the world is mine, and all that is in it." In the Old Testament, God gave the Israelites *limited* ownership, more properly called "stewardship," of a small bit of land for private use, and other land to be owned communally. The poor were to be allowed access even to "private" farmland, for gleaning. Those who treat vast tracts of land as their gated, private playground had best not seek justification for it in Holy Scripture.

Newberry rails against the evils of socialism and communism as if they were synonymous. Why does Newberry set up the straw man of communism? So that in knocking it down, he can claim the Bible endorses the other extreme: **selfish individualism**. Newberry's worldview is the opposite of a true Christian outlook: he sees social cooperation as demonic, and individualism as a virtue! He boasts of a "divine spark within each of us" that is activated by "individualism, and the competitive spirit."[57] Then Newberry adds: "Do we want to be part of a group-based, socialist America, or do we want to be part of an individual-based, self-reliant America? Do we want to be secure in our group affiliation, or free to soar as individuals?"[58] **This is not gospel, this is Antichrist.**

That's right: such enshrining of the individual is **not** a philosophy approved by Scripture. In fact, traditional Christianity views such prideful "soaring" of the individual as a Satanic trait! Isaiah 14:13 is read by conservatives as a speech chiding Lucifer for his pride: "You said in your heart, 'I will ascend to the heavens; I will raise my throne above the stars....'" The flawed ethic of "soaring individualism" perpetrated by hyper-religious capitalists is soundly condemned by their own Bible. Ironic.

Jesus: Bootstrap Individualism or Group-Based Socialism?

Jesus preached the opposite of prideful individualism: he calls us to selfless sharing, and his ministry was "group-based." Even when, once for a brief mission, he divided his disciples up, he still sent them out in pairs, not individually.

Jesus sees wealth as an opportunity to bolster relationships: "Use worldly wealth to gain friends for yourselves...." (Luke 16:9) And we've already mentioned the "socialism" in Acts 2: "All the believers were together and had everything in common." The entire Christian movement lived out the opposite of Newberry's philosophy of "individualism and competitive spirit." If Republicans were honest, they'd be worshipping Ayn Rand, not Jesus Christ!

Ayn Rand in a Blender with the Christian Right

Republicans have indeed embraced Ayn Rand's philosophy of selfish, individualistic greed.[59] They've taken her godless ethic and put it in a blender with the Bible. "Christian" Congressman Paul Ryan, a darling of the Right, stated: "The reason I got involved in public service, by and large, if I had to credit one thinker, one person, it would be Ayn Rand."[60] Ayn Rand's writings are clearly incompatible with Christianity, yet TEA Party Christians are enamored with Rand Paul—named after Ayn Rand—and Paul Ryan. (Credit Charles Colson for publicly chastising his fellow conservatives, stating that Ayn Rand's Objectivist philosophy is the "antithesis of Christianity" and that her followers are "undermining the Gospel.") In 2005, Ryan invoked (and cited) Ayn Rand's writings when he told an audience, "Almost every fight we are involved in here on Capitol Hill... comes down to one conflict: individualism versus collectivism." Ryan, like Newberry, sides with the wealthy, successful "individual" against the less fortunate "collective" rest of society—with the one notable exception of favoring corporations over individuals.

Blend in Some Tea

Joseph Farah, founder of the conservative *WorldNetDaily.com*, stated the following in an article about the right-wing TEA Party:

"When Jesus talks about clothing the naked, feeding the hungry, he's talking to us as individuals." The Bible, he claims, does not "suggest that government is the institution" that should "help the poor...."[61]

Mr. Farah, how do you know Jesus was just "talking to us as individuals"? You and I weren't there when Jesus gave that strong warning that those who fail to feed the poor are going to hell. All we can do is look at the text and the context. In the very passage Farah cites, Jesus was speaking to a **group** of his followers (Matthew 24:3), not one-on-one, and in the story he then tells of the King bringing judgment, the King also speaks in **plural**—again to a group—using the words, "those" and "them," (Matthew 25:34&40) and *sentences* **them as a group** (two groups, actually: those who are blessed, who fed the hungry, and those who are cursed for being stingy and uncaring). Of course Jesus, at times, spoke to individuals and asked for individual hearts to change. But when it comes to social and economic justice, Jesus made no statement to the effect that this was to be personal behavior only, or that government is not to be involved—Farah is putting words in Jesus' mouth, found nowhere in the text or the context.

Jesus usually taught within the Temple or synagogues, to large crowds and even to political leaders. Jesus was rarely just "talking to us as individuals." His society was ruled by Scriptural laws that clearly and emphatically demanded the nation take care of the poor. The religious law of Jesus' day, including its requirement for social programs, was not voluntary, it was mandatory. Whenever the prophets spoke of justice, they were addressing the government leaders, as in Micah 3:9-11: "Hear this, you leaders of the house of Jacob, you rulers who despise justice [and who] judge for a bribe... you lean upon the Lord and say, 'Is not the Lord among us?'"

Myth of the Solitary Christian

Jesus, and Paul, did speak a great deal about God's "kingdom" and "church," using the word *ekklesia*, a Greek word which means "gathering" —a group-based affiliation, not a cult of individualism. Indeed, the central doctrine of the Christian church is the need for sacrifice of the individual for the betterment of the kingdom. In Mark 8:34, Jesus said, "Whoever wants to be my disciple must deny themselves... for whoever wants to save their life will lose it...." And Paul adds in 2nd Corinthians 8:14-15 an encouragement to communal giving: "Your plenty will supply what they need..." so that "he who gathered much did not have too much, and he who gathered little did not have too little." Ayn Rand be damned.

As long as the whims of the **individual** (under the guise of liberty) are enshrined above the needs of **the many**, we will have a society where the fortunate few live in opulence and children starve.

In Judeo-Christian tradition, sin entered the world when Satan told a lie: *that an individual could stand alone and grasp the power and knowledge to make oneself a god*. The root of the problem for Newberry, Ryan, Farah and their ilk is that they have bought into the lie that "soaring success" comes by solitary achievement. **How can someone become wealthy by their own efforts alone?**

Bill Gates stands on the shoulders of others who invented the integrated circuit, the computer, programming languages, and even operating systems that pre-dated MS-DOS. Multi-millionaire Fred Smith, war hero and founder of FedEx, started with a four million dollar inheritance, and would admit that FedEx would not be possible without government infrastructure—the airports and highways which our tax dollars paid for. As a writer, I work mostly alone. But I could not sell my books without a distribution system. I use the government-designed/built postal system and the internet to market and sell my product—and the internet was developed thanks to government-sponsored programs. And my writing skills were taught to me by wonderful public school teachers, paid for by, you guessed it, the "evil government"! Success is communal.

Government in the Bedroom but Not the Wallet

A major intellectual inconsistency for the Christian Rightwing: they demand government control of the bedroom, but not the purse. They insist on government enforcing a conservative morality regarding sexuality, abortion, gambling and other issues... but they want *no* imposed ethics regarding economic justice. Former House Speaker Newt Gingrich writes in *Rediscovering God in America:* "There is no attack on American culture more destructive and more historically dishonest than the relentless effort to drive God out of America's public square." Without recounting the immense moral flaws in Gingrich's own personal history, we point out the other hypocrisy here: Newt wants religion in government, "in the public square," for his political purposes, with one glaring exception: he wants to exclude God from social justice!

Blind Spot

Some years ago, evangelical author Dr. James Dobson produced a "Christian" political pamphlet outlining what he perceived as the biggest threats to the American family, entitled "Nine Key Issues that Will Shape Our Future." His list begged for a Tenth Key, but economic justice, poverty and the erosion of real wages were nowhere to be found on his list! Dobson could name nine dangers to the American family, like "homosexual marriage" and pornography, but poverty, greed and economic justice didn't register on his concern meter at all. **There is a giant blind spot in the eyes of the**

Christian Right—especially among leaders with comfortable upper class lifestyles. They have become the Christian Wrong.

Newberry is quite convinced that one cannot be both a Progressive Socialist and a Christian; I am convinced that it is harder to be a free-market, hands-off capitalist and be a Christian! As difficult as passing a camel through the eye of a needle. Speaking of which....

Another Watered-down Teaching

The best example of how eyes are blind to the Bible's warnings about wealth is the *camel and needle* metaphor, prompted by Jesus' encounter with "the rich young ruler." From **Luke 18:8-25**:

"A certain ruler asked him, 'Good teacher, what must I do to inherit eternal life?'" Then the rich man claimed to have fulfilled all the moral commandments, so Jesus challenged his perfectionism by adding, "You still lack one thing. Sell everything you have and give to the poor...." The man became sad "because he was very wealthy." Jesus concluded, "How hard it is for the rich to enter the kingdom of God! Indeed, it is easier for a camel to go through the eye of a needle than for someone who is rich to enter the kingdom of God."

Wealthy folk, troubled by this dire warning, had to find a way around it. Many have since latched upon a single ninth-century commentary which claimed there was a smaller "night gate" in Jerusalem's wall, called the Needle's Eye, for pedestrians to pass through when the main gates were closed—and that a camel could get through this "Eye" on its knees if stripped of its cargo. A pleasant thought that lets the wealthy believe, "Okay, it will be hard to get into heaven as a rich man, but I can do it!" Problem is, there's no archaeological or historical evidence for the existence of such a gate so named! Most good Bible commentaries point this out.[62]

You don't need archaeology or commentaries to see the problem with such an interpretation. Look to the Scripture itself: the disciples responded to Jesus statement by saying, "Then who can be saved?" And Jesus answered: "By human power, it is impossible, but with God, anything is possible." If Jesus had intended some cutesy story about camels making it through a small gate, he would not have said "It is impossible." The disciples, too, saw it as impossible (if such a gate existed, their reaction would have been different). Jesus meant putting a camel through the eye of an actual, tiny knitting needle!

Read the passage carefully. It becomes obvious that Jesus warned the rich man that being wealthy and self-righteous—while others starve—makes it all but impossible (except by God's miraculous grace) to win God's approval. Many preachers and commentators have overlooked the word "impossible" and used the "camel escape clause," refusing to accept Jesus' hard teachings on wealth.

More of What Jesus ACTUALLY Said
If the verses and parables above were not enough, I have more. The refuge for those who encounter a Bible passage that challenges their politics is to say, "You took that verse out of context." But when you find a *hundred* verses that all give the same message, they collectively *become* the context.

What does it mean to "take a verse out of context"? It does not refer to the practice of citing single verses for reference—that is a necessary method of Bible study and discussion, to focus on a particular verse. "Out of context" means that the verse quoted, when standing alone, presents a false or different meaning than the entire paragraph from whence it was extracted. Read these verses in their larger contexts... the meaning is unchanged. The sheer volume of teachings against greed and advocating care for the less fortunate **together create a *collective context* proving my thesis.**

Below are yet more Scriptures, beginning with words of Jesus:[63]
•**Matthew 6:19 & 21:** "Do not store up for yourselves treasures on earth... for where your treasure is, there your heart will be also."
•**Matthew 25:35-41:** "I was hungry, and you gave me no meat; I was thirsty, and you gave me no drink... Naked and you clothed me not.... [So] go away into everlasting punishment." •**Luke 12:15:** "Watch out! Be on your guard against all kinds of greed; a man's life does not consist in the abundance of his possessions." •**Luke 16:13:** "You cannot serve both God and money." •**Luke 4:18:** Jesus announced His ministry by quoting the prophet Isaiah, saying: "The Spirit of the Lord is upon me, because he has anointed me to bring good news to the poor." •**Luke 12:33:** "Sell your possessions and give to the poor. Provide purses for yourselves that will not wear out, a treasure in heaven that will not be exhausted, where no thief comes near and no moth destroys." •**Mark 10:23:** "How hard it is for the rich to enter the kingdom of God!" •**Matthew 16:26:** "What will it profit a man if he gains the whole world but forfeits his life?" •**Matthew 19:21:** "Jesus answered, "If you want to be perfect, go, sell your possessions and give to the poor, and you will have treasure in heaven. Then come, follow me.""

Yet More Scriptural Evidence
In addition to the words of Jesus, the rest of the Bible also is filled with warnings about greed, and teachings on economics and generosity. (And there are many more Old Testament verses listed in the next section on Judaism):
•**James 2:6:** "But you have insulted the poor. Is it not the rich who are exploiting you?" •**Proverbs 29:7:** "The righteous care about justice for the poor, but the wicked have no such concern."
•**Galatians 2:10:** "All they asked was that we should continue to

remember the poor, the very thing I was eager to do." •**Proverbs 14:31:** "He who oppresses the poor shows contempt for their Maker, but whoever is kind to the needy honors God." •**Revelation 3:17:** "You say, `I am rich; I have acquired wealth and do not need a thing.' But you do not realize that you are wretched, pitiful, poor, blind and naked." •**1st Timothy 6:9-10:** "People who want to get rich fall into temptation and a trap and into many foolish and harmful desires that plunge men into ruin and destruction. For the love of money is a root of all kinds of evil." •**Leviticus 25:23&35:** "'The land shall not be sold forever, for the land is mine," saith the Lord.... "If one of your countrymen becomes poor and is unable to support himself among you, help him as you would an alien or a temporary resident, so that he can... live...."'" •**Hebrews 13:5:** "Keep your lives free from the love of money...." •**Psalm 82:2-4:** "How long will you defend the unjust and show partiality to the wicked? Defend the weak and the fatherless; uphold the cause of the poor and the oppressed. Rescue the weak and the needy; deliver them from the hand of the wicked."

Remember, these are only a fraction of the hundreds of scriptures dealing with economic justice, charity and giving, or warning against usury, greed and accumulation of wealth. And many of these verses (like Psalms 82, above) were addressed to the leaders of the nations, not just a call to personal charity, but to national economic justice. The majority of scholarly commentaries agree. For example, under its definition of the biblical word "Wealth," the widely-respected *Interpreter's Dictionary of the Bible*, states: "The early church's attitude consistently reflects Jesus' teaching. This is vividly illustrated in the account of the sharing of possessions in Acts 4:32." That moderate commentary from 1962 says that the Bible has a "sharp warning" against wealth and concludes, "Unfortunately, later efforts to accommodate and rationalize its rigor drastically obscure the stark New Testament attitude [toward wealth]."

Greed, the Opposite of Love

Defenders of greed are quick to point out that Jesus once said "the poor will always be with you." This quote is often misread to mean that since poverty is an ongoing, intractable problem, we can quit worrying about it. Ironically, when Jesus made that statement, he was saying the opposite: he was chiding Judas, a greedy thief, for being critical of the generous lady who gave the lavish gift of anointing oil, and Jesus did so by referencing a verse from Deuteronomy 15:11: "There will always be poor people in the land. Therefore I command you to be open-handed towards your brothers and towards the poor and needy in your land." Jesus pointed to this verse to show that the opportunity to give to the poor is *always* present and called for, but on that particular day, he needed to be celebrated as the Messiah ("the anointed one") and anointed for burial. It was not intended as an escape clause for the rich; rather, it was a statement encouraging generosity—"open-hands." Yes, Jesus understood that some people will be poor no matter what you do for them. But Jesus did *not* say that just because some poor people can't be helped, we are off the hook with all. The gospel writers even added that Judas had been stealing from the common treasury, and was motivated by his own greed, not by concern for the poor.

God Favors the Poor

If you believe that God came into the flesh, manifest as Jesus, then you can't escape this truth: God chose solidarity with the meager working class. He became a peasant carpenter whose closest friends were poor fishermen. Everything Jesus owned he carried on his back. He had no home, no horse, no property. At his death, the Roman soldiers fought over his belongings: two pieces of clothing.

Even before his birth, the prophecies about Jesus portray him in economic terms, as bringing equity and justice for the lower classes. His own mother, Mary, when she learns she is pregnant with a revolutionary Messiah (future anointed leader/king), sings a song exclaiming that God "has filled the hungry with good things but has sent the rich away empty." (Luke 1:53).

On one occasion, Jesus allowed expensive oil to be poured on his feet. He attended religious feasts, parties and banquets with rich folks. From that, we can deduce that God affirms a time for joy and celebration. But these are meant as exceptions that prove the rule of frugality, charity and stewardship. The rest of Jesus' lifestyle and teachings stood on the side of the poor against the rich.

James, the brother of Jesus, wrote these powerful words in his Epistle (James 2:5-9): "Has not God chosen those who are poor in the eyes of the world to be rich in faith and to inherit the kingdom? But you have insulted the poor. Is it not the rich who are exploiting you? Are they not the ones who are dragging you into court? Are they not the ones who are slandering the noble name of him to whom you belong? If you keep the royal law found in Scripture, "Love your neighbor as yourself," you are doing right."

You cannot truly love God without having compassion for the poor! It is a central, pervasive, emphatic teaching of the Old and New Testaments. If you can't see that, something is wrong: you need either a heart transplant or an eyelid-ectomy.

Consensus on Economic Justice in World Religions

The next section is an overview of what the other great religious teachers have said about our duty to the poor. Religions do differ significantly on concepts like creation and death, sin and salvation, the nature of gods and devils... but on the topic of charity toward the poor and economic justice, they are in near-unanimous agreement with Christian teachings. I've devoted more pages to Christianity due to the limits of my expertise—I am a Protestant pastor, not an expert on world religions. Excuse my bias... but Judeo-Christian ethics have been the most influential on Western civilization. Odd, though, that in the political realm, the ones who claim to be the most Christian, who claim to take Scripture literally, are also the ones who deny or ignore the emphatic teachings about social justice.

Summary

Conservatives are eager to meld church and state—except when it comes to economics. They ironically refuse to apply this historical context: biblical culture treated religion and politics as **one**. The Bible does not make caring for the poor a purely voluntary, individual responsibility, as Republicans claim. Priests were lawgivers; society, church and government were integral; the Temple imposed taxes as a mandate, not as a voluntary option.

"Christian" defenders of greed make their libertarian case in the guise of fine-sounding phrases like *individual liberty* and *freedom*. The TEA, Republican and Libertarian Parties all fail to see how concentrated wealth creates the very kind of oppressive power they claim to oppose. Newberry and his bedfellows want "the haves-lots" to be free. They don't seem to give a damn about the enslavement of the "have-nots."

The hypocrisy goes deeper. These so-called Christian politicians want generosity to the poor to come from individuals, not government. **But in many cases, it turns out they mean individuals *other* than themselves!** The Republican Governor of Texas, Rick Perry, is known for publicly mixing Christianity and politics, but in a year that he made over a million bucks, he gave a whopping $90 to his church.[64] According to his tax returns, this presidential contender, over several years when he earned $2.68 million (plus perks), gave only half a percent to churches and religious organizations.[65] The same year that Newt Gingrich (or is that, *Grinch*) presented himself as a Christian candidate for the Presidency, it was revealed he and his wife had spent $500,000 at the jewelry store, Tiffany's.[66] Starving kids everywhere, but half a million on baubles. Jesus said in Matthew 23: "You hypocrites... you are full of greed and self-indulgence." He also said, "Blessed are the poor, for yours is the kingdom of God. But woe to you who are rich, for you have already received your comfort."[67]

Lloyd Marcus, a spokesman for the Tea Party Express, asserts: "Jesus was not for socialism. Yes, the Bible advocates giving, but out of the goodness of our own hearts, not out of government confiscation of wealth.…" Show us a single verse to support your claim, Lloyd! I'd agree that God *prefers* we give freely out of loving hearts—but Marcus is dead wrong on the rest.

Voluntary charity still begs the question: *What do you do if the majority of people are tight-fisted and unwilling to give freely? Are you morally free to let children starve in the street?*

I once spoke privately to wealthy Republican Congressman Jo Bonner as he exited a Rotary Club meeting. With a smile I said, "You know it's my job as a pastor to remind you to help take care of the poor and the oppressed." He snapped back, "No, that's *your* job!" His job is apparently to take care of the rich and the powerful. He is typical of the Republican and Libertarian response to poverty: *Let the churches bear all the cost of helping the poor!* Sadly, that concept is rebutted by two words: **We don't.** I spent a lifetime helping the poor as a minister, and while I appreciate the charitable work of churches, I know that most churchmembers give less than 5% of their income to their church, and most churches, in turn give less than 10% of that in direct aid to the poor. A half a cent is not nearly enough, as evidenced by the fact that millions are still starving. Christians spend more on themselves, on plush "Christian Life Centers" that serve as their own gyms and country clubs, than on the hungry. But before you judge Christians and churches too harshly, polls show that they are still *more* generous than the general population! **So obviously, a just society requires more than the vagaries of voluntary giving.**

And why should society let the "pagans" off the hook? Why should only *generous* people carry the burden of income inequality? Fairness demands we spread the burden—or as the New Testament puts it, spread the opportunity for joy in giving.

In closing, let's review: •Jesus made it clear that love should be the chief motivation for sharing our wealth. But he also supported the principle of having government share in the task of taking care of the poor. Jesus paid taxes. •Social-conservatives want government to enforce all the *other* ethics of the Bible, using government law and enforcement power to do so. Their lone exception to legislating ethics: **money**. Why? •Jesus spoke more about *justice, money, giving, charity, and generosity* than he did about all the other "moral" issues put together. In almost every one of the 66 books of the Bible you will find support for love and charity, and warnings against wealth and greed. This is particularly true of the words of Jesus. •The practice of the early church was economic socialism and extreme generosity. The passage in Acts 2, explicitly stating that the early church was socialistic, exposes the duplicity of Tommy Newberry, Newt Gingrich, Ryan Paul and the rest. Jesus said: "From everyone who has been given much, much will be demanded; and from the one who has been entrusted with much, much more will be asked."[68] Don't elect him to office, he might be a socialist!

How is it that some Christians have missed this mountain of Scriptural evidence? Professor Dalton Kehoe explains that human psychology demands that we hold ourselves in high esteem, that humans "want to believe they are right," and therefore will filter and arrange facts to fit one's ideal image of self. Most humans will accept an illogical premise more quickly than adapting their thinking to a new paradigm; people will ignore what a holy book actually says, rather than look in the mirror and see self as greedy, wicked or self-centered. No one wants to think they don't have God's approval, or that they are selfish, or that they don't deserve their salary. They will latch onto the less painful option: *I work hard and am rich; I've seen lazy poor people; therefore all poor people are lazy; I am rich because of my hard work and virtue; they are poor because of their flaws*. That self-mythology is the only way to explain how intelligent people, with good motives, can ignore the teachings of the Book they (and I) so revere.

The rich young man who encountered Jesus, at first smug in his belief that he had appeased God, left "sorrowful" after Jesus exposed his greed. That is not a typical response; most humans would leave *angry*, in denial, defending their virtue. If you are a rich person reading this, you may be a fine person—better than me, in fact. But on this one matter, I beg you to read, contemplate and pray about the truth of these Scriptures. If the truth brings you sorrow, you are actually on the road to change. I believe Jesus was *pleased* that the man went away sorrowful... it showed remorse and regret, the first step in accepting a higher ethic.

~~~

Chapter 5: Does God Endorse Socialism?
Part B: What have Other Religions Taught?

The defenders of free market capitalism and the *status quo* tend to put great stock in tradition and authority. What greater authoritative tradition is there but religion? So please continue to explore with me the grand irony we are finding in our overview of world religions and the ethics of economics.

Hinduism:

Hinduism is considered by some to be the oldest religion. Judaism also lays claim to that title, asserting a verbal tradition all the way back to Creation, but some of the *written* Hindu Scriptures (the Upanishads) do pre-date the written Jewish scriptures. Either way, since we began Part A with Judeo-Christian tradition, we begin this quick overview of world religions with Hindu's ancient words.

Hinduism is the most complex of world religions, in part because they have so many different holy books and splinter sects. At first glance, Hinduism may seem to endorse wealth as a virtue. This is because the notion of *karma*—reaping what you sow—implies that successful people must have earned their wealth as a reward. Since they view life as a progressive evolution through life to death to rebirth and, via reincarnation, spiraling upward, they tend to believe that wealth is the evidence that a successful person is being repaid by karma for good work in a previous life. So Hinduism views material success and wealth (Artha) as a virtuous, desirable aim in life—there is even a "goddess of wealth," Lakschmi. The Hindu God Vishnu lived a luxurious life, served by that very goddess.

But there are limitations and nuances to this teaching. Wealth, Hinduism teaches, is merely a temporary means, not an end goal, and money must not be allowed to dominate someone's life. Hindu scriptures warn against "attachment" to wealth and against greed, selfishness and a lack of mercy toward the poor. Wealth is encouraged mostly so that the wealthy/successful person can serve others: his household, the poor, and other mission causes.

This emphasis on household wealth/success, or *Artha*, is based not only on karma, but also emphasized the duty of the patriarch or "head of the household" to support the extended family.

Artha is also considered one lesser step in a four step process of evolution toward full godhood. This material-based "householder" phase is a temporary, transitional step toward higher spirituality that, in the end, will reject materialism and money. The Upanishads emphasize that money must be earned in a righteous manner.

In Hinduism, ideally wealth does not belong to one person, but to the whole extended family. Hindus are also expected to give away any excess wealth to the poor. Giving money to the needy improves one's *karma* (to gain merit in the next life). As a person grows older, and moves beyond the householder period, they are expected to let go of mammon and evolve to the next level.

Some quotes from Hindu scripture:
"Running after that cur, money, I have forgotten you, O Lord. What a shame! I have time only for making money, not for you. How can a dog who loves rotten meat, relish the nectar?"
~*Basavanna,* Vachana 313

In the Upanishads, Maitreya asks his master: "My lord, if this whole earth belonged to me, with all its wealth, should I through its possession attain mortality?" And the master replied, "No. Your life would be like that of the rich. None can possibly hope to attain immortality through wealth."
~*The Upanishads*, The Book of Brihadaranyaka, Vedanta Press

We now live in an age where the gap between rich and poor is far, far beyond what the early sages imagined. The Upanishads are thousands and thousands of years old, and the definition of "wealth" has changed. Modern day "middle class" people would have been considered wealthy then. The ethic that I propose here would not be in conflict with Hinduism, as I do not view success and material comfort as intrinsically evil. It is *lavish* excess, waste, greed and over-attachment to money and materialism that we both condemn.

Buddhism:
If Hinduism gives any quarter to the Republican capitalist wealth machine, Buddhism takes it away. Buddhism was a reform movement sprung from within Hinduism; Buddha particularly rejected the caste system, which had created an upper class of elites. Buddha taught equality, compassion, charity and humility as key virtues, and he and his subsequent followers envisioned an egalitarian society as the ideal.[69] Buddhist scripture teaches, much as Jesus would later, that if you have two coats, "you have to take off and give away one." Buddha said, "The fool laughs at generosity. The miser cannot enter heaven. But the master finds joy in giving, And happiness is his reward." Buddha famously taught the cause of human suffering is desire, but a better translation would be the word "craving," which Buddha summed up as greed, hatred and delusion.[70]

We continue to address the objection by American libertarians and conservatives: "Charity is fine at home, but not the province of government." The fallacy in this thought is that it sets up good people as suckers, placing all responsibility for taking care of the unfortunate on them, and giving license to the greedy and self-indulgent to wash their hands of responsibility. Like most religions, including Judeo-Christian teaching, Buddhism teaches that humans must live in society and cannot be let loose to live by a jungle-law. Most Buddhists believe that religious ethics cannot just be private and personal, but must become a part of government and society-at-large or it has no pragmatic value. One of the best interpreters of Buddhism, Dr. Babasaheb Ambedkar, is quick to remind us that Buddha was not firstly concerned with systems of ethics and morality, but with a higher spirituality. Nevertheless, Ambedkar goes on to say that in seeking the higher spiritual plain, we MUST live out a religious ethic in the meantime, and do so communally and compassionately, not in a Darwinian jungle. He writes: "Is the fittest (the strongest) the best? Would not the weakest, if protected, be ultimately the best for advancing the ends and aims of society? ...[W]hat is the way to protect the weak? Nothing less than to impose some restraints upon the fittest. In this lies the origin and necessity for morality... imposed... on the fittest/strongest."[71] He argues that government must impose a moral law, or else the chaos of the jungle ensues. The immorality among "thieves" is also the same immorality "among businessmen" and upper "castemen," an immorality "marked by isolation and exclusiveness. It is a morality to protect group interest. It is therefore anti-social.... A society which rests upon the supremacy of one group over another... inevitably leads to conflict." Rule by the rich and powerful "leads to discrimination and denial of justice." A ruling elite "leads to stratification of classes. Those who are masters remain masters, and those who are born in slavery remain slaves.... The privileged remain privileged, and the serfs remain serfs. There can be liberty for some, but not for all... equality for a few, but none for the majority." He thus reasons that the "only way to put a stop to conflict is to have common rules of morality," enforced by government. So Buddhism ultimately calls us to have government that protects the individuals and frees people from being "serfs."

At a distance, Buddha may seem like a navel-gazing dreamer, but he was no naive idealist. He wrote, "Good men and bad men differ radically. Bad men never appreciate kindness shown them, but wise men appreciate and are grateful. Wise men [express] gratitude by some return of kindness, not only to their benefactor, but to everyone else." And while his teachings do focus on the individual pursuit of the True Self, Buddha was not preaching Individualism or Libertarianism. He saw humanity as interconnected, and taught the need for unity and equality.

More Buddhist scriptures:
"I see men of wealth in the world acquiring property, from delusion they give not away; out of greed a hoard of wealth they

make, and hanker sorely after more sense pleasures.... Heirs carry off his wealth... wealth does not follow him who is dying.... Long life is not gained by wealth... Rich and poor feel the touch [of death]...." ~Majjhima Nikaya ii.72-73, *Rattapala Sutta*

"Riches ruin the foolish, but not those in quest of the Beyond. Through craving for riches the ignorant man ruins himself as he does others." ~Dhammapada 355

In a later chapter we will examine the disease of greed, an addiction as powerful as heroin dependency. Buddha understood the insatiable nature of greed and the desire for excessive wealth: "Were there a mountain all made of gold, doubled that would not be enough to satisfy a single man: know this and live accordingly."[72]

Asian Religions:
Taoism and Confucianism are each more of a philosophy than an organized religion in a Western sense. Nevertheless, they add to the unanimous worldwide support for the ethics outlined in this book:

The Tao Te Ching (words of Lao Tzu):
from Chapter 29: "Do not race after riches, do not risk your life for success, or you will let slip the Heaven within you."
from Chapter 46
"There is no crime more onerous than greed,
No misfortune more devastating than avarice,
And no calamity that brings with it more grief than insatiability
Thus, knowing when enough is enough, Is really satisfying."
And from Chapter 53:
"When rich speculators prosper, While farmers lose their land; when government officials spend money on weapons instead of cures; when the upper class is extravagant and irresponsible, while the poor have nowhere to turn—all this is robbery and chaos. It is not in keeping with the Tao." ~~

Confucius (K'ung-tzu):
Like most religious and philosophical leaders, Confucius listed generosity and kindness among the top five most essential traits. "To be able under all circumstances to practice five things constitutes perfect virtue; these five things are gravity, generosity of soul, sincerity, earnestness and kindness." He also wrote: "With coarse rice to eat, with water to drink, and my crooked arm for a pillow—is not joy to be found therein? Riches and honors acquired through unrighteousness are to me as the floating clouds." And: "If a man can subdue his selfishness for one full day, everyone will call him good."

Confucius would also have scoffed at the suggestion that

government should be divorced from virtue: "He who exercises government by means of his virtue may be compared to the north polar star, which keeps its place and all the stars turn towards it." He taught that ethics/morality must be the driving force behind good government. Confucius even went so far as to envision government's role in social welfare, asserting that the government's first duty is to take care of the most needy, the "...old men without wives, old women without husbands, old people without children, and young children without fathers." He saw the welfare of the people as the first order of government: "The essentials of good government are: a sufficiency of food, a sufficiency of arms, and the confidence of the people. If forced to give up one of these, give up arms...."[73]

Islam:

In modern times, Islam is the one religion most involved in "theocracies," where the religion and the government are deeply intertwined. However, I must say critically that these theocracies rarely practice what they preach: Islamic countries, particularly the oil-rich ones, have some of the greatest gaps between great wealth (Saudi princes, for example) and abject poverty. At least the U.S., with our flaws, has a healthy middle class and is extraordinarily generous (both with governmental foreign aid and private charity).

The point is, we can't fault Islam itself for this particular failing. Islam emphatically teaches the importance of giving to the poor, and as already implied, endorses the idea of government being involved in the equation of charity.

According to the Qur'an, charity is one of the most important parts of life and worship. To become a complete Muslim one has to fully carry out in practice the instructions given by Prophet Muhammad, particularly a set of formal duties or *Ibadah* (worships) which are sometimes called "The Five Pillars of Islam." Of the "Five Pillars" that support and frame the Islamic faith, one is an injunction to help the poor. Almsgiving (*Zakah*) is intended not only to help the poor, but to help the giver by fostering self-sacrifice and to protect them from greed. Officially, Islam accepts within its fold only those who are willing to give away some of their wealth. Every Muslim whose finances are above a certain specified minimum must pay 2.5% of their cash balance annually to the deserving (in *addition* to giving to the Mosque, taxes, etc.). One of the most important principles of Islam is that all things belong to God, and that wealth is therefore held by human beings in trust. The word *zakat* (singular of Zakah) means both *purification* and *growth* as well as giving. They teach that possessions are purified by setting aside a proportion for those in need, and, like the pruning of plants, this cutting back balances and encourages new growth. Each Muslim calculates his or her own zakat individually. Although this word "zakat" can be translated as "voluntary charity" it has a wider meaning.

The *Hadith*, commentary on the Qur'an that is also viewed as holy writ, offers more confirmation of the importance of sharing wealth with the poor and being charitable and generous: "God has no mercy on one who has no mercy for others." "None of you truly believes until he wishes for his brother what he wishes for himself." "He who eats his fill while his neighbor goes without food is not a believer." "A man walking along a path felt very thirsty. Reaching a well he descended into it, drank his fill and came up. Then he saw a dog with its tongue hanging out, trying to lick up mud to quench its thirst. The man saw that the dog was feeling the same thirst as he had felt so he went down into the well again and filled his shoe with water and gave the dog a drink. God forgave his sins for this action."

But because Islam encourages, even prefers, a theocratic government, Islam blesses a giving or "re-distribution" of wealth that goes beyond voluntary offerings. The Qur'an provides specific guidelines for ordering society, human conduct and an equitable economic system. We find in the Koran, Chapter VIII/41: "And know that whatever ye take as spoils of war, lo, a fifth thereof is for Allah... for the messenger and for the kinsman (who hath need) and orphans and the needy and the wayfarer." So even the spoils of war are to be shared, 20%, with the needy. •"Anyone who is stingy, is stingy only with his own soul. God is Wealthy while you are poor." ~Qur'an 47.38 •"Woe is he... who has gathered riches and counted them over, thinking his riches have made him immortal!" ~Qur'an 104.1-3

The last words of Muhammad: "Whatever we leave is for charity."[74]

Baha'i Faith:

Small in numbers but broad in vision, the Baha'i faith seeks to embrace all religions and to find unity among them. And the one clear point of agreement it claims is central to all religions is the importance of charity and kindness to neighbors. Abdu'l-Bahá taught that poverty and extreme wealth have no place in a compassionate society, as poverty demoralizes and extreme wealth corrupts.[75]

Abdu'l-Baha in *The Secret of Divine Civilization*, writes: "Wealth is praiseworthy [only] if it is acquired by an individual's own efforts and the grace of God, in commerce, agriculture, art and industry, and if it be expended for philanthropic purposes. Above all, if a judicious and resourceful individual should initiate measures which would universally enrich the masses of the people, there could be no undertaking greater than this, and it would rank in the sight of God as the supreme achievement, for such a benefactor would supply the needs and insure the comfort and well-being of a great multitude. Wealth is most commendable, provided the entire population is wealthy. If, however, a few have inordinate riches while the rest are impoverished, and no fruit or benefit accrues from that wealth, then it is only a liability to its possessor."

The other great teacher of Baha'i, Baha'u'llah, wrote: "Busy not yourself with this world, for with fire We [the gods] test the gold, and with gold We test Our servants." ~Hidden Words of Baha'u'llah 54.

"Tell the rich of the midnight sighing of the poor, lest heedlessness lead them into the path of destruction, and deprive them of the Tree of Wealth. To give and to be generous are attributes of [the Divine]...." ~*The Hidden Words*, Bahá'u'lláh, no. 49, p. 39.

Judaism:

The Jewish religion, from its beginnings, dictated tithes and offerings to be used to help both the poor and to support the temple, the priests/leaders... a part of this was mandatory, and since they had a theocratic form of government, a portion of the various tithes and offerings were indeed a **tax**. Later Judaism had a "temple tax." **Deuteronomy 12:6:** "...bring your burnt offerings and sacrifices, your tithes and special gifts, what you have vowed to give and your freewill offerings, and the firstborn of your herds and flocks." When the Torah speaks of "tithes and offerings," a tithe was mandatory, while offerings sometimes connoted a more voluntary "free will gift" above and beyond tithes. While a "tithe" means a tenth, they had more than one tithe levied, and the total expected in gifts, offerings, tithes and taxes could exceed 30% of a person's income.[76] The ancient Jewish book of Tobit, an extra-biblical but respected text written before the Christian era, also mentions three different tithes/taxes (Tobit 1:6-8). A failure to pay was considered a violation of the Law (Malachi 3:6-12). So it is nonsense to say the Bible (Jewish *or* Christian) speaks only of voluntary re-distribution!

Of course, God "loves a cheerful giver." Some have used this New Testament verse (and there are similar sentiments in Jewish teachings) as a way to excuse government from imposing taxation that benefits the poor, claiming that *forced* sharing violates God's will. By the same failed logic, we might as well legalize murder, if we only want people to abstain from murder if they can do so "cheerfully"! The Bible does **not** say, "But if you don't have a cheerful, loving heart, we won't *force* you to give or force you to refrain from murder." No, in addition to moral laws, "laws of the heart," the ancient Jews had *civic* laws against murder—just as we do. And laws about giving. God loves a voluntary cheerful gift... but Scripture still calls for induced giving (taxation).

Jewish law was quite liberal on economics: first, no *interest* was allowed to be charged to the poor. (What would VISA and BofA think about that one?) Additionally, every seventh year, in the year of Jubilee, debts were forgiven. Unlike the practice in modern churches of voluntary tithing, the Jews were expected to give as a point of law. And the Jewish laws came with a strict expectation of obedience. As a theocratic government, violation of so-called "moral laws" were punished as strictly as any secular law. Adultery, for example, could result in being stoned to death.

We have laws for the good of society that do indeed force people to do what is right. Some Republicans are adamant about imposing moral laws drawn from Scripture. Alabama Supreme Court Judge Roy Moore famously posted the Ten Commandments in his courtroom. But Judge Moore and many other Republicans failed to support Republican Governor Bob Riley's efforts at tax reform to help Alabama's poor. (Alabama taxes the poor at a rate higher than 40 other states.) Conservatives who boast of following Jewish Law conspicuously omit from that Law the most-often repeated mandates to give to the poor. The Jewish religion has always emphasized the importance of treating the poor, the immigrant, and the oppressed with great care. Yahweh always takes the side of the poor.

The Exodus Example

The central drama for Judaism is Moses leading the people out of Egyptian bondage to the Promised Land. The Exodus story focuses on economic freedom and justice. The chief complaint against the Egyptians was that they worked the Jews for long hours in harsh conditions for low wages. After years of poverty and cruel working conditions, Moses set the slaves free, and with God's blessing and assistance, they "plundered" their rich masters. As the Jews exited, they took Egypt's golden treasures as recompense for their cheated wages—with God as an accomplice to this redistribution! Exodus 12:35-36: "The Israelites did as Moses instructed and asked the Egyptians for articles of silver and gold and for clothing. The Lord had made the Egyptians favorably disposed toward the people, and they gave them what they asked for; so they plundered the Egyptians." In modern English, *plunder* means to take goods by force. The Hebrew word used for plunder meant exactly the same, used in exactly the same way more than thirty times in Scripture. The meaning is unequivocal. God forced the Egyptians to give their wealth back to the workers.

Ironically, Republican Presidential candidate Rick Perry recently speechified about government: "We should not be asking for Pharaoh to give everything to everybody, because it's slavery."[77] Defending Pharaoh, candidate Perry managed to get the point of the story totally backwards: because of their years of slavery, God rewarded the Israelites with the Pharaoh's wealth.

Republicans stand on the wrong side of the Jews-in-Egypt struggle. They impose wealth pyramids: slaves at the bottom, the fruits of their labors flowing upward, like an inverted funnel, to Pharaoh's capstone (i.e. the CEO). In Exodus, God turned the pyramids upside down. The slaves plundered the masters, with divine permission. This plan to plunder was first laid out by God to Moses via the famous burning bush, in Exodus 3:21-22. So **God endorses economic re-distribution when it is for the cause of justice.**

Hebrew Scripture on Economic Justice

The Judeo-Christian scriptures speak a great deal about economic justice... in fact, the Bible speaks more about money and giving than about love! A sampling of yet more Hebrew verses on economic justice: •**Exodus 23:6:** "You shall not pervert the justice due to your poor...." •**Psalm 112:5, 9:** "Good will come to those who are generous and lend freely, who conduct their affairs with justice.... They have freely scattered their gifts to the poor, their righteousness endures forever; their horn will be lifted high in honor." •**Exodus 22:25:** "If you lend money to one of my people among you who is needy, do not be like a money-lender; charge him no interest." •**Psalm 41:1:** "Happy are those who consider the poor; the Lord delivers them in the day of trouble." •**Leviticus 19:9-10:** "When you reap the harvest of your land, do not reap to the very edges of your field or gather the gleanings of your harvest... or pick up the grapes that have fallen. Leave them for the poor and the foreigner. I am the LORD your God." •**Ecclesiastes 5:8, 10:** "If you see the poor oppressed in a district, and justice and rights denied, do not be surprised.... Whoever loves money never has enough; whoever loves wealth is never satisfied with their income." •**Job 20:18-19:** "He will not enjoy the profit from his trading. For he has oppressed the poor and left them destitute; he has seized houses he did not build. Surely he will have no respite from his craving; he cannot save himself by his treasure." •**Leviticus 25:23:** ""The land shall not be sold forever, for the land is mine," saith the Lord. "And you are strangers and sojourners with me."" •**Deuteronomy 15:7:** "If there is a poor man among your brothers in any of the towns of the land that the LORD your God is giving you, do not be hard-hearted or tight-fisted towards your poor brother." •**Proverbs 21:13:** "If you close your ear to the cry of the poor, you will cry out and not be heard." •**Amos 5:11-12:** "You levy a straw tax on the poor and impose a tax on their grain...you have built stone mansions, you will not live in them... many are your offenses... those who oppress the innocent and take bribes and deprive the poor of justice...." •**Proverbs 22:1-23** (excerpts): "A good name is more desirable than great riches; to be esteemed is better than silver or gold. Rich and poor have this in common: The LORD is the Maker of them all... [but] the rich rule over the poor, and the borrower is slave to the lender.... One who oppresses the poor to increase his wealth and one who gives gifts to the rich—both come to poverty.... Do not exploit the poor... do not crush the needy in court, for the LORD will take up their case...." •**Proverbs 28:8:** "He who increases his wealth by exorbitant interest amasses it for another, who will be kind to the poor." •**Deuteronomy 15:10:** "Give generously to the poor, not grudgingly, for the Lord your God will bless you in everything you do..." (NLT). •**Proverbs 23:4:** "Do not wear yourself out to get rich; have the wisdom to show restraint." •**Isaiah 3:15:** "What do you mean by crushing my people and grinding the faces of the poor?" declares the Lord, the LORD Almighty." •**Proverbs 17:5:** "He who mocks the poor shows contempt for their Maker...."

Summary of Faith and Financial Ethics:

Simon Greer, president of the Jewish Funds for Justice, reminds us that the Jewish Bible is firm on the need to protect the vulnerable, which "sometimes requires government action." We are "all made in the image of the divine...," Greer asserts. "The only sensible conclusion is that we need mechanisms like effective government... to solve the pressing problems" of society, especially including those at the bottom of fortune's ladder.[78]

Zechariah the prophet includes the poor on his list of protected persons: "Do not oppress widows, orphans, foreigners, or the poor," (Zechariah 7:10, NLT). Isaiah called these "words of the Lord," found in Isaiah 1:15-17: "When you spread out your hands in prayer, I will hide my eyes from you; even if you offer many prayers, I will not listen. Your hands are full of blood; wash and make yourselves clean. Take your evil deeds out of my sight! Stop doing wrong, learn to do right! Seek justice, encourage the oppressed. Defend the cause of the fatherless, plead the case of the widow."

The greatest sin committed by the ultra-wealthy critics of the poor is that they ignore the suffering inflicted on innocent children. Maybe some poor adults are lazy or made bad choices. But the children of poor parents did not get to choose which home they would live in. In God's eyes, they are just as precious as the children who live in the mansions of Bill Gates or Warren Buffet or the Rockefellers.

I am not a "hellfire and brimstone" pastor. But I cannot ignore the strong language which Scripture uses to warn those who abuse the poor, especially those who fail to help the widow and the orphan. We close this section on Judaism with a quote from the Apostle James, who was an ardent Jew first and a Christian second: "Religion that God our Father accepts as pure and faultless is this: to look after orphans and widows in their distress...." ~James 1:27

By now, I've cited enough examples to prove beyond any shadow of a doubt that Christianity and Judaism, and most other religions: **a)** warn strongly against greed and the hoarding of wealth; **b)** command the fortunate to share their wealth with the less fortunate; **c)** permit government to be a partner in the re-distribution of wealth.

To seal my case, one more account from Scripture: a hero to both Jews and Christians, King David endorsed plunder. What is even more striking is *how* David distributed the plunder even to those who had not "earned" it. The Amelkites had stolen treasures from David's country and had kidnapped David's wives. As David led a revenge-raiding party, 200 of his men were "exhausted" and stayed behind. He successfully recaptured his wives and took not only the plunder that belonged to him, but also the flocks and herds the Amelkites had previously stolen from other tribes. This plunder was considered the "spoils of war" and a reward to the soldiers who risked their lives in the battle. From 1st Samuel 30:1-24, we read what David did with that plunder: "Then David came to the two hundred men who had been too exhausted [lazy? cowardly?] to follow him [into battle]. They came out to meet David and the people with him. As David and his men approached, he greeted them. But all the evil men and troublemakers among David's followers said, 'Because they did not go with us, we will not share with them the plunder we recovered.'" (The Bible called those who did not want to share *evil*.) Then the communist-socialist David replied, "No, my brothers, you must not do that with what the Lord has given us.… The share of the man who stayed with the supplies is to be the same as that of him who went down to the battle. All will share alike.' David made that a statute and ordinance for Israel from that day to this."

There it is, plainly in the Bible, government-mandated socialism: "All will share alike." So much for the claims of the religious rich that God hates socialism. Yet Tommy Newberry smugly, flatly, arrogantly asserts: "The Bible never condemns wealth." Flat wrong. I've cited multiple Scriptures that prove otherwise. He further claims, "Contrary to the appeals of socialists, their ideology is incompatible with both the letter and the spirit of the Bible."[79] No, it is Newberry who is the contrarian. It is *his* ideology that is completely at odds with both the letter and the spirit of scripture. You cannot read the hundreds of scriptures in this chapter and rationally conclude otherwise.

Despite their holier-than-thou hubris, many right-wing "Faith and Family" politicians really do not know Scripture very well, and the parts they do know, they fail to follow. As Psalm 14 asks: "Will evildoers never learn—those who devour my people as men eat bread... you evildoers frustrate the plans of the poor, but the Lord is their refuge."

~~~

Chapter 6: The Gap
The growing, gaping abyss separating rich and poor

The gap between rich and poor is growing without relent. [This] lifestyle is not sustainable. ~Swiss President Micheline Calmy-Rey

Looking at the world as a whole, the gap between rich and poor is more than alarming: it is outrageous, horrific, grossly absurd, putridly offensive... it exhausts my thesaurus of all adjectives of astonishment and revulsion. After a quick google of figures easily found on the internet, even Jethro Bodine can cypher that the net worth of the six richest families in the world (the Gates family, the Sultan of Brunei, the Walton family, Mukesh Ambani, Carlos Slim, and Warren Buffet) is **greater than the entire gross domestic product of the 50 poorest nations on Earth** —combined! Pull the fire alarms, this is an emergency: a half-dozen individuals controlling all the resource-equivalent of fifty nations, filled with millions of deprived citizens.

Recently in India, multi-billionaire Mukesh Ambani built a *billion*-dollar, 27-story home. That was 27 *floors*, not *rooms*. According to *Forbes* magazine, it features a health club, gym, dance studio, a ballroom, guestrooms, numerous lounges, a 50-seat screening room, an elevated garden, three helipads, and underground parking for 160 vehicles. Yet all around Ambani's indulgence, 665 million Indians have to "defecate in the open," as the Associated Press put it (here in the South, we'd say they literally "don't have a pot to pee in"). I can't fathom how Ambani's conscience let's him sleep at night, when nearby, a 35-year-old maid, Nusrat Khan, **works hard and raises her four children on $67 a month in a shack with no running water or toilet.**[80]

Numbers are Boring, Flat

Numbers do not fully illustrate the size of the gap, nor convey the emotion, the human pain, that goes with it. Numbers are two-dimensional; people are three-dimensional. Graphs plot only lines on a page. **Statistics** are flat symbols, reported on thin pieces of paper; **reality** is like the tree from which came the paper: a tall, round, living organism, with beautiful branches stretching out. If Mukesh Ambani were a single giant tree standing in a field, and the working people were a forest of trees cut down in order to provide "humus" for his growth, to understand the vast gap between his income to ours, then envision the clear-cutting of *thousands* of forests in deference to one lone tree. The 800 green acres of New York's Central Park boast 25,000 trees.[81] That means to provide a *billion* trees, you would have to cut down every tree in 40,000 central parks!

Or would you cut down every single tree in England (estimated to have about a billion trees) to keep one single tree alive? That's the ratio we are talking about when we look at a billion dollars vs. one dollar. I know, a tree is worth more than a dollar... and a human life is worth more than a tree... I'm just struggling to convey the sheer size ratio of "a billion to one" and how disproportionate the gap really is. Ambani has $63 billion in personal worth, and since $90 is enough to buy a human on the slave market, if humans were trees, it would be like Ambani cutting down every tree in England in order to stand as the one lone tree there.[82]

Slavery in Our Time

The numbers correlate to real human beings. Forty million people are enslaved in India alone. Ambani's wealth could easily free every one of these, his fellow citizens. Here's the actual report from the United Nations: "An estimated forty million people in India, among them fifteen million children, are bonded [enslaved] laborers, working in slave-like conditions in order to pay off debts. The majority of them are Dalits. At least one million Dalits work as manual scavengers, clearing feces from latrines... with their bare hands. Dalits also comprise the majority of agricultural laborers who work for a few kilograms of rice... a day."[83] Ambani's $63 billion would pay their wages, all one million of them, for **172 years**... that's right, he could buy the labor of a million people for 172 years even if he never earned another penny in the meantime!

The Gap in the U.S.

By Indian standards, the poor in America live well... but the gap here is still a gaping maw. The standard of living for the middle-class, with hi-tech conveniences, has risen a bit since I was a child. Several economists and politicians have boasted that technology has improved the plight of the U.S. middle class and even the poor by giving the lower classes TV's and DVD's and computer access (in the U.S., that is). But this only creates another problem: raised expectations. Children learn how underprivileged they are by watching television. Widespread visual media, produced in affluent contexts of New York and Hollywood, portray opulence, showing the children of the poor that they *are* poor, because they don't have the nice things shown on the screen. Expectations rise, but incomes fall.

Incomes for the working poor have stagnated, welfare aid has been drastically cut, but incomes of the upper classes have soared over the last 30 years. The gap grows both in numbers and in perception. According to the *Harvard Business Review*, in the United States the poorest 10% receive less than 2 percent of total income, while the richest 6% get nearly a third of the national income.[84] The Walmart tycoons —Sam Walton's family—are worth over $100 billion dollars, yet they pay their average employee just $18,000 a year. At that rate, a regular Walmart employee would have to work for over 55 THOUSAND YEARS to earn as much as the Waltons![85]

In my state, nearly one-third of the children under five-years-old live in poverty, yet a family of four who makes less than a $100 a week will still pay state income tax on that salary... plus a variety of other taxes. On the Alabama income tax form, the deduction for children was set during the Great Depression at $300... annually! Today it is unchanged. I couldn't raise a child on $300 a *month* much less $300 a year! But in Alabama, Federal income taxes are fully deductible on the state form... a beneficial break to the wealthy. Why is this unfair for the poor? The wealthy pay a lot to the federal government, and thus get a fat deduction on their Alabama income taxes. But if you are poor (annual salary of $18,000 or less, with children), you get NO deduction on your state taxes. And if you are wealthy in Alabama, you also pay very little in property tax on your mansion. But if you are poor in Alabama, you pay the same sales tax on your groceries as the mansion-dwellers.[86]

It's not exactly breaking news that we have a valley between the filthy rich and the poor. So let me begin with what is less-often reported: *Why* is there a Gap?

What Causes the Gap between Rich and Poor?

The primary cause of the Gap is a **psychological** aberration: people are most sympathetic to others like themselves. So the upper class tends to take care of its own, whether it's a corporate board of well-dressed, well-to-do winners setting executive salaries, or the well-fed Senators setting governmental policy. One reason we find irrational explanations for excessive pay is that the analysts, ironically, can't imagine something as *irrational* as emotion or class-identity affecting how high-level salaries are set. But emotion and personal bias do enter into salary-setting. I have witnessed this illogical phenomenon first-hand.

In my thirties (as the "token" young person), I sat on a corporate committee that set salaries across-the-board for a particular headquarters. We were in the midst of a recession, so the mindset was that we should be frugal in giving raises. One of the more generous "suits" sitting around the large boardroom table pointed out that the inflationary cost-of-living (CPI) was 3%. So he stated, "Let's keep this simple: everyone's done a good job, so let's give a cost of living raise of 3% and a tiny merit raise of 2%, for a total of 5% across-the-board." Everyone in the room loved a simple number and a simple formula. A 5% universal raise was about to receive a unanimous vote—until I spoke up. Although the raises would not apply to me personally, I was the only person in the room who was having to borrow money to put diapers on my children. So I raised my hand and meekly spoke for the under-represented, "Ya know, at the grass roots in this organization, there are a lot of people who make less than $30,000 annually [this was 25 years ago] who are unhappy with the fact that those at corporate headquarters have had salaries skyrocket—I know many who have seen their salaries frozen for years while the executives get a big raise every year." Suddenly there was a look of hostility in the room.

Stern voice: "Well, I don't know whose banner you're carrying, Lance, but what could be more fair than 5% across the board for everyone?"

This is when I began to see that **class-identity surpasses logic.** "Fair?" I rebutted. "Don't you see: if you make $100,000 and get a 5% 'cost of living' raise, your salary has gone up $5,000! We have a secretary here at HQ, she's been with us faithfully for ten years, and she makes $20,000... 5% to her would be only $1,000. How is it 'fair' to give one employee $5,000, and another $1,000, especially when it is mostly based on the cost of living? They both pay the same price for a loaf of bread."

The math seemed obvious to me: flat-percentage raises give a five-times-larger raise to those who already have a big income, compared to those at the bottom who are struggling to pay their bills. Extrapolate this over ten years and we find one reason why the income gap widens:

Executive: $100,000 x 5% x 10 years = **$62,886** total increase
Worker: $20,000 x 5% x 10 years = **$12,438** total increase
(Note that the 5% is not even linear... it multiplies the *previous* year's fatter raise as well, so the gap compounds algorithmically.)

So, everyone around that table (save me) was arguing that *$62,886 equals $12,438*. These people were not math illiterate. They were supposedly the tops in their field, sharp "executive-level" minds. How could they not see that their plan rewarded those who *already* were better-compensated than the working-class? How could they claim this was fair? **Because people in power make self-interested emotional decisions, not rational decisions.**

Remember, I was not even arguing that the executives were overpaid, or that the secretary should make the same wage as the CEO. I was only pointing out that their "fairness" was increasing the already existing wage gap. Increasing the Gap by $50,000! (Applying their so-called logic over 10 years) Everyone else in the room identified with the executive-level pay. My lone voice representing the far-larger number of lower-paid employees in the organization was quickly voted down. And this is the case with every corporate board and governmental-commission—**the poor are rarely represented in the room**. (Somewhere in a file, the Minutes reflect that I voted on behalf of the working class, even though my future promotions were in the hands of the very people I voted against. Even with token minority representation, it is very hard to vote against the herd, against Power.)

Usually, the people in a board room are paid a large salary, while the majority of wages they oversee are hourly. Ask those executive level board members what their hourly wage is, and they will grossly underestimate. Even assuming the CEO really does work 60 hours a week (martini lunches do not count), do the math and you'll see they are making $10,000 per hour and more, even before you count their lush perks and benefits. $10,000 vs. $8 an hour.

"But you are comparing apples to oranges!" the executive argues. Actually, I thought I was comparing humans to humans.

Their emotional belief that they are worthy of their high pay becomes a rolling snowball, ever-increasing in size. So we have glacier-sized executive pay. The CEO of Walmart makes over $16,000 per hour! And how is his job performance? Most of my friends say, "I hate shopping at Walmart!"

Governments Grow Gaps

Progressive governments do make efforts to help the poor; we hear loud whining (usually from Republicans) about such government "giveaways" to the poor. Yet, far more government money is given to the rich, expanding the Gap between "have-nots" and the "have-lots."

Consider the chief deductions in the Federal tax code. Other than the "Earned Income Credit," almost all of them—nearly one trillion dollars in annual tax breaks, according to CNN—are given to the wealthiest (not even counting *corporate* tax breaks/subsidies... see Chapter 10). Pension, health and other insurance tax breaks rarely benefit the poor or lower middle class. The book, *Retirement Heist*, details how corporations raided workers' pension plans to enrich executives.[87] Companies like Walmart have had a history of purposely hiring part-timers so they could avoid paying health insurance for low-level employees. Executives get golden policies—tax-exempt. "At least 25 top U.S. companies paid more to their chief executives... than they did to the federal government in taxes," report the New York Times.[88]

Capital gains tax breaks certainly are a bonanza for the wealthy. The mortgage interest deduction mostly rewards upper middle class and above: first you have to own a home, then you need enough total deductions to exceed the "Standard Deduction" to benefit from itemizing, and then it helps to be in the high-tax-bracket with a $500,000 home. According to CNN, "The mortgage interest deduction was claimed on just 22% of all returns in 2009. High-income filers tend to benefit disproportionately...."[89] So a host of government policies transfer money from the general public to the rich, thus feeding the Gap.

Is It Really that Bad?
Even Jesus said, "The poor will always be with you." Why fret over the inevitable? I don't envision creating Utopia (a word which comes from Greek words that literally mean, "No place"). And trying to "level" society shows a foolish disregard for human psychology, and for efficiency of markets. Those who are smart, talented and work hard should be rewarded in ways that will result in economic tiers. But it is **the *size* of the gap** (and the shrinking of the middle class) that is so troubling. The wild extremes of poverty and wealth that have emerged in the last forty years are unjust and unhealthy.

On March 9, 2011, *Forbes* magazine released *The 2011 Billionaires List*, reporting that it "breaks two records: total number of listees (1,210) and combined wealth ($4.5 trillion)." During these tough times for most workers, there are several hundred new billionaires... over a *thousand* billionaires now on the planet.[90] How did your salary compare? And many experts say that *Forbes* lazily under-reports the true number of billionaires, since many try to hide a portion of their income for tax and PR purposes.

Over the last thirty years, the top 1% saw a quadrupling of their already-higher income, while the bottom 90% saw almost no increase in real dollars.[91] Another stat that should wake up anyone still complacent about this crisis: the bottom 90% of the U.S. population must share only 27% of it's net worth… and that's 2007 data—the gap has grown more since then.[92] Worldwide, the numbers are even more shocking.

More Rebuttal of Thomas Sowell
As mentioned previously, economist Thomas Sowell defends this atrocity, confusing data with truth, painting in black-n-white when the full picture has greys and colors. The pain and struggle of people's lives cannot be dismissed by mere number-crunching. But Sowell tries. He disputes the obvious fact that the rich are getting richer and the poor are getting poorer by first claiming—but never proving—that the statistics are "lies" and "a house of cards." Then he retreats and confesses that it is not "the numbers themselves usually in dispute. It is the *analyses*... at issue."[93] Most of the statistics in his book pre-date the new millennium, and the gap has

only grown since then. All the numbers then and now show that all incomes have stagnated except the top 10%. So Sowell "analyzes" these facts to twist them into fallacies of his own... ironically in his book entitled, *Economic Facts and Fallacies*.

For a bright man, Sowell's argument seems silly and dumb: the Gap between rich and poor **isn't** growing, he argues... *because the poor have DVD players!* Seriously: his primary argument is that the standard of living, *the quality of life*, has increased over the last forty years... and thus we can just throw away those pesky statistics that show how rich the fat pigs at the trough have grown. In a book with "Facts" in the title, he ignores the plain fact that income has expanded exponentially for the most affluent.

The Gap has been around for thousands of years, but the movement of vast wealth from the working classes to the pockets of the rich accelerated greatly from 1980-2011, triggered by the advent of inexpensive desktop computers (1981), the Internet (1982), and the election of union-busting free-market evangelist Ronald Reagan (1980). In 1980, CEOs at the largest companies received **42** times the pay of the average worker. By year 2000, the gap hit a high, with CEOs making **525** times the average worker.[94] After the crash of 2008, the gap shrunk a bit, but only for a moment. Median pay for CEOs of large corporations rose 27% in 2010—while workers' pay gained, at best, 2%.[95]

Ronald Reagan, Enemy of the Middle Class

One person chiefly responsible for this atrocity is Ronald Reagan, who ushered in "Trickle Down Economics," banking de-regulation, and waged war on the Air Traffic Controllers' union. But he is beloved by the working class because, after all, Reagan was an actor, a polished Hollywood pretender who knew how to look good and sound sincere even as he laid the groundwork for the rise of the rich.

In the seventies, the number of labor union members hit an all-time high. Then Ronald Reagan began a 30-year trend of union busting. Today, unions are nearly extinct, restricted by law on what they can and cannot do. For what little power and effect they have on national policy, unions might as well be dead. The Pew Research Center examined news reports from 2010 on the economy, and found that leaders from organized labor unions were only cited in 2% of such stories.[96] Once politically-influential, unions were largely responsible for the rise of the middle class from 1935-1975.

The decline of unions runs tandem with the decline of the middle class that began with the election in 1981, when Reagan chose Donald Regan as his Treasury Secretary, plucking him from the investment firm, Merrill-Lynch. Thus began a 30 year period of putting former Wall Street execs in charge of our economy, and over 30 years of de-regulation and bubble-making, resulting in the biggest rip-off of wealth from the lower and middle classes in human history.

In 1982, the Reagan/Regan team de-regulated the Savings and Loan, which became ripe with rip-offs costing taxpayer over 100 billion dollars as S&L's collapsed across the country. Consider that a "dress rehearsal" for what happened under George Bush, which cost the country trillions of dollars with a similar banking collapse and Wall Street-engineered rip-off. Reagan next appointed Alan Greenspan (who had a hand in the Keating S&L fiasco) as head of the Federal Reserve. Corporations grew in size and strength, not by "making a better mousetrap," but by buying out the competition. Mergers, once infrequent, became the norm. During Reagan's term in office, his de-regulation fueled a takeover frenzy. Before 1980, hostile corporate takeovers were rare to non-existent... but then soared.[97] This ushered in the era of gargantuan CEO salaries as well as the raiding of pension plans and corporate cash reserves by those engineering the leveraged buyouts. Reagan was such a great salesman, many Americans still buy his lie that cutting taxes on the rich is the path to economic paradise. We now have the lowest taxes since 1950, yet an economy in shambles, high unemployment and stagnant wages for all but the uppermost brackets.[98]

Amazingly, despite overwhelming evidence to the contrary, we still hear politicians extolling the virtues of Reagan, supply-side economics, de-regulation. If you wanna continue "liking" Reagan as a person, fine, but he was no friend to the middle class. The income share of the top 1% has risen more dramatically in the years since 1980 than at *any time in human history*.[99] During the same period, despite huge productivity gains from computer technologies and millions of women moving into the marketplace, middle class wages went unrewarded, and Welfare was *cut*.

Sowell's Ivory Tower

But Sowell is undaunted by these facts. His remaining refuge is that none of those numbers matter to him because "by 2001 most people defined as poor had possessions once considered part of a middle class lifestyle."[100]

This exposes the elitist attitude of folks like Sowell, who sit comfortably in their plush ivory tower and say, "All is well! The poor have cake to eat!" He celebrates the fact that 98% of the poor now have a VCR or DVD player "which no one had in 1971."[101] You're damn right no one had a DVD player in 1971... they weren't invented yet! *God forbid that the poor should grumble, we've been nice enough to let them have modern technology.* Sowell would have made a fine plantation slavemaster (yes, I know his race!), rocking on the front porch with a mint julep, saying, "Aren't those po folks so *lucky* I brought them out of Africa, here where they can have modern technology like mule-pulled plows for them to man!"

Indeed, we could quickly destroy Sowell's argument by citing Third World poverty, where billions couldn't use a DVD if they had one, as they have no televisions... most don't even have electricity.

The same technology that has, admittedly, blessed us "po folk" with DVD players has, even more so, raised the "quality of life" for the rich; they now have surround-sound, 3-D, wide-screen, Blu-Ray home theaters. And the rich had little to do with the forward march of technology that brought these technological comforts: the engineers who did the pioneering work on electronics were middle class. The manufacture of the DVD player is also done not by executives, but by Asian workers. Yet the rich are the biggest beneficiaries. The huge increase in both manufacturing productivity and in life-quality luxury reaped by computers has fueled crazy profits to those who own Apple, Microsoft, Sony, etc.—how many lower middle class folks own Apple stock? If anyone should be grateful for the widespread availability of DVD's, it's those at the top of the economic pyramid.

My point is the exact opposite of Sowell's: because we *have* had this enormous leap forward in technology, productivity, and other "robot-built" efficiencies—a leap made possible by thousands of middle-class scientists, professors, and workers—shouldn't the entire planet share in these remarkable blessings?

Yes, I concede we've had a slight improvement in quality of life. I do agree that air conditioning is a fantastic blessing! But as society baked a bigger and better-tasting pie, the gluttons eating it are not the middle class or the poor, but the upper classes—in proportions never seen in human history. The Gap has grown.

Gadgets are Hushpuppies

Dr. Zan Holmes, the renowned United Methodist preacher from Texas, once told me the story, from his black preaching tradition, of the origins of hushpuppies: in the Antebellum South, the slave-cooks would be frying up fish after dipping them in cornmeal and onions. The hunting dogs and their pups would gather at the screen door of the kitchen, whining and yelping as they smelled the meat cooking. Rather than share the more valuable fish, the cook would roll up small wads of cornmeal, deep fry them, and then toss the meatless balls to the dogs to "hush the puppies." This, Dr. Holmes added, was how blacks viewed the earliest attempts at racial justice in the South: token, meaningless gestures were made by the white power structure in attempts to quell the demand for equal rights.

"Hushpuppies." Zan concluded. "I eat 'em, but they aren't very satisfying."

Thomas Sowell believes that DVD hushpuppies should satisfy the poor. While we have more material conveniences, our overall quality of life has not improved. Gadgets do not compensate for the erosion of paychecks. **Society's *expectations*—and *anxieties*—have risen** due to those very "luxuries" that Sowell cites as examples of our good fortune. If anything, when you have a product like a video player that is found in 98% of homes, that product then becomes a "cultural necessity," thereby putting a greater burden on the income/budgets of the poor. As the entire level of technology rises, the perception of poverty rises with it; poor children may indeed have a small TV/VCR at home, but when they walk by the wide-screen HDTV and Blue-Ray picture in Walmart, they feel, in relative terms, poorer than the kids of my generation did.

When I was a child, we had an old black-n-white TV; I didn't feel poor until I saw my uncle's big color television console. A related point: my parents only had three channels of television, but they *never* feared being unable to pay the cable-TV bill—they had no such bill! Technological prosperity is not always a blessing. Americans may now have 50 to 500 channels... but they also have a "cable provider" bill each month to worry about. Our homes, and our bodies, are not equipped to deal with a loss of air conditioning, so the utility bill is a serious concern, especially here in the South. Most working class people I meet live in constant fear of losing their jobs to foreign markets, harbor anxiety about their debt load, wonder which bills they can't pay this month, and dread the soaring cost of health and education for their children.

Inflation Hardest for Families

Speaking of health and education, another point Sowell and his ilk overlook is how inflation hits families the hardest. Health insurance and medical costs have risen at twice the rate of inflation; so not only have wages stagnated, the costs of keeping a family healthy have soared. Ironically, since the cost of a high-end video system with Blu-Ray player for Richie Rich has gone *down*, the government factors that into their CPI, so as to make inflation look less daunting. Meaningless metrics. A parent is more concerned about the cost of a gallon of milk, or the cost of medicine, than about the cost of video.

The cost of education has risen even faster than milk or medical care. My parents didn't worry about our college: their meager income qualified us for Pell Grants for tuition (and we worked jobs in college to pay our living expenses). As I write these words, rich politicians are trying to scale back the Pell program, even though tuition is ten-fold what it was in my day. In my own family, with a household income of about $60,000 in 2009 and two daughters in college, we still did not qualify for Pell grants. $60,000 can no longer keep a family in a middle class standard of living without incurring debt... and lots of it. But it was enough to disqualify us for aid.

Most of my career, I made a small income as a pastor, but by the time my children reached college age, I had hit the peak of my career and no longer qualified. Scholarships tend to disregard a lifetime of low pay and accumulated debt, and instead disqualify middle class parents based on their most recent tax year, during their peak earning years. Lifelong family savings accounts are drained by tuition costs. College tuition and fees rose over the last 30 years at a rate nearly three times that of general inflation, so now a degree from Middlebury College or George Washington University will cost you a quarter of a million dollars.[102] Sowell never mentions this, even though he is a college professor himself.

The Poor are Fine: They have Credit Cards!

Sowell claims the poor are doing better over the last forty years than the statistics on income indicate, because those below "poverty level spend $1.75 for every dollar of income."[103] His logic: we are better off because we can **borrow** our way to prosperity.

Debt is a curse on the poor, not a blessing, as 30% of income merely goes to pay interest in many households. Madison Avenue has tempted Americans to become slaves to consumerism... and consumer debt. The average household debtload is about $85,000, according to *USA Today*. By comparison, my lower middle class parents never owed more than $10,000 at any given time. Poor? Perhaps, but they died **debt-free**. Their children, however, are now indentured servants—in debt in amounts that would horrify them.

Sowell deserves the epithet of "callous elitist" because of his disconnections from reality, like this one: "Most of the millions of people in the often-cited statistics on households in the bottom 20 percent" of the U.S. economy are not "genuinely hurting."[104] Bull. I spent much of my career ministering to those in the bottom half of the economy, and most of them are swimming furiously upstream, trying to keep their heads above water. Statistics don't reflect the pain and anxiety these persons feel over job losses, debt burdens, struggles to pay their health insurance bills, both spouses working yet trying to keep a house clean, the constant juggling of priorities. *Do I send my child to a good college, or do I buy them braces... I can't do both*. Even that worry may seem petty to the billions in the Third World whose fear is about sheer survival. But Sowell would have us gloss over the anxieties of the shrinking middle class, the unrelenting fear of the working class, with a wave of his hand: *They have DVD players... all is well!*

Pick and Choose Statistics

And he wants it both ways. When statistics overwhelmingly show that the rich are getting away with murder at the expense of the rest of us, he calls those statistics "lies," but then goes on to use other statistics when it suits his argument. I, too, find statistics to be pliant and misleading—especially Sowell's. I know firsthand the hard work and pain of an unrewarded middle class without seeing a data sheet.

Thus I have little interest in quibbling with Sowell over his various numbers. While other experts are near-unanimous in seeing the widening gap between rich and poor, Sowell convinces himself it's fine to have the most tedious work in society done for pennies per hour in foreign sweatshops while others wallow in millions. His statistics are out-dated and cherry-picked. Instead, allow me to debunk his pretzel logic and deluded conclusions.

At first glance, Sowell marshalls fine-sounding arguments. Some of his points I will concede: the free market *does* provide an opportunity for a poor person to strike it rich. That doesn't mean it's possible for everyone—or even a majority—of the working class to ever get ahead financially. His logic is like saying, "Because *one* person won a million in the lottery, *all* persons should win the lottery." Some who start life in poverty do manage to rise to middle class or above. Sowell wants to celebrate this tiny minority as an excuse to ignore the plight of the rest, the vast millions who continue stranded in economic slavery. He fails to see that the possibility of good fortune for a few does not change the real-life pain of the many.

Sowell states that "income statistics greatly under-estimate the economic resources available to people in the lower income brackets...." Greatly? Slightly, perhaps. Some "po folk" work second jobs, take tips and other unreported income, and barter. Ironically, Sowell then turns around and denigrates the poor as lazy because so many of them are under-employed—forgetting his previous point that some work in the "underground economy" and have unreported income. He further slurs the poor by citing their higher ratio of unemployment vs. the wealthy—forgetting that poor families with young children choose to have one spouse stay home with the children rather than play the zero-sum game of paying for daycare so mom can work at Burger Doodle for pennies. If mom could get a job as a part-time "consultant" for $65,000 a year, as Texas Governor Rick Perry's wife did, then she could afford a nanny to watch the kids while she goes to her meetings.[105]

Few ivory-tower analysts understand the financial burdens on families... so many little expenses never get put on their spreadsheets. For example, schoolteachers tell me how they grieve when a field trip is announced, but due to lack of school funding, the children must bring $5 or $10 to pay museum admission or transportation—and those that can't afford it get left behind.

Dependent deductions allowed by the IRS do not reflect even a tenth of the cost of raising a child. The rich get a bigger deduction for a country club membership than I do for raising a child. Most people in poverty have children, but the tax code penalizes marriage and offers far bigger tax breaks to stock speculators than to parents.

Fewer Children? Feel Blessed!

Sowell gives us another reason why the poor of today are better off: they have fewer children than previous generations of the poor. Yet more Sowellian logic: *The statistics on poverty are misleading... the quality of life is better for the poor... because they have fewer children!*

The reason they have fewer children is because they can't *afford* more children. After our second child was born, we took a hard look at the burgeoning cost of college... and decided to kill our third child. Okay, I overstate... no, we didn't choose abortion, we simply chose not to have more children... an economic decision that Sowell flips to use as proof of good times. I'm surprised he didn't just say, "Sterilize the poor, then *Laissez les bons temps rouler!*"

Wake Up and Smell the Coffee

TIME magazine reported that of each $100 in retail sales, only 66 cents goes to the average Ugandan coffee farmer for his coffee.[106] That is less than one percent of total value going to the person most responsible for the product. Who do you think worked the hardest to bring that coffee from seed to marketplace? Not the barista at Starbucks, not the executives at Folgers nor their ad agency, not even the shipping company. The one who sweated and labored the hardest, the one most responsible for creating and picking the coffee bean, is paid the least. And if you argue with that, you have not visited a coffee plantation. I have. But a visit is not enough. If you've not spent a year working in dusty, hot fields, contending with insects, watching your hands turn to scratches and callouses, and laying down at night with aching back and broken spirit, you have no basis on which to defend the justice of capitalism as you sip your latté.

According to the Associated Press, workers in a Honduras shirt factory make 24 cents for each shirt they sew... even though the name-brand shirt sells for $50.[107] The workers make an average of

55 cents an hour in miserable conditions, but are routinely fired if they try to establish a labor union. Many of the guilty companies, with gargantuan profits, are U.S. firms. Our minimum wage laws do not prevent U.S. corporations from exploitative wages in other countries.

Those Lazy Poor

My passion is not driven by envy of the rich and their possessions, but rather by my indignation that they not only dance on the graves of the poor, they do so with smug sanctimonious platitudes: "I earned my millions," "The poor are lazy," "It's their own fault." These are the "damn lies," not the statistics that show that Walmart has over a million employees paid less than $10 per hour,[108] yet as ABC News reports, the CEO of Walmart makes $$16,826 *per hour!*[109] Or the fact that over one-fifth of all children in the United States live below the poverty line.[110]

Sowell emboldens the dancing rich with his absurd and abstract notions... and sadly, he is not alone. Corporate boards ignore the most troublesome statistic of all: in 1950, the ratio of the average executive's paycheck to the average worker's paycheck was about 30 to 1. Since the year 2000, that ratio has exploded to more than 300 to one.[111] This is a **ratio**. It is unrelated to inflation. It proves that executives were once hired and happy at 30 times the rate of the worker's pay; now they are paid 300 times, with no justification other than greed. The statistics showing an astronomical gap between executives and the rest of us are not "damn lies," but have been verified and cross-referenced by a variety of sources.

Summary

Money means entirely different things to the wealthy than it does to the poor and middle class. Sure, *all* people see money as the means to food and shelter, and thus security. But for those of us who are not rich, money is connected to pure fear and pain. Most working-class Americans live with a gnawing fear about tomorrow. We fear for our very survival. We fear that if we lose our jobs, we will lose everything of value: the respect of our children, the feelings of success and achievement, safety, health—and ultimately, we fear losing the most important elixir of life: hope. Lack of money and the real fear of not having enough robs people of hope and of a future.

Studies have shown that the poor buy lottery tickets in disproportionate numbers, and pundits imply this is a function of ignorance in understanding statistics. I doubt the educated classes understand lottery odds any better than the poor. No, the poor buy lottery tickets because **they can purchase hope for a dollar**.

Tragically, the only, tiny wisp of hope our society offers most people is a lottery or casino—more illusion than promise. Upward job mobility, for most Americans, is no more of a realistic hope than winning a Pick Six ticket.

Another class of people, however, views money through the prism of plenty. They could lose their job without a moment's concern. This privileged class worries about money only as a game, an abstract of the board game, *Monopoly*: one bad roll of the dice is disappointing, but soon they'll go past "Go" and "Collect $200" or land on "Opportunity" and find they've collected a stock dividend. Or in a rare calamity, like the financial collapse of 2008, they simply brush the pieces from the board and start over, pulling the cord to their golden parachute. Money for them is as easy and painless as gathering up the orange $500 bills when an opponent lands on Boardwalk. Because of this abstraction, they are easily detached from the misery of the working class... they just don't "get it."

And yet, the wealthiest do understand one thing about the rest of us: because we do struggle and have real fears about our financial futures, we are susceptible to political manipulation. The oligarchs manipulate us politically with *fear*—the topic of our next chapter.

~~~

Chapter 7: The Fourth Reich of the Rich
Politics and fear-mongering: best friends of dynasties

The danger is not that a particular class is unfit to govern. Every class is unfit to govern.   ~Lord Acton, 1881

Their final objective... is to capture political power so that, using the power of the state and the power of the market simultaneously, they may keep the common man in eternal subjection.
             ~Vice-President (1941-1945) Henry A. Wallace

Amazing Connections

Henry A. Wallace was not some wild-eyed radical. An humble farm boy from the midwest, he quietly and calmly saved the world! His father, Henry C. Wallace, was a professor at Iowa State College, where he taught a remarkable student who would separately grow up to revolutionize agriculture. That student, a 19-year-old son of slaves, befriended the seven-year-old Henry A. and instilled in him a love for growing things and a deeper appreciation of God's hand in nature... that college student's name was George Washington Carver! And Henry A. Wallace grew up to become Vice-President under FDR. While helping a crippled Roosevelt fight the Nazi menace, Henry A. also fathered the "Green Revolution" that saved billions from starvation.[112] Having developed hybrid corn himself, Henry established an agricultural research station in Mexico, which hired Norman Borlaug. Borlaug developed miraculous hybrids of corn, wheat, and rice—eventually winning the 1970 Nobel Peace Prize for preventing worldwide famine. Gene Lucht wrote: "Norman Borlaug, Henry Wallace and Herbert Hoover ...did more to fight world hunger than any other trio in history."[113] Vice-President Henry A. Wallace, a man who helped save the world from Nazism and massive starvation, in turn, warned us of plutocrats—rich fascists: "If we define an American fascist as one who in case of conflict puts money and power ahead of human beings, then there are undoubtedly several million fascists in the United States.... They demand free enterprise, but are the spokesmen for monopoly and vested interest."[114]

Plutocracy—Rule by the Rich

Newsman Bill Moyer, similarly calm and not prone to hyperbole, recently warned, "Over the past thirty years, with the complicity of Republicans and Democrats alike, the plutocrats have used their vastly increased wealth to assure that government does their bidding."[115] Of course, plutocracy is not just a *modern* threat. If pressed, Moyer would admit that political control by the wealthy has been a scourge on humanity for millennia. Moyer is just reluctant to accept the extreme theories that come along with this topic; neither he nor I endorse the anti-Semitic paranoia that sometimes accompanies the phrase "The Fourth Reich of the Rich." Plutocratic rule is not a lone dynasty linked across history, nor a singular conspiracy attributable to any of the following: Jewish bankers/Saudi princes, Texas Republicans/European Freemasons, Nazis/Communists, Catholics/Atheists. Indeed, we can readily see stark contrasts and conflicts of interest among these "usual suspects" in fruitcake theories. Does anyone really think Nazis and Jews conspired together!?

A Conspiracy of Greed

A single "master conspiracy theory" simply doesn't match the facts of history or of human psychology. The rich and powerful are too egoistic and competitive to bow to one leader or world-view. There is no chorus line of ideologues. **But one thing binds *all* plutocrats across *all* history: the code word G-R-E-E-D.**

Regardless of the religion or politics of any particular plutocrat, all have the same temptation: **to use their money to gain more power, and their power to gain more money.** A vicious self-reinforcing circle. When lust for money and lust for power meet, they mate like the hellish description of the incestuous impregnation of Satan and Sin in *Paradise Lost*, yielding, to use Milton's phrase, "odious offspring": plutocracy, the Reich of the Rich.

Yet, this enduring Rule of Greed does not have a pure lineage across history, it does not hold ideological hands nor depend upon a singular secret conspiratorial cabal. No, the Evil Empire is a multi-headed Hydra, each face different though all sharing a body of gold.

New-Feudalism

Both liberal and conservative writers have recognized this "conspiracy of greed." Des Griffin, author of *Fourth Reich of the Rich*, was a staunch "Christian conservative," adamantly opposed to progressive politics and socialism, yet he warned us of the coming neo-feudalism, a time now upon us when only two classes remain: indebted serfs owned and ruled by rich feudal lords. Griffin quoted the liberal Georgetown Professor, Dr. Carroll Quigley, who admitted that the rich and powerful "had a far reaching aim" to establish "a world system of financial control in private hands able to dominate the political system of each country and the economy of the world as a whole. This system was to be controlled in a feudalist fashion by... secret agreements...."[116]

You may dismiss Griffin as an anti-Semitic kook, but Professor Quigley was widely respected and intimately connected to heads of state and to world financial leaders. In his 1992 acceptance speech,

President Bill Clinton pointedly named Quigley as a key mentor. Griffin and Quigley wrote those words forty years ago. Today, the world is divided into two classes: those with economic freedom, and those without it. Their prophecy is fulfilled. The idea of a "Fourth Reich of the Rich" is no longer the ranting of a "conspiracy theorist."

Peasants Ruled by Feudal Lords

Money controls the world. Money controls the mouthpieces at FOX news on the right, and CBS news on the left. Money controls the political process; Katy Bachman at *Brandweek* estimates "political media spending will hit $5.6 **billion** during the 2012 election." Money even warps academia—not a lot of poor people attend Harvard and Yale. Most college presidents earn *twenty* times what a schoolteacher earns, so they too belong to the Fourth Reich, not the middle class.[117] "Ivy-League Economics Professors are often on the payroll of Wall Street and other corporations, to the tune of millions, as board members or consultants," stated Charles Ferguson, who gives examples in his documentary *Inside Job*, showing how these same academics gave false-positive reports of their benefactors' industries. "Many prominent academics quietly make fortunes while helping the financial industry shape public debate and government policy," he adds. Academia for hire... for *bribe*.

And 98% of our media in all its forms are controlled by big-money elites: Madison Avenue advertising, most magazine and publishing businesses, television and movies and music.

The Reich of the Rich

Using the word *Reich*, the German word for "rule" or "ruling party," may be inflammatory to some because of its association with Nazism. I am not one who carelessly accuses my enemies of being another "Hitler." Hitler stands alone in the annals of evil. But I purposely use the phrase "Reich of the Rich" to connote something broader and more insidious than a singular dictatorship. Dictatorships come and go, they tend to die with the leader, but what Hitler had in mind was "a thousand-year Reich," **an empire and a *system* that would be ongoing and all-powerful.** I don't fear any one single billionaire. I fear a worldwide system, call it a "leaderless confederacy of the rich," which makes it increasingly difficult for the grassroots to control their own destiny.

Ancient as the Fourth Reich is, rule by the rich is growing to new proportions, moving toward a formidable dynasty of almost unlimited power. Cold-blooded powermongers have always been amongst us. But **factors unique to our post-modern age** include:

- The gap between the the mega-rich and the working class has never been so vast, with unprecedented amounts of wealth in the hands of a few. The exponential rise of wealth, as we discussed previously, can't really be grasped by the human mind.
- "Big Brother" spy technology and hi-tech armaments offer the rich elite frighteningly-sophisticated ways to control us.
- Globalization and a diminished nationalism has some value, but may be leading us to an era where the normal checks and balances of nation against nation fail to limit the rise of singular power and control. Russia and China are no longer so much enemies as they are business partners who conspire with U.S. moguls and European bankers for control of the masses.

The world is quickly shifting away from communism *and* away from democracy, becoming a "plutocracy," or "oligarchy," or "timocracy," all words which allude to "rule by the rich or elite."

The Day Democracy Died

Even some conservative voices are crying out against this invasion by land and by sea. Paul Craig Roberts was Assistant Secretary of the Treasury in the Reagan administration, yet he warns: "Now that the five Republicans on the Supreme Court have overturned decades of U.S. law and given corporations the ability to buy every American election, Democrats and Republicans can be nothing but pawns for a plutocracy.... The American public cannot even get reliable information about their plight, as the 'mainstream media' has been concentrated into a few corporate hands...as dependent on corporate money as are politicians."

Roberts refers to the Supreme Court ruling of January 2010, *Citizens United v. Federal Election Commission*, which trumped a century of campaign finance regulations that had limited the power of corporations and the wealthy to buy elections. Even some Republicans are alarmed at the danger, like John Bonifaz who warns that corporations now can "effectively own our democracy."

Author Greg Palast wrote: "The Court ruled that corporations should be treated the same as 'natural persons', i.e. humans. Well, in that case, expect the Supreme Court to next rule that Walmart can run for President."[118] The absurd equation (Corporation = Human) gives faceless companies an entitlement to free speech... which means unlimited monies pouring into political ads via PACs.

In the 2010 election alone, $3 billion was spent with commercial broadcasters (this does not include money spent via print, billboards, direct mail and other campaign media).[119] No wonder the major networks did little to protest the Supreme Court ruling. Additionally, Republicans work feverishly to eliminate PBS and NPR at the Federal level, as Governors Chris Christie and Rick Scott worked to destroy their state public broadcasts.

To win even a minor election requires thousands of dollars, so the average citizen is effectively locked out of politics. Niether you nor I can win a national campaign without help from deep pockets. That fact should set off alarm bells: we *are* ruled by a plutocracy, and the few exceptions one might cite are merely "the exception that proves the rule." Politics is a rich man's sport. And most of the countries of the world—be they tyrannies, democracies, even communist countries—are ruled by the richest of the rich.

DC Rich

American politicians are extremely wealthy... or have close friends who are. George W. Bush had both: personal wealth (from his government-subsidized baseball franchise) and wealthy friends, like the ENRON crook Ken Lay and computer importer Michael Dell. Mr. Dell's compensation package exceeds $150 million annually, thanks in part to government contracts, tax breaks and subsidies, and overseas tax havens... but don't worry, he gives back to "the government." Dell has given nearly a million bucks to Republican politicians.[120] Half of U.S. Congressmen are millionaires, as is every President in my lifetime.[121] Of the 43 U.S. Presidents, 34 have been millionaires (in today's dollars).[122] (Lincoln was one of the few Presidents who was not filthy rich.)

We no longer have a "citizen's Senate," we have a "tycoon's Senate," and the House is not far behind. The ten richest members of Congress have a combined net worth of $2.8 billion. That's billion with a B. You may be surprised to learn that seven of the ten are Democrats. All ten of them voted to extend the Bush Tax cuts, which benefitted the top 1% of Americans more than all other taxpayers combined.[123] The tax rate for millionaires is now half of what it was in 1945—and the Inheritance Tax has been eliminated (see Chapter 10). So the plutocracy is getting exactly what they are paying for.

The higher the profit of a particular industry, the greater the chance that they tried to manipulate politics to their advantage. The top campaign contributor to Bush the Younger was MBNA—at the time the country's second largest credit card issuer. Not surprisingly, during Bush's tenure, MBNA had a major hand in writing the "bankruptcy reform" law which made it much more difficult for middle class families in financial trouble to find relief.[124] As a group, the top campaign contributors to Barack Obama were from the financial sectors.

Both Sides Against the Middle

Obviously, these companies are not giving out of a sense of civic duty or patriotic commitment. Most corporate donations and PACS give to *both* sides of the political aisle! They are not expressing their "free speech" preference for a particular ideology, corporations are blatantly buying access and influence.

On some matters, politics and policy can be morally complex, with reasonable arguments on both sides (abortion and death penalty, for example). But when it comes to economics, the issue is crystal clear: the rich have bought off both political parties, who are complicit in ripping off the middle class. We can argue about which side of the aisle did the "best" job in ripping us off, but that's an academic rabbit trail. As Saint Paul put it, "All have sinned and fallen short...." The system is corrupt on both ends. The mega-rich corrupted it with bribes and continue to play both sides against each other in a game of political distraction.

But we, the hard-working middle class, have the votes to change it. This will require a huge educational effort. We are just as much in need of a revolution today as we were in 1776. Again, this is why I am writing in a non-academic, informal and personal style, passionately begging you to tell others about the bi-partisan con job, and about this book and the website: **www.FireTheRich.org**.

Why do both Parties cooperate with the Fourth Reich plutocrats in legislation that harms the middle class? It is not that they hate the middle class, or have some conspiracy to destroy us. They simply realize that the middle class is where most creativity, productivity and wealth actually originates. We are the golden goose that lays the golden eggs. And in that fable, the owner of the goose gets greedy and squeezes the goose for more golden eggs—in the end, impatiently killing the goose. Third-graders react to the old fable this way: "How could anyone be so stupid as to kill the goose that is laying the gold!?" Yet the plutocrats are foolishly killing the middle class, driven by greed and a lust for power.

Tragedy and Hope

Why are we not reduced to a slave-planet by this loose confederation of plutocrats? Because of competing factions not drawn along party lines: agendas shaped by differing corporate, geographic and even religious interests. Even if secret societies like Freemasonry or the Bilderbergers had a singular plan to rule the world, they have never been successful in holding together competing power groups. If the plutocrats have established a New World Order, they get a failing grade for "order." Ours is a world in chaos and tension. Some quick examples of how monied powers can't always agree:
•Global warming legislation would profit the nuclear and alternative energy industries, while hurting others, like coal and big oil.
•Hollywood is a huge monied industry that tends to lean left, while most manufacturing and energy companies lean right.

- Rich attorneys oppose tort reform, corporations lobby for it.

But at any point where diverse powerbrokers encounter a legislative agenda that chooses **profits over people**, there you will find shared agreement amongst the oligarchs.

In a glimmer of hope, sometimes the conflict among the wealthy works for the greater public good. Some corporations are beginning to see that what is good for the consumer and the employee (health and job safety, clean/green products, equitable pay and benefits) can create a more robust economy in the long run. And sometimes, people of virtue stand up for the average Joe. Yes, I do believe some wealthy folks want to do the right thing!

The Bipartisan Screwing of America

Occasionally, the excesses of the Reich are so extreme that even reporters on the Left *and* the Right take notice. In the same month (August 2010) one of the most **conservative** magazines, *Reader's Digest*, and one of the most **liberal**, *Rolling Stone*, both published articles warning us of how Congress has screwed us over in favor of making big banks richer. You know you are in trouble when *Rolling Stone* admits Obama friends, like Tim Geithner and Larry Summer, are just as guilty of favoring the rich as were Republicans George Bush and Richard Shelby. G. W. Bush sold us out to ENRON, Bechtel, Halliburton and Big Oil, but when it comes to pandering to Wall Streets bankers and brokers, many Democrats outdo Republicans. Rabid Leftwing investigative journalist Mait Taibbi has admitted this is a bipartisan con job. When asked about how big money has corrupted both capitalism and politics, he said: "The Democrats are worse than Republicans on this."[125] (That does not mean he's gentle in his criticism of the Republicans, calling Senator Richard Shelby, head of the banking committee, a "monster.")

On the Left, magazines like *The Progressive Populist*, *Mother Jones*, and *The Progressive* have argued that de-regulation by Clinton, banking/Fannie Mae bills by Senate Democrats Chris Dodd and Charles Schumer, with House Rep Barney Frank, and more recently bail-outs and failed oversight by the Obama administration, all helped keep billions flowing out of taxpayers' pockets into New England mansions.

Even voices from the conservative side admit that Republicans have gone too far in throwing taxpayer money at bailouts and robbing the middle class. *Reader's Digest*, ultraconservative pundit Pat Buchanan, and even Fox's Bill O'Reilly, loudly voiced opposition to the Wall Street bailouts. TEA Partiers scream at Obama, but when pressed, many in the TEA Party will concede that their movement began because of anger at George Bush, who had favored the rich with big government spending and bailouts, with huge tax cuts for the wealthiest. TEA Partiers are being thoroughly screwed by both Left and Right. Wake up and smell the Lipton!

It is past time to uproot the two-party system. We need a viable, populist Coalition Third Party. Many fine people in the early TEA Party movement thought they were signing on for just such reform, but we have since learned that it has been secretly funded by rich Republicans such as the Koch brothers, making the TEA Party a puppet of the Republican "protect-the-rich" agenda. All the political parties are bought and paid for by the Fourth Reich of the Rich.

The Glass Menagerie

We can point to numerous laws and policies over the last hundred years that benefit the upper classes, disastrous legislative actions that prove who runs the country. For example, the repeal of the Glass-Steagall Act set the stage for the crash of 2008 and the largest fleecing of Americans in history. In the aftermath of the crash, this is how Senator Feingold describes the window-treatment "reform bill": "They wouldn't even let us have a vote on those amendments... because they didn't want it.... [T]he unholy alliance that is the revolving door between Wall Street and Washington is running the show." Of the end result of so-called reform, the candid Senator added: "Did you notice that Wall Street didn't seem upset about this at all? That's all you need to know."[126]

Fear-Mongering: Weapon of the Rich

For millennia, kings, popes and potentates used violent force to control the masses. In civilized countries, strong arm tactics have fallen out of fashion. So they now rely on another ancient weapon of suppression: fear. Fear is a friend to the rich and the comfortable, causing the masses to ignore logic, fairness, and justice. Poisonous fear can drive people to subvert their own best interest.

The fears exploited by the rich in my lifetime have been threefold: **racial fear, fear of communism, and fear of God's wrath**. All of this is quite ironic: the rich have the most to lose from communism, and the most to fear from God, who judges greed harshly (see Chapter 5). Working class whites, paradoxically, worry about minorities and immigrants "taking our jobs," when they have a shared economic interest with minorities. Policies and programs that help minorities also tend to benefit lower-to-middle-class whites. But the plutocrats stir up racial tension (watch *Fox News* with a critical eye and see how they handle race) to pit us against each other. It works.

A Third Way

So one way to defeat the Fourth Reich is to reverse their game:

build a consensus party. We need to look for commonalities, and overlook differences, to focus on electing national leaders who are dedicated to saving the middle class. Adversarial relationships are not a smart endgame, not in business, politics or neighborhoods. When someone stirs up middle class Whites against Blacks or Hispanics, the only winners are the upper class. The stresses on the middle class and the stresses on the ethnic poor all come from the same source: plutocrats who control the Two-Party system and the economy.

Economic justice should be our first political concern, rather than debates over gun control or abortion or capital punishment. Ideological and religious issues that are irreconcilable must be set aside; we've debated for decades and settled into compromises that may not make either side happy but are *workable* comprises. We can still continue to work for our pet causes, but a Third Party should focus first on electing national candidates who will stand up against the monied powers. A Third Party may finally be viable. More on this in the final chapter, "**Solutions**."

But first we have to wrest control away from the greed-addicted, power-corrupted Elite Class of the Ultra-Wealthy. And the antidote to their "control poison" is *courage*.

Blame the Victim

The Fourth Reich uses a variety of tactics to keep fear and loathing among the classes below them aimed laterally or downward... even though our anger should be aimed upward at those in power. In the aftermath of the housing crash, despite the plain facts—that minority homebuyers were victims, not perpetrators—conservative media outlets began to put the spin out that the "crash" had its roots in ethnic loans. Much of middle America fell for the yarn spun by Wall Street's cronies that the main culprit in the financial collapse was Fannie Mae's efforts to help minorities get home loans. Yes, some did default on these sub-prime, under-$100,000 mortgages. But measured by actual dollars lost, wealthier white homeowner defaults cost lenders far more than ethnic defaults. The bigger truth is that the mortgage meltdown was a direct result of Wall Street/banks' manipulations: over-leveraged derivatives betting on home mortgages. The "underclass" wanted to *stay* in their homes, *wanted* to pay their mortgages—that's why they saved up to buy a home in the first place. A year before the Wall Street implosion, the country entered into an economic downturn— with many causes, some of them cyclical, but one large cause being the surge in gasoline prices. Consumers retreated in their spending on other items, sales decreased, corporations began layoffs, and a vicious downward spiral began. As always happens in a recession, the poorest people, with the smallest cash-cushion, are hurt the worst. So naturally, a good number of minority housing loans went into default.

In the big picture, those losses were a drop in the bucket. The bankers, Wall Street investors and insurance moguls began a "bailout" raid on the public treasury that dwarfed a few minority home-repos. The beauty of this race-baiting tactic (from the perspective of the rich and, in this case, the Republican Party) was two-for-one: **1.** it continued to foment and focus class resentment downward, rather than upward **2.** since Bill Clinton and Barney Frank had been cheerleaders for the Fannie Mae plan to empower minority and "lower class" home ownership, the Republicans shifted blame to the Democrats—though plenty of Republicans had previously jumped on board the Fannie Mae train too. And the vast majority of Republicans supported Bush's bailout of the rich. So again, the minority housing issue is a red herring or straw man, pick your metaphor. The real profiteers behind the Great Robbery of 2007-2009 were not the minorities, but the bankers and investors. And the real causes of the crash were the speculators taking outlandish risks with *our* pensions and savings, knowing that if the bubble burst, the U.S. government would take the fall. Which was exactly what happened.

Race-Baiting and Fear-Mongering

The race-baiting associated with the economic crash continued, aided by the election of a scape-goat, Barack Obama. Tea Partiers (mostly white and middle class) became incensed that the new President was spending billions of tax dollars to keep the economy from spiraling into a full-blown depression. Never mind that George Bush is the one who *began* those TARP bailouts, never mind that Bush had incurred more deficit spending than any President before him. Now, suddenly, white people were livid at the new President for doing the same things Bush did. No, wait, there was *one* difference: Bush signed those executive orders with a white hand; Obama held the pen with black fingers.

My words here may disturb Tea Partiers. Which is a shame, because I am *sympatico* with the populist aspect of that movement. I even agree with the core idea behind the T.E.A. Party: we are "Taxed Enough Already." (The *middle class* is overtaxed; the wealthy have tax shelters, slick accountants and offshore bank accounts.) I don't wish to paint all Tea Partiers with the broad brush of racism. Many fine and patriotic Americans are angry for the right reasons—fed up, as I am, with dishonest fat-cat politicians, government bloat and inefficiency, and Wall Street extortion. But there is no denying that a portion of Tea Party members are preoccupied with racial issues, as evidenced by the repeated emails I get from my right-wing friends—emails that attack Barack Obama in blatantly-racist ways and constantly harp on immigration issues in the most one-sided and inflammatory ways. Most of these emails are too unpleasant to share here, but a quick example: one chain-email sent to me contained a picture of a dark-skinned "illegal immigrant" in an unflattering pose, flipping his "bird finger" during a Cinco de Mayo parade, and another picture in the email showed a dark-skinned man burning the U.S. flag. This was designed to inflame passions against ethnic minorities, even though more *white* youth have burned flags than the rare radical Hispanic. I am no particular fan of Barack Obama. He has been guilty of putting questionable persons into positions of power over our economy, our banking regulations, etc., starting with Timothy Geithner and Larry Summers (i.e. foxes appointed to watch the hen house). But for the likes of Donald Trump to question Obama's intelligence reeks of racism. Or read the words of Alabama Republican Scott Beason, who called blacks "aborigines."[127]

George Wallace and Welfare Cadillacs

When I was young, growing up in the state of Alabama, the wealthy found a champion in George Wallace, the multi-term governor who stirred up racial hatred and fear, turning the anger of lower-class whites away from the upper-class and toward "negroes in their welfare Cadillacs." In the small Southern town in which I lived, there were indeed welfare-recipients who drove Cadillacs. They parked old, dilapidated Cadillacs and Buicks in the dirt driveways next to their unpainted, ramshackle rented shanties, in front of the outhouse. (The upperclass in our town were fortunate to have a trade-in market for their big, gas-guzzling cars after the odometer flipped past 99,000 miles.) When you lived in a shack with no bathroom, gaps in the floor, with no insulation or running water, the one consolation was to have a ten-year-old status symbol parked in the drive. And yet, this became the "proof" of welfare abuse in the minds of Wallace-era racists.

Most blacks in our town did not own transportation at all. Black maids, cooks and nannies did, however, ride in Cadillacs: when wealthy white women would pick them up, carry them to the white two-story mansions, and employ them for a dollar an hour or so. The "domestic servants" were never allowed to ride in the front seat beside their white bosses... they were second-class citizens. As a boy, I found it humorously ironic that the white women were serving as chauffeurs to their black patrons! *Driving Miss Daisy* in reverse.

The upper-class whites lived in luxury, the blacks lived in squalor and took the jobs no one else wanted. So the core mythology—that blacks were somehow taking advantage of the taxpayer—was absurd. The reason minorities accepted such low wages, usually in cash with no taxation costs, was because the government, in essence, subsidized the labor pool through food stamps. Whites benefitted the most from this arrangement, having a kitchen slave for pennies.

Today, the people taking the least-desired work—fruit-picking, toilet cleaning, unskilled construction work—tend to be of a different race: Hispanic or other recent immigrants. In time, it became politically incorrect to overtly denigrate blacks. So now the whipping post of the affluent is "illegal immigration."

The New George Wallace

Alabama Governor Robert Bentley continued the Wallace tradition of scapegoating minorities when he signed a fascist immigration law in June, 2011, saying he was "proud" of the legislation which, among other things, effectively makes it illegal to be a Good Samaritan to Hispanics. This is the same Governor who previously told a mostly-black audience, "Anybody here today who has not accepted Jesus Christ as their savior, I'm telling you, you're not my brother...." I would suggest, Dr. Bentley, that you re-read the teachings of Christ, as you have evidently forgotten them.

Rich fascists distract us with a new myth, with the fear that illegal immigrants are taking our jobs and free-loading on the government. The truth is the opposite: illegal immigrants often are employed using fake I.D.s, but their wages are still taxed. That means the money they paid *into* Social Security will never be drawn *out* by these illegals—many will never qualify for Social Security, as they will either end up back in Mexico, or never reach retirement age, due to the high stress lifestyle and lack of medical care illegals endure. So in effect, illegals are subsidizing the Social Security for rest of us!

Those who supported the heavy-handed anti-immigrant bills of Alabama and Arizona claim they are not racist by asserting their concern is only with *illegal* immigrants, with armed Mexican drug peddlers. But no one is suggesting we coddle criminals. The Russian mafia has guns too, yet we seem to have little fear of white immigrants. The fear seems focused on dark skin—even though less than 1% of Hispanic immigrants own guns. They can't *afford* to own guns... if they were successful in the drug trade, they wouldn't need to be crossing the border for farm jobs!

Once the Red Scare, Now the Blue Fear

In the opening Presidential Debate for Republican candidates in

June 2011, immigrants and terrorists continued to be used for fearmongering. Candidate Herman Cain made it clear he doesn't trust Muslims, but if that weren't enough, Newt Gingrich piggybacked on Cain's remarks to connect the *Islam scare* with "Nazis and Communists." You can't teach an old dog new tricks. Fearmongering of communism has long been used by wealthy conservatives like Newt to justify trillions spent on military defense—including enough nuclear weapons to blow the world up 100 times over. The plutocrats, along with the military-industrial complex, used the "red scare" as a great fear inducer to control the masses, and as an easy way to counteract progressive populists. *Populist = Communist*. Completely untrue, but it had a nice ring to it!

With the collapse of the Soviet empire, it became harder to sell such a weak, straw man argument. We began to laugh at the demagogues who tried to brand progressives as Reds. So the new tactic has been to re-define populism as "socialism," and socialism as a stand-in for the red villain—with conservatives like Tommy Newberry (see Chapter 5A) labeling it as re-packaged communism. Oddly, the media has used red for the states that vote Republican, and blue for Democrats... so we have a new, *blue* scare: Socialism. Which the plutocrats caricature as *social leveling, dumbing down, stealing from the rich, destruction of incentive, central planning* and other nefarious plots by atheists in league with Satan.

Fearmongers Don't Fear the Reaper

But the truth is, the Fourth Reich propagators of fear don't really worry about socialism or communism or even Satan. They fear **democracy**. They fear the ballot box. They fear loss of political power, which might lead to loss of their luxuries.

They are smart people, skilled manipulators, though childish in their motives. Playing a child's game of *Monopoly*, they are not satisfied owning Boardwalk and Park Place, they also want to own Pennsylvania Avenue, the Utilities, the Railroads... they want it all.

Life is not a game. I see no joy in financial "winning" if that is defined as having everyone else lose. And the fearmongers will never be happy with democracy, with fair representation or a chicken in every pot. They are driven to be a winner-take-all. They spend millions to control the House, the Senate and the Oval Office, using any tactic—lies and fears—to control all three.

Summary

The Fourth Reich of the Rich has been around for centuries. Thomas Jefferson warned: "Banking institutions are more dangerous to our liberties than standing armies." Jefferson's warning is not so much about banking as it about the power of money to corrupt the financial process. He was not alone. Abraham Lincoln similarly warned, "The money power [national and international banks] preys upon the nation in times of peace, and conspires against us in times of adversity. It is more despotic than monarchy...."

I need not waste space here with details and examples of how the wealthy control our political system anymore than I need to prove the existence of gravity. The proof is in the fact that billions are spent to influence politicians and control legislation through corporate donations, individual donations, PACs and Super-PACs, corporate gifts/trips/perks, a horde of lobbyists, and the promise of high-paying jobs or board positions for "retired" elected officials. Take a look at how many former Congressmen end up with seven-figure salaries from the Halliburtons, Bechtels and GEs of the world. The politicians themselves will be quick to claim that those billions do not force them to vote a particular way. "I am my own man!" one Congressman self-righteously proclaimed. But **if the financial industry were not getting results from the expenditure of these millions in political-payback salaries and bribes, er, donations, would they continue to make those donations year after year?** They spend a fortune on politics because they double or triple their investment. Who is funding that rigged casino payout? You and me.

They no longer even make the feeble claim that these political donations are an expression of civic duty or ideological support for a particular politician; the rich individuals and corporations are giving to *both* parties at the same time! When political donations are given across the ideological spectrum, it is painfully obvious they are not exercising a constitutional right to free speech advocacy for deeply held political beliefs. It is bribery, plain and simple.

I began this chapter with quotes from Henry Wallace, and now close with another from the farmer-turned-Vice President: "A fascist is one whose lust for money or power is combined with such an intensity of intolerance toward those of other races, parties, classes, religions, cultures, regions or nations as to make him ruthless in his use of deceit or violence to attain his ends."

It is time for a new and higher ethic if we wish to save the American Dream. It's past time to reject fear and bigotry, to quit goose-stepping to the fascists of the Fourth Reich of the Rich.

~~~

Chapter 8: Greed is Heroin
Why Greed is the world's most dangerous addiction

You are not here merely to make a living. You are here in order to enable the world to live more amply, with greater vision, with a finer spirit of hope and achievement. You are here to enrich the world, and to impoverish yourself if you forget the errand.
~Woodrow Wilson

Some businesspersons look with condescending disdain at those of us who value the arts and humanities more than dollars. They hear the words of President Wilson, quoted above, and misread it to think their mission in life is to "enrich the world" by making themselves obscenely wealthy. Wilson, a progressive, believed that art, music, compassion, education, philosophy and religion are the higher virtues. Money is at best a tool, a *means* to enable a better society—it should never be mistaken as an *end*. But Wilson was like salmon swimming upstream, fighting against a river that has been flowing for thousands of years. The river is *Greed*.

Greed Expunged from the History Books

The river of greed flows tandem with the history of murder. In Genesis, Cain killed Abel out of jealousy, or so we are taught, but look closer at the story: the jealousy began when God favored Abel because of Abel's generosity with material goods. Abel gave the "first-fruit" offerings which Cain had greedily witheld. Cain's story does not end well, a fact that "Godly capitalists" have forgotten. This, and hundreds of other warnings against greed found in the Bible, are either forgotten or set aside in favor of remembering King Solomon's wealth.

The story of greed (and violence) in America is also ancient. The Mayans and the Incas were not "noble savages," innocents living in paradise. They hoarded gold and they warred and they sacrificed real innocents on altars, bloodily. But the history of "civilized greed" in America begins with Columbus.

According to a young priest who accompanied his expeditions, the primary motivator for Christopher Columbus was a lust for, and bloody search for, **gold**. Father Bartolemé de las Casas wrote in 1650 that, in contrast, the Native Caribbeans, "put no value on gold or other precious things... [and] are extremely generous with their possessions...." Columbus himself confirmed this, reporting to the Queen that the natives met them on the beach with friendship and charity, giving them gifts and other kindness. Columbus and crew requited their generosity with slaughter, enslavement, and theft. Columbus and the Spaniards put the natives to work, mining gold in such harsh conditions that a third of them died in the process of trying to satisfy Columbus' greed.[128] I quote Howard Zinn, who in turn quotes Las Casas: "'[The natives] suffered and died in the mines and other labors in desperate silence, knowing not a soul in the world to whom they could turn for help.' [Casas] describes their work in the mines: '...mountains are stripped from top to bottom and bottom to top a thousand times; they dig, split rocks, move stones, and carry dirt on their backs to wash it in the rivers, while those who wash gold stay in the water all the time with their backs bent so constantly it breaks them....' After each six or eight months' work in the mines... up to a third of the men died. 'While the men were sent many miles away to the mines, the wives remained to work the soil, forced into the excruciating job of digging and making thousands of hills for cassava plants. Thus husbands and wives were together only once every eight or ten months.... As for the newly born, they died early because their mothers, overworked and famished, had no milk to nurse them, and for this reason... 7000 children died in three months. Some mothers even drowned their babies from sheer desperation....'"

Columbus was not by faith or disposition a cruel man. What turned him into a monster guilty of "genocide"?[129] A desire for adventure? He'd already arrived in the Americas, fulfilling his yearning for discovery; even empty-handed, he could have returned to Spain a hero. Despite his investors expectations of profits, even without a grain of gold his discovery would have been greeted with joy for the prospect of colonization of new lands. The open-hearted natives would have cooperated with colonization in exchange for mere glass trinkets. Violence and theft had not been required. Columbus admitted as much.

So what drove Columbus to endorse mass cruelty, theft, slavery and murder? One word: **greed**. Gold has that effect on people. Any honest reading of Columbus' years with the "savages of the West Indies" reveals that the true savages were the Europeans, whose lust for gold and land overtook all other concerns, even the tenets of their own religion.

C'bus & the Conquistadors: Jazz Quartet Plays Tonite in NYC

Today's savages on Wall Street, our energy pirates and corporate conquerors are not as brazen at mass murder and torture, but they rob and enslave women and children just the same. And they do so while wrapping themselves in similar greed-driven justifications as did Columbus and the Conquistadors: Religion and Nationalistic Elitism-disguised-as-Patriotism. Those "Columbus Day" tunes are still being strummed in our time, by Goldman-Sachs CEO Lloyd Blankfein claiming "we are doing God's work," by the Walmart tycoons wrapping themselves patriotically in the American flag while selling Chinese goods, by BP Chairman Carl-Henric Svanberg bragging, "We care about the small people." These elitists believe they are special, they have God's favor. Another elitist who speaks for God, Pat Robertson, more a capitalist profiteer than a preacher, even blamed the disaster in Haiti on a religious curse. Ironically, Haiti is one of the islands still paying for the sins of "Christian" Columbus.

If the modern savages truly followed their religion, they would sell their excess and give to the poor; it they truly loved their country, they would not do business with foreign dictators or pay bribes or sell arms to questionable allies; if they truly believed the founding fathers, they would embrace "all men are created equal" instead of living in gated communities and sending their children to private schools away from the "riff-raff." Some of the denizens of the Upper Estate really do desire to act rightly... but they are blinded by one of the most powerful and deceptive forces of history: greed.

The More You Have, the Greedier You Get

The ancient Romans had a proverb: *Money is like seawater—the more a man drinks, the thirstier he becomes.* This aphorism applies to any addictive substance: the more you get, the more you want. Addiction, by definition, is a substance or action that provides temporary pleasure but longterm thirst for more. Greed is, truly, a form of addiction. Addiction destroys the addict and the persons around the addict. And to extend the drug metaphor: the more drugs you take, the worse the collateral damage of one's addiction. The more money one hoards, the greater the harm of greed. Are only the rich greedy? Of course not. But greed is more destructive in proportion to the amount of money hoarded. And studies have shown that the rich are, indeed, prone to be less compassionate. "We have now done 12 separate studies measuring empathy in every way imaginable, social behavior in every way, and ...on compassion and it's the same story," stated social scientist Dacher Keltner. "Lower class people just show more empathy, more prosocial behavior, more compassion, no matter how you look at it." An academic article entitled, "Social Class as Culture: The Convergence of Resources and Rank in the Social Realm," published in the journal *Current Directions in Psychological Science*, showed that the wealthier people become, the more likely to think selfishly, and the more they justify their success as self-achieved.[130]

So there seems to be a contradictory emotion that overtakes reason when wealth piles up: the bigger the mountain of money, the bigger the greed... an entitlement attitude sets in. CEO and Wall Street insider Seth Merrin confesses: "Do Wall Street people expect to be paid large bonuses in years [even] when their company lost $27 billion? The answer was, Yes!"[131]

Entrepreneurial Passion Transmogrified into Greed

Ayn Rand would argue that greed is a benefit to society, as it motivates people to work harder. Money motivates, which is why fictional characters Dagny Taggart and Gordon Gecko speak a speck of truth when they say that greed is good. An entrepreneur begins with a passion to build an innovative product or company that benefits society... maybe there is a touch of "good greed" there, a strong desire for money that pushes people to get out of bed early. Most streams in life don't run un-mingled; good runs with bad. With addiction, it is often a matter of moderation: one glass of wine now and then is good for the heart; ten glasses every day and alcoholism steps in and ruins your life. The same holds for greed. Over time, money motivation turns to money addiction. Greed warps the personality so that money becomes the *only* goal, the only yardstick of success, and they begin chasing profits without care to the consequences. This is why greed/money is a flawed motivator compared to, say, a desire for personal achievement or, better yet, a desire to improve life for family, friends and community. Greed leads to the ingrown, narcissistic life. Greed is unfulfilling. The theme song of greed is, "I can't get no satisfaction."

Insatiable

Greed never has "enough," never finds satisfaction, often spirals out of control. Actor Charlie Sheen made untold millions, and when money proved unsatisfying, he turned to cocaine, prostitutes and other hedonistic pursuits that also failed to satisfy. But most dedicated "greed addicts" stick with their first love—even though money never satiates. They are not satisfied by a million, yet they grasp for another million, regardless of the cost to society.

Sadly, greed is the one addiction that has society's blessing if it wears the mask of business respectability. We have various sayings bandied about which mindlessly pardon terrible ethics simply because profit is involved: "Business is business." "*Caveat emptor.*" "Don't take it personal, it's just bizness." "A man's gotta make a livin'." Our society makes profits the only measure of a successful business, and thus any *means* is justified by the monetary *ends*.

As a pastor, I received condescending lectures from churchmembers who were also "businesspeople" (condescending in that they view me as a naif, as if I'd never had to pay a light bill or put groceries on my own table—ignoring the fact that I have run my own, for-profit businesses). When I refused to heartlessly lay-off a longterm employee, they chided me for not making *dollars* the church's main concern. Of course I understand the value of money and that a church cannot run without it, but I strongly argued, "The church is *not* a business. The product we offer is *love*, and we offer it for free." (And yet, every church I served saw significant increases in financial giving.) In retrospect, I wish I had made a wider argument: "A church should not operate like a business; a business should operate like a *church*!" Companies should have a conscience, a core set of values, a concern for employees and customers that goes beyond dollar bills, with a goal of uplifting the entire community, not merely concerned with making a million more this quarter than last. The entire system of American finance is predicated on "growth," which is another word for "more profits regardless the consequences," another phrase meaning *greed*.

Greed is Bad for Business

I will go further and cite examples of companies that, when blinded by greed, actually *hurt* their own profitability. We can cite an unending list of examples where greed has cost corporations cash, and society... human lives: •The BP Gulf Oil Spill of 2010 was a direct result of greed.[132] Only greed explains why a successful company like British Petroleum, awash in cash, threw caution to the wind and expedited deep sea drilling—killing eleven workers. As I write this, the shoreline just miles from my home is awash in dead baby dolphins, symbols of the carnage of greed. •The Big Branch coal mining disaster under Massey Energy Company killed 29 workers. Massey had been cited over a thousand times for safety failures, many of which stemmed from penny-pinching.[133] Yet they paid CEO D. L. Blankenship $17,835,837 in total compensation the same year as the median worker made $33,190.[134] Blankenship, safely at a desk, made 537 times the mineworkers! •The Union Carbide chemical leak at Bhopal killed over 10,000 men, women and children... for the price of about a dollar a life, a back-up safety system may have prevented the accident, but Union Carbide would not spend the money.[135] •The Ponzi-scheme called ENRON, upon collapse, lost $50 billion and robbed thousands of workers of their pensions. •In order to save money, the Fukushima nuclear reactor was built a stone's throw from the ocean, just five-and-a-half meters above sea level in a location where the average tsunami had been eight meters high for the past thousand years. To make matters worse, the generators were installed in the basement instead of safely up the hillside, and spent fuel rods were stored too close. Greed resulted in the worst radiation contamination since WWII.[136] •Greed is not always revealed by major calamity, but by slow erosion of a company's reputation. Greedy CEOs have ruined companies by raising prices and lowering quality, killing the golden goose of a good brand name. GM, Ford and Chrysler, especially during the seventies and eighties, allowed quality to decline while prices soared, opening the door for imports. Sears & Roebuck is one example of a retail brand in decline—one of the best-loved brand names in America until greed, and higher prices, took over. The list goes on.

Fairy Tales that Teach Fact

In the previous chapter, we considered the fable of the Golden Goose, the means of production killed by impatient greed. It's a parable to inspire personal virtues of patience and moderation and longterm good over short-term gain, lessons sorely needed for our economic plight. A healthy goal for business should be, *Let's be in business 20 years from now*, not *Let's squeeze all the profits we can out of this business and leave a drained corpse behind*. As a society, we need to think longterm and nurture our "golden geese," protecting them from the ravenous wolves of greed. I'm mixing metaphors, but when it comes to combatting greed, we would do well to employ all the best metaphors! We should remember and re-tell the many fables, parables and fairy tales that try to warn us against greed.

Indeed, one of the most instructive parables is the classic fable of King Midas. Midas was a wealthy king who *already* had mountains of treasure. In asking for the magic touch to be able to turn plain objects into solid gold, Midas was an archetype for our modern affliction: **greed carried to the point of absurdity**. Midas enjoyed turning the chairs, tables and even fruit in his room to solid gold with his magic touch, but when he killed his daughter by touching her, thus changing her into a golden statue, we are reminded that greed only brings destruction and death. But we are also left with a sense of pity for the king as he grieves his daughter, forgetting that the parable is an allegory and forgetting that the sin was not in touching his daughter, but in being unsatisfied with his immense wealth even before gaining the "Midas touch."

We smugly condemn King Midas: "I would never be so foolish as to value gold more than my child!" Yet we build more lavish and luxurious buildings to care for our money (banks) than we do to care for our children. Some of the shabbiest structures in America are our schools and daycares, and some of the ritziest, marble-and-gold gleaming mansions are our banks. This sad fact is emblematic of a sick society that values gold more than grandchildren.

King Midas is not a fictional character. Our institutions are ruled by real-life Midases: little kings with colossal riches, yet never satisfied. Any wise observer can see that beyond a certain point, wealth becomes destructive to both the wealthy person and those around him. Bernie Madoff is a recent example: he could have been comfortably wealthy as a legitimate broker, but greed overcame him and he started a Ponzi scheme. His greed resulted in prison for himself and tragedy for his family. Everything he touched turned to gold... and then ash. Some do not learn from wise fables.

Who are the Villains of the Fable-Come-True?

I am not saying the rich are all evil villains. Most wealthy people *want* to be "good" and even view themselves as good, because most do give away some of their wealth. But I challenge anyone who makes over $200,000 annually, with assets over a million, to accept this simple challenge: if anything about the Midas parable resonates with you, ask yourself if greed is creeping up on you.

The *American Heritage Dictionary* defines greed as, "An excessive desire to acquire or possess more than what one needs or deserves...." And *Webster's* adds, under *avaricious*, "...eagerly desiring wealth, even at the expense of others." Greed, by definition, seeks to accumulate wealth for selfish interest without any care about the consequences upon others. Thus, it is the opposite of love.

I've known missionaries living hand-to-mouth in Third World countries whose own wealthy family members, back in the States, never sent them a dollar of support. How can such blind greed be explained? For centuries, we recognized greed as one of the "Seven Deadly Sins," but in today's culture, greed is no longer considered a vice. From Ayn Rand to John Stossel, there are mainstream voices who support the philosophy that *greed is good*. So let me dispute that notion and rebut the oft-stated myths about greed:

Myth Number One: *Greed is good because it motivates people to work harder and thus improves the overall economy.*

Wrong! Money is not the only motivator. Money is not even the *best* motivator, except for those who have lost touch with their natural creativity and drive. Humans have an innate motivation, as the Bible says, "to be fruitful and multiply. My childhood friends and I would get very excited and energized about building things together: a raft, a go-cart, a tree-house. We'd work tirelessly in the hot sun for not a penny—motivated by the sheer pleasure of achievement and of working together on a common goal.

The best motivators are the desires for love and security. Because you love your family and wish to keep them safe and secure, you get up each day and go to work in order to earn a salary. A healthy and good desire to be productive, to earn an income, is *not* greed, it is a God-given impetus to be fruitful and to provide for those you love.

Greed is an **unhealthy motivator**. We often witness greed dividing families as siblings squabble over inheritance. We see greed destroy marriages when one or both partners are unwilling to share wealth. Greed, once it is full-blown, has no concern for the economic health of the society; avaricious investors look for the fast buck instead of investing in longterm productive enterprises; greed prompts corporations to run roughshod over the mom-n-pop small businesses, harming communities; greedy conglomerates rape the land of its non-renewable resources and pollute the environment for future generations. Avarice throws caution to the wind. **Most of America's environmental catastrophes, worker deaths, economic calamities, crashes and scandals are the direct result of greed.**

And the addict is the first one harmed by the addiction. Greed is no different. Ask yourself: *Are my attitudes about money hurting myself, my relationships with family and friends? Has a lack of generosity created problems for my business? Am I unsatisfied with the good things I already have?* Which leads to our second point/myth:

Myth Number Two: *Greed brings happiness by increasing one's luxuries.* No, if vast wealth and luxury brought happiness, we would not see so many rich movie stars commit suicide or end up on drugs. The Betty Ford Clinic is only one of many therapeutic rehab centers catering to the rich and famous. Ask the folks who run celebrity rehabs if wealth buys happiness. They'll tell you of a waiting list of so-called "beautiful people" who are rich... and deeply miserable.

The great sage of India, Mahatma Gandhi, taught that the more material things you cast off, the happier you will become. "Renounce and enjoy!" was his credo. Kerala, a province of 30 million people in southern India, adopted Gandhi's challenge: in 1930, many of the richest upper class Brahmin renounced their wealth and status and shared with the poor, and today that province has one of the smallest wealth to poverty gaps in the world. Despite the poverty around them, the average life expectancy and the literacy rate in Kerala approach our own.[137]

Myth Number Three: *Greed is an imaginary construct of religion... if you don't believe in religion, you don't have to fear greed.*

Greed is real. Greed is not just a religious term. My objections to greed are not only rooted in my faith, but also stem from real life observation and experience. A large segment of the uppermost class interact with money as if it were a drug, a psychological addiction that is as real as a physical heroin addiction.

In my years as a minister, I've dealt with addicts, sometimes intimately and painfully involved in their disastrous lives. Addiction is the ingestion of a substance that triggers the pleasure centers in the brain, creating an obsession to repeat the behavior. There's key difference between addiction and healthy pleasures: the same dosage will, day after day, **become less satisfying**. On a hot day, a cool glass of water is deeply satisfying, all that I need. The next day, hot again, two glasses of water will *again* be all I need. But not so with drugs.

This explains why a million dollars would bring me overwhelming joy and satisfaction today, but over time, I would long for more. Addiction is why a million wasn't enough for Bernie Madoff. Addiction explains why it is so hard for the wealthy to let go of dollars (via charity) or to accept the ethical arguments proposed in this book. **Addiction closes the mind.** It is very hard to "reason" with an alcoholic. If you are a greedy person, open your mind.

Addiction also closes the heart. I have known people who, in order to feed their ever-growing crack addiction, would steal from their grandma or their own children's piggybanks.

As a percentage of income, middle class folks are far more generous than the wealthy, a fact which should cause head-scratching: once someone has all the money they need to meet their own needs, why would they then not be *more* generous with the remainder than those of us in the lower classes? Addictive behavior may explain this statistical anomaly.

The Smartest Addict in the World
Greed is the only explanation as to why otherwise-intelligent people say the dumbest things about economic ethics. The *Parade* magazine columnist Marilyn vos Savant presents herself as the world's smartest woman, based on a listing in the *Guinness Book of World Records* for having the highest IQ on the planet. Yet in one of her "Ask Marilyn" columns, she demonstrates strangely-flawed logic. In the column, a reader asks if it is moral to spend exorbitant amounts on luxury items, such as $1,000 on one pair of shoes. Marilyn says *Yes*, giving a justification that defies logic: *The artist who made the shoe would then take the $1,000 and spend it on some other things, thus stimulating the economy*. Why would a genius like herself not see the obvious fallacy in her argument? I have a nice, comfortable pair of leather shoes that I bought for $19.95. I even received compliments on these $20 shoes! Would it not be far more ethical to buy a twenty-dollar pair of shoes for oneself, and donate the remainder of the $1,000 to *fifty* barefoot children, so that they could be wearing shoes instead of just *one* person? In Marilyn's scenario, for all we know, the cobbler is wealthy (selling shoes for a thousand bucks a pop!), so he stuck the grand in the bank—The End. In my example, 50 people now have shoes on their otherwise bare feet and **money circulates**. Marilyn, a math whiz,

misses this entirely. I can think of no other explanation for her sudden mental lapse except that of an addict trying to justify her own greed. The rich really do believe it is okay for them to eat a $1,000 gold-dusted hamburger (actually sold in Manhattan) while children are starving.

Others have seen the holes in her logic, too. David Swanson wrote these words: "Marilyn's July 21, 2002, column begins with this question: 'Do you think it's proper for people to spend money on luxuries for themselves when there are poor people in the same city?' This question [asks] whether someone [with] extra money should (a) spend that money on luxuries for themselves, or (b) give that money to someone else in the same city whose basic needs have not been met.… In Marilyn's response, she [never] considered the possibility that the rich person might do something… to help the poor. She seems to view the alternatives as (a) spending the money on luxuries or (c) leaving it in the bank. She proceeds to address the question of whether buying luxuries might in itself conceivably do any good for the poor people. Here's her answer: 'Yes. Say a person buys a pair of $1,000 shoes… jobs are created and maintained… and our rich friend has a pair of shoes in his closet that will fall apart just as fast as any other shoes….'" If the $1,000 instead had gone to the poor, Swanson goes on to point out, and "some of *them* were to buy reasonably priced working shoes, instead of our rich friend buying obscenely expensive shoes, …jobs [would] be created and maintained." He adds, "Is money somehow less in circulation in the economy if poor people spend it than if rich people do?"[138]

Yes, thank you David, not only would 50 people benefit rather than one, but the same amount of money ($1,000) would still circulate into the economy! In my scenario of 50 people buying $20 shoes, the chances are much higher that the money will go into circulation rather than being squirreled away.

From the perspective of the ultra-rich, (who, like Marilyn, view themselves as smarter than the rest of us), it seems *right* to have a few oligarchs "generously" trickling their largesse onto the peasants below. Shoeless children in India have a different perspective. Marilyn defends her greed with the failed logic of Reagan's trickle-down economics. Can we once and for all put a nail in the coffin of Reaganomics? The *Pittsburgh Post-Gazette* editorialized in July, 2011 that the argument "not to tax the wealthy because they are job creators is patently false." After thirty years of supply-side trickle-down tax cuts for the rich and the only ones better off are the 1%.

Dispassionate Diagnosis

Allow me to repeat a paragraph from the Preface: Guilt or shame are unpleasant emotions that cause us to lash out defensively; no one likes to be called greedy. But imagine if greed were a purely-physiological disease, a viral epidemic destroying our planet. If you could remove guilt and shame from the equation for a moment, and just see greed as an infectious agent, perhaps your attitude toward someone offering a diagnosis might be less emotional. Greed *is* a disease, and in particular, it affects the eyeball: it blinds people to seeing themselves in the mirror as they truly are. The cure is to find the courage to rip the scales from one's eyes, to calmly look into one's own heart, to see the greed there—and then to change.

If greed is an addiction, it may not be simple or easy to change. The bondage of addiction is so powerful, it takes teamwork to be set free from it. AA, rehab, methadone and all the other treatments work only if the addict decides to change and has a support network. Better cure rates happen with a "Higher Power" helping as well. The model of greed as an addictive disease explains two things: one, why it is so hard to convince the self-deceived that greed is bad, and two, why we need a coercive power (yes, big bad government) to limit the damage that "greed addicts" inflict upon society—just as we need DUI laws to keep drunks from killing innocent motorists.

Summary

Greed is over-rated as a motivator. I have met many people across the years who are not motivated much by money, yet are quite ambitious, high-achievers. I've known successful people in a variety of occupations who find fulfillment in the work itself, and while they may need and want higher pay, it is a secondary concern. I've known and worked with ministers and leaders of non-profits—well-educated and highly-intelligent—who are motivated by a desire to help people and improve society, regardless of the (usually low) pay.

The wolves of Wall Street, unsatisfied with the first $100 million, who then put everything at risk to grab the next $100 million. Addiction causes strange thoughts and strange behaviors. Money addicts become *emotionally* opposed to the arguments made in this book. Addicts don't generally respond well to anyone who wants to make them confront their addiction. Which is why fables and fairy tales like the Golden Goose and King Midas are spun—sometimes a story can break through to the heart in ways that statistics can't.

Scrooge in the Mirror

It has been 150 years since any writer has used a fable to ignite the public conscience about poverty—or exposed the addictive power of greed—as movingly as Charles Dickens. His story of Tiny Tim and Scrooge, *A Christmas Carol*, has been perennially re-told. It holds the record for the most Hollywood reduxes. Even re-cast with Muppets or cartoons, the message remains: a heart-warming and heart-wrenching treatise against the greed and indifference of a man whose name has become synonymous with greed: Ebenezer Scrooge.

In a pivotal scene, Scrooge is shocked into seeing the error of his ways by the phantom of his long-dead parsimonious partner, Jacob Marley. Marley's ghost came floating into Scrooge's bedchamber with a chain clasped about his middle and draping behind him like a long tail. The chain was made of the tools of his lifelong trade: cash boxes, keys, padlocks, ledgers, deeds, and heavy purses wrought in iron. Scrooge was puzzled, but we know that the chains represent the addiction of greed. We continue with Dicken's own words:

Marley explained: "I wear the chain I forged in life. I made it link by link and yard by yard; I girded it on of my own free will, and of my own free will I wore it. Is it a pattern strange to *you*? Or would you know the weight and length of the strong coil you bear yourself? [Yours is] as heavy and and as long as this... a ponderous chain." Scrooge glanced about him on the floor, in the expectation of finding himself surrounded by some fifty or sixty fathoms of iron cable: but he could see nothing.

"Jacob," he said imploringly. "Old Jacob Marley, tell me more. Speak comfort to me, Jacob."

"I have none to give," the Ghost replied....

"But you were always a good man of business, Jacob," faltered Scrooge, who now began to apply this to himself.

"Business!" cried the Ghost, wringing his hands. "Mankind was my business. The common welfare was my business; charity, mercy, forbearance, and benevolence were all my business. The dealings of my trade were but a drop of water in the comprehensive ocean of my business! At this time of the rolling year," the spectre said, "I suffer most. Why did I walk through the crowds of fellow-beings with my eyes turned down, and never raised them to that blessed Star which led the Wise Men to a poor abode? Were there no poor homes to which its light would have conducted me?" Then the ghost of Jacob Marley floated out the window, leaving Scrooge to reflect....[139]

When you look in the mirror, do you see the chain of addiction, and the ghost of Scrooge?

~~~

Chapter 9: Money for Nothing
Bankers, mortgages, usury, and derivatives

Labor is the superior of capital, and deserves much the higher consideration. ~Abraham Lincoln

I believe that banking institutions are more dangerous to our liberties than standing armies. ~Thomas Jefferson

A S#!+ Sandwich

Perhaps a salesperson does deserve a huge commission if he is capable of selling a "sh!t-sandwich" at any price, even more so if he can sell it at steak-sandwich prices. Or maybe not, since intentionally violating health codes is a crime. This is exactly what Wall Street hedge fund managers sold America: a meatloaf-and-sh!t sandwich. My daughters will be disappointed in my vulgar language here, but with apologies, it is a **very purposeful, serious and appropriate metaphor, one necessary** to get the reader's attention... the equivalent of yelling "Fire!" in a movie theatre when there is, in fact, a fire. And you must understand, I am merely quoting the exact language used by Goldman-Sachs in their own internal email to describe their own product: CDO derivatives, a highly-leveraged re-packaging of sliced-n-diced mortgages. Regarding the sale of one package of such derivatives, a senior G-S executive actually called it, "one shitty deal."[140] His words, not mine! If taxpayers and pensioners would fully understand what they have been asked to "swallow," they would have the same visceral revulsion at our lack of economic justice as you may be having right now with my metaphor. I am unrepentant, I still yell: *Fire!*

How the S#!+ Works

Early in this book, I borrowed the "sausage metaphor" that other writers have used to explain derivatives. The subject deserves repeating, and Goldman-Sachs' "one shitty deal" statement begs that I offer a stronger metaphor than pork sausage. Here's how some of the mortgage derivatives made Wall Street billions while nearly destroying our entire economy:

It was not enough that hedge fund managers were being overpaid millions for crunching numbers and clicking computers, they inflated their salaries further with over-hyped and leveraged investment packages. But even that wasn't enough: driven by insatiable greed, they began to sell a crappy product at high risk *and* got the government to cover their mistakes with hard cold cash (TARP, etc.). Normally, derivatives would take a pound of cheap ground beef, a half-pound of ground round, and a lump of filet mignon, mix them together, add some salt, and bake, then sell the slices... the concept being that the higher-risk of the cheaper mortgages would be diluted by more solid investments—the "steak." But to bake *over-leveraged* **derivatives**, you take some crappy high-risk mortgages almost guaranteed to fail, then dilute the stench by mixing the "sh!t" in with some chopped steak (solid collateral, lower-risk mortgages), then grind 'em all together into a new meatloaf, covered with the spice of a math algorithm to fool people into thinking you won't "taste" the small amount of crap mixed in! Bake 'em and slice 'em up and serve the meatloaf on an investment sandwich, now over-leveraged and priced in the BILLIONS. But the greed didn't even stop there: some began to leave out the filet mignon, using nearly-100% dog poo— spiced and sliced and hyped with the sales pitch that "This dog poo sandwich is safe to eat because the ingredients came from *different* dogs!!"

This is not much of an exaggeration of what happened with mortgage CDO's. Again, excuse my crude language... but if you are feeling angry revulsion, tasting an unpleasant stench in your mouth, it would be very wise to aim your emotions *not* at the messenger (me, the book author), but at **Wall Street**—and at the Feds who bailed them out with your tax dollars after your pension "ate" the losses as the over-inflated housing market crashed! And no, this is not just a one-time anomaly, over-leveraging still goes on: *This Week* mag reported in the first week of February 2012 that the top 25 hedge fund managers made a combined $25 BILLION DOLLARS just one year after the Crash was behind us. Crap!

Money for Nothing

But let's back-up and consider that it is not just con artists and CDO's that are robbing us blind... it is also as simple as a thing called *interest*. The rock band, Dire Straits, wrote a song with self-parodying lyrics about the easy life of rock stardom: "Money for nothing, get your chicks for free." (As a guitarist myself, I can tell you that most musicians work hard for peanuts.) But there is one sector of economy that does offer "money for nothing," one process that requires little work yet brings in free money: **banks and interest on loans**. Interest, money "earned" on deposits at the simplest levels, makes sense. If I forego the use or pleasure of my money by putting it in your bank, I should be rewarded for the deferred gratification with a percentage of return at least equal to the erosion from inflation. But the interest paid on bank savings accounts has been less than the rate of inflation, robbing the average American everyday.

But the greater theft is on the other end: loaning money at high and compounded rates. The banks and credit card companies do very little "work" (the hardest work is done by low-paid customer service phone operators and by computers that handle the calculations). They use our money, and government money, with little to no risk, yet charge us anywhere from 5% to 24% annually, plus fees, for the privilege. And that is not even mentioning the far-higher rates charged by "pay-day lenders" and pawn-broker-type title-loan companies that prey upon the poor. Mainstream banks and especially VISA, Discover and American Express charge outrageous interest and fees that beg us to come up with a stronger term than "usury."

Why Usury Was a Crime and a Sin

For most of civilized history, usury—the charging of excessive interest on loans—was viewed as a serious spiritual sin and a civil crime punishable by death! Ezekiel 18 states, "If he has exacted usury or taken increase, shall he then live? He shall not live! If he has done any of these abominations, He shall surely die...." Psalm 28 equates usury with extortion. Leviticus 25:35: "You shall not lend him your money for usury, nor lend him your food at a profit."

The word usury comes from the Latin *usura*, which simply means "interest," so its root definition is the charging of interest on loans. In modern times, it has come to mean excessive or unlawful interest.

The Bible defined usury as any profits made from anything but the simplest and lowest interest charges: compound interest was even considered a sin in any form. The reason the Bible viewed loaning as evil is because usury creates excessive profit and gain without any true productive labor or work. And debt kept the lower classes from ever escaping poverty. Usury was a sin associated with avarice, greed, trickery and manipulation. The First Council of Nicaea in 325 A.D., forbade clergy from engaging in usury, defined as loaning money on interest above one per cent per month. Later ecumenical councils applied this regulation to the laity. Now we have banks, via credit cards, *legally* engaging in usury at 20 times that amount!

Usury has often been defined in terms of interest rate, or APR. So when we see a bank only charging 4% for a home mortgage, we may not see a problem or accuse them of being usurious. But a low advertised rate is usually reserved for those with perfect credit ratings and huge down payments on a home that provides solid collateral; the bank is making money with almost no risk. What we don't see advertised is how many "points" and various fees they add to that, which can mean thousands in profit, or how often they jack the APR up to twice the advertised rate on some customers.

The most egregious examples of usury, apart from outright loan sharks, are what banks rake in via **credit card interest.**

The Plastic Money-Making Machine

I have sterling credit, a high FICO score, yet Chase VISA offered me the following "promotional rate" that sounds like a bargain: transfer a balance (or write a convenience check) and get 0% APR! Wow, what a deal. But of course, read the fine print: the "free" interest would only last from March through August, (six months), when "at the end of the promotional period, your APR will be 16.24%. This rate will vary with the market based on the Prime Rate." In other words, the rate could go even higher if the Prime goes up... but even at 16.24%, you must also factor in an upfront "balance transfer fee" of 4%. $400. That means I am now paying back a $10,400 loan even though I only borrowed $10,000. In six months, the "bargain" becomes a 16.24%+ loan. Indeed, in 2010, Americans paid, on average, about 16% for credit card interest.[141] If you don't like the word "usury," I have another word for it: criminal.

Yet from 2009-2012, the Fed was loaning banks money at less than 1%. That's a 1600% "mark-up" at a time when small-business retailers are happy to get 30% gross profit on their wares. And that doesn't include the high fees for overlimit or late payment, as much as $39 a whack the credit card banks enjoy. Again, this outrageous unethical fleecing continues even after congressional "reform." The CARD Act (Credit Card Accountability, Responsibility, and Disclosure Act), implemented in 2009, still allows loan sharks, bankers, VISA, Mastercard, Discover, etc., to charge outlandish rates. Those industries are, not surprisingly, some of the biggest lobbyists and donors to political campaigns. In a Third World country, we'd call this a bribe or payola. In America, we call it "reform."

Credit Card Cons

Most readers have experienced one of the many ways credit card companies con us out of our hard-earned bucks. Some examples:
•Late charge: the U.S. mail is slow to deliver the bill. We set it aside for a few days because we have a *life*. Then we pay the bill and the mail is again slow, and the processing center is slow to process, and suddenly we're a day late and a $30 fee is imposed. The payment was made, and the lateness cost the bank less than a dime, but for some reason, they feel entitled to charge us thirty dollars—a profit margin so outrageous, a bank robber incurs a higher expense-to-profit-ratio when he gasses up the getaway car! Our lawmakers enshrined this robbery in the so-called CARD Reform Act.

Remember: •The credit card company had already profited by charging the merchant a fee for our use of the VISA. •Some credit card companies charge *us* an annual fee for *their* privilege of ripping us off. •Then they charge you interest on any unpaid balance, usually in the range of 12%-24%. •The greedy companies are still not satisfied. They also try to extract outrageous additional charges for services they could be providing for no extra charge: fees to protect you from lost cards/identity theft/fraud, insurance for loss of job, fees to "protect" and report your credit rating. •But my "favorite" scam: **the wonderfully-generous offer of 0% cash advance**. Mentioned above, but now let's actually look at the numbers. First, the fine print begins with a balance transfer fee of "5%, or a minimum fee of $10." The "minimum fee" is a marketing ploy to put the figure of "ten dollars" in your head... subconsciously, you think, "Oh, no problem, I'll gladly pay ten bucks for zero percent." But in most cases, you would pay far more than ten dollars up front and far more than zero percent in the long run. If you borrow as little as $2,000, you will be paying $100 right up front! This "5%" is far worse than 5% interest. 5% on $2,000 for an entire year is only $75, because in a normal loan with a $100 per month payment, each month you are paying down the principal upon which you pay the 5%.

But with the "wonderful offer" for a balance transfer from a credit card, you paid a 5% upfront fee. If you didn't make a payment for six months (during the zero-interest period), you will will eventually be paying interest on that $100 fee itself![142]

Here are two actual offers I received, because of my "excellent history of payment," from these "loan sharks":

Discover Card: 5% up-front Cash Advance Fee, 6 months free interest, then an interest rate of 11.24 *variable* based on Prime Rate
Chase Card: 4% up-front Cash Advance Fee, 11 months free interest, then an interest rate of 16.24 variable based on Prime Rate. Remember, these are not rates for a high risk individual. At the time these were offered, I had a long-standing relationship with both credit companies, paid bills early and more than the minimum, and possessed a credit score in the top 20% range of Excellent rating. Let's compare these to a simple interest non-collateralized loan at the fair rate of 8% (from my local credit union):

Simple Interest Loan from Credit Union or Local Bank:
$5,000 borrowed, paid in equal payments of $101 for 58 months, at 8%: A healthy but reasonable "profit" for the local bank of **$635**
vs.
Discover "Free Interest" Loan:
$5,000 borrowed, paid at the same monthly payment: $101
•Add $250 fee of 5% charged up front. $5,250
•6 months: 0%, 6 payments of $101 ($5,250-606=$4,644 balance)

- Remaining payments of $101 per month, on declining balance$4,644 at 11.24% (assuming the variable rate doesn't go up) = **$1,470 interest**

So the Discover "free" offer costs twice as much and takes 63 months to pay off!
- Total interest paid to a fair Simple 8% Interest Loan: **$635**
- Total cost of Discover's "FREE" interest offer: **$1,700**

The local bank and the credit card loaned the same money, both took the same (slight) risk, yet Discover made a far greater profit. And this was a "favorable" rate; Discover charges some customers more than **23%** for cash advances. If you borrowed $5,000 at that rate, paying $101 a month, it would take you over 13 years to be rid of your small debt, and Discover would have collected $10,800 in interest—twice your original loan! That's why usury is a sin. At the same time I received these offers, Discover was offering a savings account, boasting that they would pay me 1.15% interest if I gave them my money. Discover is doing a better job than rock stars "Dire Straits" at getting "money for nothing," ironically by claiming to offer *you* "money for nothing." Incidentally, another line in the same song reads, "Bangin' on the bongos like a chimpanzee." Yep, they are saying a monkey could do it!

Swimming with the Loan Sharks

Another prize for "loansharking while calling it saving" should go to Sears *Mastercard*: again, with an excellent credit rating, I received the following offer, touted as a bargain: "You could save on interest with these checks." Here's the offer: pay 5% up front fee, receive a "promotional" rate of 2.99% for eight months, after which the APR would go up to 23.24%—or higher, as this was a variable rate based on a historically-low Prime Rate.

Borrow $5,000, here's what it would cost you, assuming a $100 per month payment: $250 fee up front means you paying on a $5,250 loan at 2.99% interest the first 8 months, then it moves to 23.24% interest until paid off... at a grand total of $6,630 that Sears collected—and of course, they get their $4,000 back in the end, too.

What's worse, many folks are not going to pay these loans off in in four years, and likely incur a $35 late fee now and then, so the profit can run even higher to Sears, Discover, Bank of America, VISA, Mastercard, etc. Again, the banks are not doing any actual "work," not providing an actual product, they are just loaning us money, some of it from our government—small loans that would not even be necessary if Americans were paid a decent wage in the first place.

Screwing Us Both Ways: Low Interest Rates Fleece Seniors

The August 2010 *Reader's Digest* succinctly points out how that due to cheap money being pumped to bankers by the Fed, interest rates paid by banks to savers can stay at only 1%. Then the banks loan the money out to the public at 6 to 8 percent with safe home mortgages and 10-25% on credit cards... profit margins as high as 2,000 percent! So with little effort or risk (mostly risking other peoples' money, with a Federal safety net), the banks are working an incredible spread, robbing the nest-eggs of retired Americans while simultaneously sucking younger Americans into lifelong debt with usurious credit card rates. There is a reason the Bible calls usury a sin. It is essentially civilized theft.

The nonpartisan Roosevelt Institute warned that the Finance Reform Bill would do little to stop "too-big-to-fail" banks from paying outlandish bonuses after gambling with taxpayer-backed funds. And when a publication as conservative as *Reader's Digest* begins to make similar observations of capitalism gone awry, we know there is truth to my treatise. Honest journalists of all stripes agree that something is rotten on both sides of the aisle in Congress.

Toothless Reforms

The one silver-lining found in the last burst-bubble was that now the shell game has been exposed. It became obvious to everyone that trillions have been stolen by Wall Street over the last 30 years. Moved by public opinion, Congress had to address this. So they began bipartisan attempts to **cover-up** the true size of the problem. Congress enacted symbolic but toothless "reforms." Just as the much-ballyhooed credit card reform act did little to stop banks from fleecing credit cardholders with excessive rates and fees, likewise the "Finance Reform Act" neither reformed Wall Street nor protected consumers. Wall Street is as reformed from greed and corruption as Bourbon Street is from liquor and ribaldry.

Yep, the senatorial monster that had helped set-up the scenario for the financial industry to rob billions from 2000 until the 2008 crash, and then bailed out mortgage lenders, banks, investment firms and insurance conglomerates with billions of taxpayer dollars, came back in 2010 to supposedly "reform" these industries. Officially called the Dodd-Frank Wall Street Reform and Consumer Protection Act of 2010, the monster's twin heads of Democrat Chris Dodd and Republican Richard Shelby made sure that most meaningful reform was watered down. Shelby should be required to post at the bottom of all his campaign ads, like a warning label on a pack of cigarettes: "Caution: Senator Shelby's campaign received truckloads of bucks from the financial industry."

Rolling Stone magazine printed a polemic on the Finance Reform Act entitled, "Wall Street's Big Win," in which Matt Taibbi wrote "Control over the economy in the past decade was ceded to a small group of criminals who to this day are engaging in a mind-numbing campaign of theft on a global scale...."[143] He understates: the control dates back much longer than a decade. But Taibbi correctly details how whore Democrats climbed in bed with whore Republicans to produce a bastard idiot child of legislation that will do nothing to stop the fleecing of American workers.

Wall Street Giving Thanks for a Turkey of a Bill

The Reform Act needed to do three things: 1. to stop Wall Street firms from Proprietary Trading (using taxpayer-guaranteed funds to prop up their high-risk gambling) via the **Volcker Rule**; 2. to stop big banks from over-leveraged derivative trading (slicing and dicing mortgages to artificially inflate values) via the **Lincoln Rule**, and 3. to place better **regulations on consumer credit-lending**, limiting the usurious rates and deceptive practices. The Reform Act achieved none of the above in any substantial way. This turkey offered just enough window-dressing to allow the Obama administration to tout it as "the biggest financial reform since the Great Depression." That's not saying much. As Taibbi reminds us, all the financial reform bills since the Depression era have been later weakened, repealed or circumvented by Big Finance. The parts of the foul bill that the oligarchs did not manage to eviscerate will be further carved-up by the final regulation-writing. Finally, this rotten turkey of a bill will be served as an even more bland and tasteless product by **lax enforcement**. The whole process is cooked by the chefs of Wall Street, not Main Street... a "reform" meal that makes me gag.

The Volcker Rule was shot down by back-room hijinx in the Senate, and the Lincoln Rule was gutted by a House conspiracy that even involved the bill's namesake, Blanche Lincoln. She had proposed her ban on derivatives to help fend off her political opponent, populist Bill Halter. A week after she defeated Halter in a runoff, she turncoated and offered broad exemptions to her own ban. House Democrats and Senate Democrats were more instrumental than even Republicans in gutting the bill, leaving a dry husk of an exoskeleton for public appearances but with no real interior muscle for animating reform. But had the Republicans been in power (and after all, they *were* in power for most of the decade leading up to the 2007-2008 disaster), we would have had pro-corporate shills like Senator Shelby, calling reform "social engineering" and attacking limits on the Wall Street thieves as "socialism." Shelby and his ilk campaign on being pro-family and pro "small-businessman," but the legislation they support almost always favors big business over family businesses.

Banking and Bubbles

Banking provides so many ways to "print money," legally, by leveraging and loaning out other people's cash, why was it necessary to go farther and create illegal schemes to reap even more obscene profits? The only answer I have is found is *greed*, as we presented in the previous chapter.

So the next question is not *Why*, but *How* did they do it? Muzzling the watchdog, the foxes ran wild in the hen house. First, with bribed politicians in both parties, the Fourth Reich pushed through financial de-regulation as well as relaxed lending standards so that housing loans could be made willy-nilly. Next, the Fed robbed senior citizens of any real return on life savings by artificially reducing interest rates, which deluged the housing market with cheap money. This created a boom in home prices. With higher housing prices, the banks made higher profits from fees and interest (remember, the banks profit regardless of interest rates, because they make profit on the *spread*... even if they loan out at 5%, if they borrow from the Fed at 1%, they are still making a bonanza).

Next, banks conspired with investment houses who developed a new level of leveraging: **mortgage derivatives** (also called CDO's—Collateralized Debt Obligations).

Derivatives are more than bubbles, they are **hyper-bubbles**. A bubble is when your house, that cost $100,000 to build, inflates in value to $130,000 "appraised value" in a few short years. Housing bubbles can be caused by a variety of market factors, some genuine, some artificial (in recent years, mostly a product of low-interest rates and easy money). Under normal circumstances, even if the real estate bubble bursts because of a recession or over-supply, history shows that your home would still retain most of its original "cost of construction" value (what we might call "real" value), as the market rebounds. And in the interim, you could still live in the home. Thus it provided real value after the "bubble" burst. There was actually something of value within the bubble—i.e., a house.

But a *hyper*-bubble differs in two ways. First, its inflated value is not 20% or 30% above the root value, but can be double or triple the "real" root value (as happened with the addition of derivatives).

Second, when a hyper-bubble bursts, it creates such an explosive reaction, such a rapid, dramatic pop, that those not prepared for the bursting are destroyed by it and lose even their original real-value equity. This is what happened in the crash of 2007-2009.

Normally, the wealthy investors are wise to the impending bubble-burst, and with their pockets full of cash, they walk away fine and dandy right before the pop. But in 2008, the Fourth Reich got extra-greedy and tried to hold on too long to too-big a bubble. The hyper-bubble popped with such seismic ferocity, their financial houses began to shake. But never fear: Presidents Bush and Obama, and Senators Christopher Dodd and Richard Shelby and their other political minions, propped up the foundation to the house of cards, and re-inflated the bubble, with trillions of tax-payer dollars!

Derivatives Explained Yet Again

Many derivatives were/are a hyper-bubble. When you peel away the veneer of financial jargon and quantum math, you discover that the derivative is a con job, a false contrivance to take money from governments and people. The brokers even confess that most of the "value" of a derivative is a so-called "notional value"; that is, the value is just a fictional notion! That's their official jargon, not mine!

If I'm a broker and can convince you that the hyper-bubble represents real money (even as I admit it is "notional value"), then I can take loans against it and draw commissions and bonuses based upon it. The best part, if I'm an investor, is that when the hyper-bubble bursts, the salaries and commissions of those who constructed the con do not burst. Paid out long ago, those bonuses are safe in an off-shore tax-free account or annuity. Even more amazing in this most recent debacle, the salaries of those responsible for the disaster never got cut! *The Week* magazine reported in June 2011 that the "inept corporate generals [still] raked in $1.15 billion" annually, over $3 billion before the house of cards collapsed. The same leaders who had brought the "too-big-to-fail" banks to near collapse were profitting from their own failure.[144] Citigroup Exec Vikram Pandit, who was at the helm when Citigroup's stock plunged 87%, was still getting about $22 million in 2010-2011 according to *Fortune* magazine. If you fail so utterly, you'd be getting a pink slip; the bankers got green.

The Mathematical Wizards

Anyone who can master mathematics with ease, and who as an ounce of self-discipline, can find highly-paid employment in the fields of chemistry, engineering or accounting/investments. But why are the mathematicians on Wall Street paid 100 times that of equally-smart engineers and chemists? They are *not* masters of the universe. Eric Dexenhaul, CEO of Dezenhall Resources, says of those Wall Street "masters": "what used to be nobly attributed to strategy can better be explained by ego [and] rampant self-delusion...."

Who can defend the insanely-large bonuses paid to math heads like Dow Kim, who made over $34 million in 2006 alone—even when their work led to financial calamity? Thomas Donohue, for one. Donohue, President of the U.S. Chamber of Commerce, explained these are "very unique kinds of people... like mad scientists. They are all mathematicians and they are very mobile."[145]

Donohue's defense is weak at two levels: first, it implies that there are not enough mathematicians to go around, which is not true. Yes, it may require a little creativity to go out to grad schools and recruit them, but there are thousands of sharp math graduates each year and only a handful of job openings on Wall Street. The much bigger problem with Donohue's defense is that the math doesn't work! Kim was crunching numbers that enabled Merrill Lynch to sell highly-leveraged, mortgage-backed CDO's. The math wizards were claiming their formulas ensured the inflated values were safe. They were not. The bubble burst. Merrill Lynch no longer exists! But have Dow Kim and his ilk re-paid their bonuses to the millions of people who lost their retirement funds on the boondoggle?

I'm not saying that math is without value. But the math that makes a hedge fund work was "discovered" way back in the 1950's, and the principle is rather simple: using statistics and percentages, you divide your risk up among a variety of industries, and you throw in some short-selling, so that the risk of losing all our investment is greatly reduced. Derivatives take it a step further by claiming that, because of the reduced risk, you can leverage the core investment even higher. Using mathematics and computers, they created scenarios that convinced investors to jump on board in such numbers that it created a balloon effect. A balloon has a thin skin of "real substance," and as long as the hot air (more investors) keeps coming in, it appears bigger and bigger and everyone is winning... until, as always happens with balloons, the bubble bursts, all the air is lost, and you are left with a shattered and shriveled "substance." Common sense usually trumps math. And common sense tells us two things:

    1. Numbers can be manipulated in a number of ways to fool the mind, such as in parlor tricks or in the old saying, "there are lies, there are damn lies, and there are statistics."

    2. Common sense tells us that derivatives based on a single industry—such as housing—have **lost the key advantage** that hedge funds have: diversification across various industries. The wildly-inflated prices of mortgage-based derivatives were based on the nonsensical notion that housing markets can't fail broadly. When there is a wide-spread recession on top of another bubble (over-inflated housing prices), housing can and did deflate across the board. Upper middle class Californians found it hard to sell their houses for what they had paid for them; struggling ethnic families in Detroit who lost their automotive jobs could no longer make their payments; hurricanes made insurance unbearable for homeowners in Florida, Alabama, Mississippi, Louisiana, and Texas. The general recession took care of everyone else and suddenly we had a housing collapse and derivatives popped. The rest, as they say, is history. So

now we know the number crunching was little more than a parlor trick, a long con, a grift. And yet, Donohue and Friedman and the other defenders of the Fourth Reich persist in claiming these mathematicians were worth millions!? There is simply no argument here: they were catastrophic failures.

Or not. From their perspective, they were highly success con men. Not unlike Madoff, they *made off* with huge amounts of money through sleight of hand at the expense of ordinary, hard-working people even while providing no true product or service. How can this be defined any other way but a con? What's worse is, our government backed the con artists!

We Need a Mob with Pitchforks

The Feds not only allowed derivatives to be created, but even *reimbursed* the Wall Street firms after the imaginary hyper-bubble burst. The thieves ripped you and me out of billions of dollars, no one has gone to jail, and many have been rewarded with huge bonuses and continue on the fat payroll of Wall Street... well, except those that quit corporate investment jobs to take jobs working for the government itself. I'm ashamed I've *not* taken a torch and pitchfork and marched on Wall Street. But alas, Barack Obama said to the bankers that he "stands between you and the pitchforks."

True. His administration was loaded with Wall Street cronies to help spin things and calm the mob.... cronies like Larry Summers, who earlier had muzzled those who had tried to regulate derivatives.

And the problems preceded Obama. Bill Clinton signed the legislation that made derivatives possible and allied himself with Chinese businessmen, actions that opened the way for the ongoing steamrolling of the middle class. Republicans are equally guilty in deed and in word: Ronald Reagan and the George Bushes trumpeted "free markets" and "de-regulation," and condemned limits on corporate and Wall Street excess as evil government. And our Congress is even worse than our Presidents in their failure to protect working Americans. The Senate failed not only in its oversight of the private sector, but also in properly regulating the quasi-government "banks" of Fannie Mae and Freddie Mac.

And the Federal Reserve from Greenspan to Bernanke, and White House Treasury folks from Reagan to Bush to Clinton to Bush Jr., all were complicit in allowing the industry to run wild.

Titanic-sized Failure, Titanic-sized Reward

The list of guilty parties in the Greatest Bank Robbery of All Time is long. Remember, they weren't robbing banks; the banks *were* the robbers... bankers, brokers, investors, insurance companies, all conspired to inflate the bubble to enrich themselves. While the crooks were making billions in salaries, commissions and bonuses, no one was regulating or preventing the firms' machinations. At AIG, Joseph St. Denis was one of several honest auditors who saw trouble on the horizon well before the 2008 crash. Imagine standing on the bow of the *Titanic* with night vision binoculars. You run to tell the Captain of the looming iceberg, but the Captain screams, "Full speed ahead." No one would listen as St. Denis sounded alarms: AIG was over-leveraged in Credit Default Swaps. The *AIG Titanic* kept heading for the iceberg. St. Denis finally resigned in protest to draw attention to the impending shipwreck... to no avail. Almost everyone else at AIG and Goldman-Sachs who had made foolish decisions that nearly destroyed the entire world economy were richly rewarded. St. Denis got nothing. And you and I were like hapless passengers trapped in steerage on the Titanic. We went down with the ship.

Words fail at conveying the injustice, the criminality, the sheer cruelty of how Wall Street, in particular Goldman Sachs, Lehman Brothers, Bear Stearns and AIG, robbed and hurt the working class in the last several years. Watch the award winning film, *Inside Job*. It offers a pictorial view of how a rogue financial industry, with politicians on the take, stole the equivalent of the entire output of every American for a year and flushed it down a toilet.[146] The metaphor works if you realize that the ultra-wealthy were like sewer rats swimming around the cesspool collecting most of those flushed dollars for themselves. TARP took taxpayer money equivalent to a year and a half of Gross Domestic Product and offered it to Wall Street and other giant corporations and fat rats. In just three years, they stole an amount equal to **the entire lifetime output of one third of the planet's population**—20 Trillion dollars.[147]

Redefining Risk: Our Money Risked, They Profit

All of my life I've heard this excuse for unbridled capitalism: *those who take the risks deserve the rewards*. But in fact, the opposite has happened. The reward-reapers risked nothing. The top five executives of Lehman Brothers made over a billion from 2000-2007, and when the firm went bankrupt, they made still more money. Charles Ferguson in *Inside Job* gave the example of Merrill-Lynch CEO Stan Oneal, who "collected $161 million dollars *after* he drove his company in the ground."

Meanwhile, average Americans lost jobs, pensions/stock values, homes, and we also lost a sense of security. We had bought into the promises of leaders like Alan Greenspan, who wrote in 1997, "The unbundling of financial products... [such as] derivatives... help firms manage interest rate risk, other market risks... credit risks."[148] The pretend-geniuses of Wall Street, emboldened by real-geniuses from academia with their quantum math, fooled us into believing that risk can be cleverly spread and leveraged so as to safely permit wild speculation. Could no one see that in an interconnected global economy, economic downturns are pervasive and inevitable? Well, they were right about one thing: they *had* eliminated risk for themselves as broker, risking investors' money but not their own.

Malcolm Gladwell describes, in his book *Outliers*, how a plane crash is the inevitable result of seven mistakes and/or malfunctions in a row that overwhelm the many failsafe systems. Economic crashes are similar. In the 2008 crash, the intersection of various trends, including fuel prices and consumer confidence, brought on a recession which triggered mortgage defaults which popped bubbles. Interconnectedness leaves no safe haven to compartmentale risk.

While Wall Street was getting rich via artificial manipulations of the market, they told us the plane was flying high and safe, repeatedly reassuring us that the stock market was a safe bet. But quietly, a variety of other voices—investigative reporters, IMF experts, economists, analysts and auditors—began to warn about the dangers posed by Derivatives, Credit Default Swaps and other bubbles. We'd previously experienced the S&L fiasco, the Black Monday Wall Street crash of 1987, the dot.com tech bubble/bust. Still, Henry Paulson and Ben Bernanke, well-warned of the looming disaster, publicly denied there was a problem even as late as 2008![149] Like a pilot saying, "You may unbuckle your seat belts and walk around the cabin," even as the plane is in a death-spiral dive.

The Crash damage was amplified by "fire and rescue." Paulson, Geithner and Bernanke (appointed as Fed Chair by both Bush *and* Obama) made costly decisions in the ensuing Federal payout/rescue —such as throwing billions at companies with no accountability for what they continued to pay executives, and forcing AIG to pay Goldman-Sachs $150 billion without negotiation—decisions that cost taxpayers over a trillion dollars. Tim Geithner, as late as 2006, wrote that "Financial institutions are able to measure and manage risk much more effectively. Risks are spread more widely...." The book *13 Bankers* reported that he boasted of the "resilience of the financial system of the United States" and of "improvements in the stability of the system." The ink was barely dry when the house of cards came crashing down. That Geithner remained in a highest position of economic leadership is astounding. He is not alone. Almost every leader who helped rob America still continues in cushy positions.

Fed Chair Ben Bernanke called the 2007-2008 crash as the worst financial crisis in the history of the world. One would think that the people responsible for causing the worst financial crisis in all of history might, such as the CEOs of Bear Stearns, Lehman Brothers, Merrill Lynch, Morgan Stanley, and Goldman Sachs, would have been fired. Fined. Arrested. But instead, most of them walked away scot free. Most retained their jobs, many got bonuses, a few changed firms, but almost all of them are still making millions this very day. The only "spreading of risk" was the bipartisan political maneuvers to spread the risk to every taxpayer. In 1776, patriots rebelled against tyranny with the rallying cry, "No taxation without representation." Today we could chant, "No risk without reward."

The List of Suspects Grows: add Grave Robbers

As stated in a previous chapter, op-eds and Letters-to-the-Editors tried to blame the ethnic poor for the economic collapse of 2008-2009. We know the collapse was caused by over-leveraging and bubble-blowing by the rich, not the poor. And the mortgage bubble was only one part of the profiteering. After the collapse, "Foreclosure mills," law firms that profit excessively or fraudulently by handling the paperwork of foreclosure, crept in like grave-robbers to pilfer the pockets of the "corpses": the poor souls who couldn't pay their mortgage in the thralls of a recession. In "the old days," local bankers had an incentive to work cooperatively with such homeowners to get through hard times. But seeing the promise of Federal reimbursement for mortgage losses, and having hedged their bets to profit from derivatives' collapse, Wall Street was happy to hasten foreclosures.

Many of these attorney-owned mills weren't satisfied with excessive profits, they wanted *insane* profits, so they fraudulently sped up the process via paperwork tricks such as back-dating contracts. Florida Attorney General Bill McCollum investigated several of the larger firms, including one founded by multi-millionaire attorney David J. Stern. The mills churn through a million foreclosure cases a year for Fannie and Freddie and other lenders—charging $1,000 and more for the simple paperwork involved. Rushing foreclosures through and collecting huge fees proved insanely profitable for Stern, who owned a $15 million 16,000-square-foot mansion, a 130-foot jet-propelled yacht, four Ferraris, four Porsches, a Bugatti—a total of over $60 million in property/assets, some of which he hid in a Virgin Island tax haven.[150] A Pasco County judge said Stern's firm was guilty of "fraudulently backdat[ing], in a purposeful, intentional effort to mislead...."[151] According to the *New York Times*, while you and I suffered in the 2008 crash, Stern made $18 million from foreclosures. With nearly seven million foreclosures nationwide in 2009-2010, mortgage mills across the country ground out a profit from homeowners' misery.

Senate Investigates Goldman-Sachof$#!+

Back to Goldman-Sachs: thankfully, a Senate subcommittee took a close look at their emails and found smoking guns. The 650-page report, *Wall Street and the Financial Crisis: Anatomy of a Financial Collapse*, shows without a doubt that key executives perjured themselves while under oath before the Senate. The report gives evidence (internal emails) that G-S executives lied so frequently and to such a degree of intentional deception, it can only be called fraud. Five years after their crime, they have yet to see prison, and knowing their entanglements with high-placed politicians, I doubt they will. The congressional testimony of G-S execs Blankfein, Viniar, Spark and Swenson were outright deceptions.[152]

Read the Senate report: "Goldman transferred risky assets from its own inventory into these CDOs; in others, it included poor quality assets that were likely to lose value.... Goldman took... the short side of the CDO, essentially betting that the assets within the CDO would fall in value or not perform. Goldman's short position was in direct opposition to the clients to whom it was selling the CDO securities, yet it failed to disclose [this]. Goldman did not disclose to potential investors when it had... taken short investments that would pay off if the particular security it was selling... performed poorly. In the case of Hudson 1, for example... when the securities lost value, Goldman made a $1.7 billion gain at the direct expense of the clients to whom it had sold the securities."[153] This is not just fraud, but "triple-fraud": a scam with more layers than Redford's classic movie, "The Sting." While re-packaging garbage as gold, they additionally sold "shorts" on the same... betting that their own product would fail! "Bet" is the wrong word: they new the product was faulty, and they knew their stooges in government would cover their losses.

You can choose the metaphor: Congress tactfully called it "poor quality assets," I started the chapter with an inflammatory word for excrement, then "garbage." Now let me try lead vs. gold: I have a young friend who literally tried to sell a pawn-shop some gold-plated lead as solid gold bullion. Had he not been a minor at the time, he would still be in jail. If you wrap up lead in a shiny box and bow and sell it as gold, that's fraud and you go to prison. Yet, we gave Wall Street billions of tax-dollars, thus enabling the firms to reward the con-alchemists with multi-million-dollar golden parachutes. The hoax alchemists got the gold mine, and we got the shaft. But let's blame the poor families thrown out of their homes!

Reaping the Whirlwind, Blaming the Poor

The report from the U.S. Senate Permanent Subcommittee on Investigations two-year, bipartisan investigation into the origins of the 2008 financial crisis is an amazing read. It chronicles corruption, greed and failure at every level—corporate and regulatory. The report calls the collapse of Washington Mutual (WAMU) "one of the most spectacular failures of federal bank regulators in recent history." Take note of this sentence: "After the subprime mortgage backed securities market collapsed in September 2007, WAMU was unable to sell or securitize subprime loans and its loan portfolio began falling in value."[154] The collapse of the housing bubble, which subprime loans was a part of but not solely responsible for, in turned triggered the fall in value—but the value was an artificially inflated one, hyped by the nature of CDO's. The losses came not just because a few poor folks were late on their loan payments. If housing had not been artificially inflated in value in the first place, the value/equity in the homes would have covered much of the losses of those who defaulted. The losses were in the **hundreds of billions**—far more than the loss of small mortgages— and a reaping of the whirlwind, the result of Reagan's de-regulation, and over-valued CDO's and over-valued real estate and over-valued WAMU. "By not sounding the alarm, [Federal regulators] enabled WaMu to construct a multi-billion-dollar investment portfolio of high risk mortgage assets, and also permitted WaMu to sell hundreds of billions of dollars in high risk, poor quality loans and securities" [i.e. derivatives/CDO's].[155]

Summary

So let's review: a young minority couple works hard, saves, and comes up with the money for a down payment on the American dream. With the economy booming, with the government and the bankers encouraging them to buy a home, they do so—even though the real estate market in 2007 had been value-inflated by speculators, the Fed and Fannie Mae. Our young couple borrows money anyway, and starts paying interest… fairly high, considering they don't have they best FICO score. Then the Wall Street exploiters slice and dice the sub-prime loans, along with mortgages at all levels, to create a new sausage. The money manipulators leverage these sausage derivatives and make **billions** in profits. Some even make short-sell and insured arrangements, betting on their own losses! Next, because of oil-speculators, gas hits $4 a gallon, consumer spending retreats, companies lay-off, and poof, *recession*. The poor homeowners can no longer make their house payments. When Wall Street's sausage turns rotten, the fat-cats get billions more in government-aid, and keep their high-paying jobs. To add insult to injury, the foreclosure mill lawyers pull out a final dose of profit.

Allan Sloan, the conservative, staid, senior editor-at-large with

Fortune 500 magazine, had the honesty to confirm what I am writing: "The biggest danger to the U.S. capitalist system doesn't come from communists or left-wing academics. It comes from... the nation's biggest financial institutions [who created] the financial meltdown that touched off the Great Recession [and] the foreclosure fiasco.... It's utterly shocking, even to a congenital skeptic like me, to see that giant institutions such as Bank of America, GMAC, and J.P. Morgan were allegedly using misleading affidavits to oust people from their homes... and repeatedly misled courts.... If you or I did that, we'd be kicked to the curb by the legal system in about two seconds. [But] these institutions and their CEOs will get what amounts to a slap on the wrist... something more systemic and serious is wrong."[156]

The larger, more important question that underlies all of this is: **Why are we paying billions for work that is mostly done by computers and provides so little value to society?** Prize-winning reporter Chris Hedges calls those who work in the financial industry "parasitic." This is not a mindless *ad hominem*: most of what Wall Street does is suck money out of the industries and workers who do the actual work. "Parasite" is a descriptive term for an organism that engorges itself off the work of another organism without contributing anything of value back to the host. We pay billions to leeches.

If you're not angry, you haven't been paying attention.

~~~

Chapter 10: Welfare for the Rich, Taxes for the Poor
Corporate subsidies and taxation myths

A financial element in the large centers has owned the government since the days of Andrew Jackson. ~Franklin Roosevelt

Corporate Welfare, The True Welfare Cadillac

As I grew up in rural Alabama, I often heard people gripe about the so-called "Welfare Cadillac" (see Chapter 7). Working people resented the unemployed for getting a fat check from the government (they imagined welfare checks to be more substantial than they actually were). A relatively-few cases of welfare fraud created a myth and a mantra: the poor are *lazy cheats*. A certain percentage of the poor are indeed lazy—about the same percentage as middle class and upper class folks! (How can you be rich and lazy? One word: *inheritance*.) All of that is moot: the welfare system has been restructured since I was a kid. In 1996, then-President Clinton and Congress enacted sweeping welfare reform (*The Personal Responsibility and Work Opportunity Reconciliation Act of 1996*). Welfare benefits are greatly reduced or eliminated entirely. The able-bodied are required to find work... even though this is very difficult for single mothers, who must not only find a job but also find daycare for their children. Moreover, improvements in computers, state-to-federal connectedness, and identification technology are making it increasingly difficult for anyone to significantly defraud welfare. Well, except for one class of people: the people who can afford accountants, lawyers and lobbyists to milk Federal subsidies and tax loopholes, or who use political connections to gain lucrative no-bid contracts, like Dick Cheney's Halliburton in Iraq and Katrina.[157]

People complain about welfare for the poor even though it is a drop in the bucket compared to **welfare for the rich**. Less than 1% of the U.S. population gets *cash* benefits, most of which goes to single women with children.[158] Critics of welfare inflate that number by including food stamps, subsidized school lunches and other children's nutrition programs like W.I.C., the federally-funded nutrition subsidy for women, infants, and children. Why fret over programs that **feed** hungry children while *not* counting Medicare/Medicaid/Social Security, which is the biggest welfare program in the world, where more dollars go to wealthy folks than to the poor?

Gimme Shelter

The rich tap a far more lucrative form of "government welfare" that dwarfs the free milk and juice given to disadvantaged children: tax shelters and tax subsidies. The oligarchs extract billions from Federal and state governments. Let's use my own state as an example... because this is also the place where I've heard the most belly-aching about "welfare Cadillacs" for the poor, yet our politicians brag about a literal "welfare Mercedes" deal for the wealthy. Allow me to use my own state, Alabama, one of the poorest in the nation, as an example. Over the last decade or so, hundreds of millions in tax breaks were given to Mercedes, Hyundai, Thyssen-Krup Steel, ALFA insurance, and other large corporations in this state. Some of these breaks come directly via grants or tax write-offs, some come indirectly by huge infrastructure investments, like a new highway built to a Mercedes plant, or dock facilities for cruise lines and ship freight, or airport expansions that cater mostly to the wealthy and the corporate customer.

• *The Wall Street Journal* estimated that the total gifts to Mercedes would exceed $300 million, which works out to a cost to taxpayers of $200,000 for *each* Alabama job created. A $119 million "incentive" was added later for plant expansion.[159]

• Thyssen-Krup Steel was promised an astounding $811 million: $461 million in upfront in state, county, and local grants; $111.5 million in state tax credits and exemptions; and $238 million in local tax abatements... with more possible later.[160]

• Honda, Hyundai and Walmart also received millions in state subsidies. (More on Walmart later in this chapter.)

• Alabama is becoming less of an agricultural state but agribusiness still gets preferential treatment by Bama government. I'm not complaining of the family farm with 100 acres or less, but corporate "factory farms" and massive timber/pulp operations. According to the *Birmingham Post-Herald*, between 1996 and 2001, Newby Farms received nearly $3 million in federal farm subsidies. 7,500-acre Newby Farms is partly owned by Jerry Newby, president of ALFA —whose insurance arm also gets special tax breaks. No wonder Newby and ALFA, which also has a huge lobbying arm, campaigned against tax reform—they like the *status quo*.[161]

My grandfather, mentioned in Chapter 1, had a small Alabama farm and never saw a penny of government help. His farm and thousands like it no longer exist. Why? Of the $190 BILLION Federal Farm Bill of 2002, guess who got two-thirds of that pie? The top 10 percent, the richest and biggest corporate farms.[162]

Whether in my state or yours, no one lobbies for those working class folk at the bottom of the economic ladder, or even the middle class, so the largest tax breaks and subsidies of the past twenty years went to the rich. Welfare for the rich.

Sleight of Hand

A magician and a pick-pocket use the same strategy: draw your attention away from what their unseen hand is doing. The "official" top corporate tax rate in the United States is 35 percent, one of the highest in the world... on *paper*.[163] "I'm a corporation. Watch my right hand as I wave the number 35%, while with the left hand, I pay only 6%." In his book, *The Price of Civilization*, Professor Jeffrey Sachs proves that the 35% corporate tax rate is a "fraud," as he reminds us that no Fortune 500 company in America pays 35% and many pay less less taxes than Ma and Pa's Smalltown Diner.[164] According to the *New York Times,* "companies have been increasingly using a maze of shelters, tax credits and subsidies to pay far less...," often *zero*, so that "the corporate share of the nation's tax receipts [fell] from 30 percent of all federal revenue in the mid-1950s to 6.6 percent in 2009."[165] Derek Thompson, a pro-business advocate, admits that 35 percent is a meaningless number since most companies "take advantage of loopholes or move [a portion] of their businesses overseas." Pharmaceutical companies, for example, pay an effective rate of only 6%.[166] Poor people in my state pay more tax on a loaf of bread than that!

The Times also reported that General Electric paid zero taxes on its 2010 profit of $14.2 billion.[167] Zero. And not much more in prior years. Jeff Immelt, GE's CEO, accepted a high-status White House position and that hasn't hurt their tax bill; GE has been a part of "fierce lobbying for tax breaks and innovative accounting that enables it to concentrate its profits offshore."[168] To rub salt in the wound, GE benefits extensively from government incentives and government contracts. Yet we still find conservative commentators bemoaning the 35% corporate tax rate, claiming it is higher than other countries. Like most carping by the rich, that number is a charade, a lie even worse than "damn statistics," because it exists for the sole purpose of swaying public opinion rather than as a real tool for revenue collection. The smoke and mirrors game of tax avoidance and tax subsidy is so complicated, no one knows what corporations really pay in taxes. Percentage-wise, the middle class is taxed more aggressively than most multinational corporations.

When you hear a pundit claim, "Our U.S. corporate tax rate is higher than Europe's," your bull-sweat meter should sound off. The same goes for, "The rich pay most of the taxes," which may be true in total dollars, but not percentage-wise, and certainly not true when the benefits the rich receive *back* from the government are factored in. Moreover, a large portion of corporate profits funnel into stocks, which are only taxed at the capital gains rate of 15%. I saw this magician's hoax in the first presidential campaign debate for the 2012 election, as the "35% corporate tax rate" was trumpeted by a Republican candidate as something to be lowered to help "stimulate the economy." None of the other candidates challenged the hoax. They were all sending a signal to corporate PAC's: "Contribute to Republicans, we'll keep the con going."

Money Grows on Trees... and Farms

Some of the largest forms of government welfare are found in the Farm Bill (millions to giant corporate farms, poultry houses, and livestock mills) and Mining and Minerals (coal and metals mining and petroleum). Begin with the ethanol scam: oil refineries can take a 45-cents-a-gallon tax credit for ethanol blended with gasoline which not only gives one of several tax gifts to the oil companies, but also "benefits corn-based ethanol, driving up corn prices, distorting agricultural decisions, and having little if any benefit in terms of greenhouse gas emission reductions or fuel savings," according to Gilbert Metcalf, an economics professor at Tufts University. Ethanol costs taxpayers over $7 billion every year, because of additional tax breaks at the state level for corporate corn "farmers." The Feds pay around $20 billion per year to corporate farm-factories in direct subsidies as "farm income stabilization," according to the USDA. Plus there is a special tariff on imported ethanol. Artificially increased demand (ethanol uses a third of the U.S. corn crop) has driven up grain prices—and those higher prices are like an additional "tax" on consumers' grocery bills. Richard Lobb, communications director for the National Chicken Council, said high corn prices are the main reason feed-costs for livestock and poultry have risen 50 percent. All of this was so egregious that in 2011, bipartisan voices began to question the logic of ethanol subsidies.

We lack space to detail all the ways major agribusiness squeezes the government teat, including dairy price supports that milk the taxpayer (sorry for the udderly-tasteless milk/squeeze puns!), the peanut and tobacco buyout programs, and other miscellaneous programs. Other Federal payouts to agribusiness are less obvious: conservation program payments from the Conservation Reserve Program; Environmental Quality Incentives Program; the Conservation Security Program; emergency and disaster relief programs—all fine-sounding causes, and of some value, but well-hidden from the average taxpayer as the plutocrats stir up racist fears of "welfare Cadillacs" and supposed rip-offs by "illegal aliens draining local resources." The poor are caricatured as leeches sucking the government dry, when the bulk of this Federal and State "welfare" goes neither to the poor nor to the struggling Ma and Pa Kettle on the family farm. By 1997, large farms accounted for 72% of farm sales, and from 2003 to 2005 the top 1% of beneficiaries (i.e. the richest) received 17% of subsidy payments.[169]

A Case Study: Whining by the Rich at Tax Reform

When, as a pastor, I supported a modest tax reform plan in

Alabama proposed by Republican Governor Bob Riley, I was accosted by several wealthy parishioners, including a timber operator with hundreds of acres of timberland. He lived in an opulent three-story mansion and was angry at my support for the poor. Thanks to a tax loophole called "current use," he and other big farm and timber interests paid the lowest rate in property taxes in the nation, in most cases less than $2 per acre! The proposed legislation would have increased that only slightly, to a maximum of $2.50 per acre.[170]

In addition to the fifty-cent an acre increase on land tax, the Alabama Tax Reform Act only asked for the state income tax rate to raise from 5 percent to 6 percent for family incomes over $150,000. But even this was too much for the greedy to bear: they fought vigorously to shoot it down, even though the tax increase was not aimed at increasing "big government," but merely to give slight relief to working families in poverty: a family of four with an annual income as low as $4,600 were being taxed, and Governor Riley's proposal would allow them to make $17,000 before state income tax kicked in (they would *still* pay sales tax of about 9%). Millions of acres of Alabama escaped a reasonable share of taxation because of the powerful lobbying efforts of ALFA.

Early in the process, Governor Riley had told me privately that as a Christian, he felt "a moral duty" to champion tax reform. Soon, *The Economist* magazine of London printed an article entitled, "What Would Jesus Do?", about the need for tax reform in the state of Alabama and applauding the efforts of this Republican governor.[171] Riley had the moral high ground, but what he did not have was the ability to get his message out. With millions to spend on media propaganda, agribusiness lobbyists tricked middle class voters into fearing their taxes would greatly increase. With so little widespread understanding of the issues of fair taxation and economic justice, Governor Riley's tax reform plan failed... even though most Alabamians would have seen a tax *decrease*.[172]

Governor Riley later told me he was frustrated that he could not get the churches to help counter the propaganda with the truth about tax reform and basic economic fairness. I assured the governor that myself and many other Methodist pastors had spoken from the pulpit in support of non-partisan tax reform. Knowing that the rich of our state enjoyed the lowest tax-rates in the nation while the poor suffered one of the highest, reform was a moral issue. To my chagrin, most of the other churches/pastors remained silent in that town. Pastors who had been quick to speak in opposition to abortion or to align themselves with Reagan and Bush, were now silent. Few were preaching the full gospel that includes Jesus' words, "As you have done to the least of these, so you have done to me."

That experience motivated me to write this book. The propaganda machine of the plutocrats is monstrous—but books can change public opinion in ways that politicians cannot. People, understandably, do not trust politicians. But if given the facts, they can vote for justice… it will require support for organizations like **www.FireTheRich.org**, to counteract the monied campaigns of corporate PAC's.

Digging for Dollars, Raping the Land
Mineral mining is another boondoggle that rapes the birthright of natural planet-resources, making a mockery of Woody Guthrie's famous song, "This land is my land, this land is your land." Governments not only help these industries with tax breaks and access highways and university geologists, but they often provide the very land and resources from which the mineral ore is extracted. The "usage fees" for Federal lands are a joke. Remember, this is not to let a company grow a soybean on government (i.e. public) land; **mining** can completely destroy the land for future use, pollutes the entire area and sometimes, via water flow, thousands of additional acres, and steals the valuable mineral forever. At least lumberjacks on Federal parkland leave us something for another tree to grow back upon. But coal, oil, gold, copper and silver is not going to "grow back" on our public lands, it's a treasure that's gone forever. And while the bulk of the profits from those extracted treasures should be used for longterm investments (building colleges or hospitals, for example), instead, it goes into the pockets of the fat-cats as yet another form of corporate welfare.

And the List Goes On...
According to *CNN.com*, there are over 130 business tax breaks currently in the tax code.[173] But remember, in addition to tax cuts on their list, there's an entirely separate list of outright grants that give your hard-earned money to the richest corporations and, in some cases, individuals, for projects that often are already making a profit on their own legs. Some of the projects are outright absurd and wasteful, but that's not even the point: the problem is that worthy or not, this is corporate welfare.

The Bias Against Small Business
My ex-wife and I once tried to open a business of our own, a tiny "mom and pop" children's clothing store. With a few thousand dollars and a lot of sweat equity, while I continued to work a separate 50-hour a week job and both of us raising two toddlers, we did indeed manage to open a small store on a shoestring (bootstrap!) budget. We soon found it impossible to buy inventory without

purchasing quantities in "lots" larger than our small-town store could handle. At that same time, Walmart ended their aggressive ad campaign about "patriotically" selling "Made in the U.S.A" products, and began importing cheap Asian-made children's clothes. Unable to afford large purchases of new product, we shifted our business model to selling used clothes (we'd buy them leftover from yard sales), but suddenly our customers could buy new clothes at Walmart for less than we could sell *used* clothes! And rather than receiving assistance from government, we faced a gauntlet of forms and fees and taxes: buy a business license; register the store name (form and fee), apply for a Federal tax number (form), apply for a State Tax number (form and fee), apply for a county permit (form and fee), file monthly sales tax, etc. Had we been any bigger than a sole proprietorship, we would have registered as an LLC (form and fee), filed employee FICA, Workman's Comp and deal with OSHA. More forms and fees. Our tiny business paid four different utility taxes, a rental tax, an annual license fee tax, a tax on equipment and inventory, and paid Social Security and personal income tax. When my wife drove to work, the car represented a tire excise tax, an EPA battery disposal tax, an motor-oil tax, gasoline tax (hefty), a title fee, a tag fee, a driver's license fee, and sales tax on the car purchase.

With all those taxes and the other overhead, from rent to advertising, we could not make a profit. The forms and regulations were more onerous for us than for Walmart, who could afford to hire a compliance officer and CPA. Our business failed.

By contrast, even as the government hindered our mom 'n pop business, look at what it did *for* our competitor, Walmart. State and Federal government gave "Wally-World" more than **$1.2 billion** in tax breaks, free land, infrastructure assistance, low-cost financing and grants—plus we indirectly subsidized the mega-corporation by paying the healthcare costs of Walmart employees who didn't receive coverage on the job and instead turned to aid/relief programs.[174]

More About Government Blessing the Big

Years after our clothing store failed, I considered opening a music store. Again, I would be willing to work hard and smart. However, despite a sterling credit rating, I could not find capital, and soon realized that the costs of insurance, building rent and utilities, interest-on-product-debt, business licenses and taxes just made it impossible to compete with mail-order stores importing directly from China and selling online *tax-free*. The rhetoric from politicians about "I support the small businessman because he [sic] is the backbone of the American economy," is pure balderdash.

Even the so-called "Small Business Administration" (SBA) has a loan process that in practical terms requires one to hire a CPA or attorney to sort out all the paperwork, and $10,000 or more in cash before qualifying for the loan. It is almost impossible these days for any middle class person trying to put children through college to have enough money to open a small business. Save up money for ten years for such a plan, and suddenly as your child starts college, you discover that the government counts *that* savings against you and denies your student financial aid. The deck is stacked against the little guy in every way imaginable.

In the final chapter of this book, I offer some possible solutions. Without jumping too far ahead, here we can see an obvious and easy way to boost the economy and help the little guy: **government should make "mom and pop" start-ups a Number 1 priority.** How risky would it be for the SBA to offer quick-app, low-collateral, 4% business micro-loans of $20,000? Thousands of people are eager to work hard at their own business and would jump at the chance to accept such a loan to kickstart their micro-business. Even if their business failed, most Americans would still strive to pay off such a loan in good faith.

Federal and local governments should end the giveaways to Walmart, Mercedes and Thyssen-Krup, and the tax-free status of Amazon and eBay retailers, and instead give loans, tax breaks and aid to small businesses, at least for their first five years of operation.

More Case Studies in Welfare for the Rich

An entire book could be written exposing the ways taxpayer money is funneled to the already-rich via government... and David Cay Johnston did that, in his book, *Free Lunch*. Some may find it old news to read Johnston's account of George Bush's taxpayer rip-off in the Texas Rangers baseball franchise case. But since both Bushes were U.S. Presidents, the parable is timeless, a case study in how political power yields taxpayer subsidies. The tale also points up the hypocrisy of right-wing plutocrats, who yell the loudest about "free markets," "limited government," and "self-advancement." Bush campaigned on a platform of limited government, while having made millions from his Texas Rangers baseball team, an investment that used and abused the powers of government to make its profit. Johnston reports that "every dollar that Bush and the other [franchise] investors pocketed when they sold the team came from the taxpayers" via multiple subsidies: wielding the government power of "eminent domain" to buy the land for his stadium on the cheap (virtually stealing it from the unwilling landowners), imposing a special sales tax to fund the stadium, getting favorable lease/rental rates from local government, and in the end, finding questionable tax breaks on the profits—reporting on his 1998 tax return a long-term capital gain of nearly $17 million, part of which Johnston argues should have been taxed at the much higher rate of "compensation." Lucky for Bush, in 1999, the IRS audited those who made less than $25,000 more often than those who made over $100,000![175]

The lawyer who facilitated the sweetheart deal with Arlington is the husband of Bush crony, Senator Kay Bailey Hutchison... and even he places the value of the subsidies to Bush at over $200 million.[176] The hypocrisy: the Texas Republican Party platform at the time stated, "Public money or public powers (such as eminent domain) should not be used to fund or implement so-called private enterprise projects." The passion which ultra-conservatives express against taxation and government intrusion is only exceeded by their passion for exploiting government. Entire books detail the frequents visits by the "pigs to the taxpayer trough." [177]

Welfare and Faring Well

In addition to outright and obvious "welfare for the rich" through cash grants, subsidies and tax breaks, let's remember the larger yet more subtle meaning of "welfare." The word is connected etymologically to the old parting phrase, "Fare thee well," meaning, "I hope you fare well in daily life—I hope you stay healthy and happy and have good things." How does the upper crust "fare" in life, compared to how well the poor survive? The answer is obvious: the rich have better health care and live longer, have unlimited opportunities for travel, education, art and leisure, more freedom, less stress, no bill-paying anxiety, and a bright future for their children. The wealthy can roam their gated estates without fear of crime, violence or invasion. The rich benefit the most from government-supported institutions, systems of banking and economics, security (police/military), medical research and hospitals, institutions of higher education, airports and seaports and more, all of which make their lavish "faring well" possible. Rightwing politicians attack government spending for the poor, then get on a jet, never admitting that millions of government dollars helped build the airport, and the highway leading to it, and Homeland Security that guards it, and the Air Force that patrols the skies it flies in. Most poor persons will never set foot inside an airplane in a lifetime.

The daily life of the working classes is not greatly changed by what sort of government we have (democracy or tyranny, they are still going to be slaving away), or by how much is spent on military defense. The poor will die in far greater numbers on the battlefield to defend the castles of the rich. The poor have the least to gain from infrastructure and other benefits funded by the trillions of dollars flowing through government.

Progressive Taxation

Progressive taxation simply means that those with great wealth should pay taxes at a higher rate. Proponents of a flat tax (usually wealthy folk like Herman Cain or Steve Forbes... or people who are have a math-phobia) argue, "Hey, if I make a million dollars and pay 10%, then I'm paying $100,000 in taxes, while if you make $100,000 at the same 10% rate, you only pay $10,000—so rich people like me are paying most of the taxes in this country!"

This book has offered multiple reasons for progressive taxation:
1. The fortunate have a moral duty to help the less fortunate, as taught by all major religions—a golden rule response, an ethical debt of gratitude to the society that gave them the opportunity for success; **2.** The privileged class has a fiducial duty to bear a proportionate burden of the cost of government, to pay for the systems and infrastructures and armies that preserve their lavish lifestyle.
3. The rich can afford it... a progressive tax on the upper class comes from "disposable" or saved income, while taxes on the lower classes come out of survival-budgets that have no margin.

Don't take my word for it; listen to multi-billionaire Warren Buffet: "My friends and I have been coddled long enough by a billionaire-friendly Congress. It's time for our government to get serious about shared sacrifice." In an op-ed piece in *The New York Times*, Buffett explained that his federal tax bill "was only 17.4 percent of my taxable income —and that's actually a lower percentage than...the other 20 people in our office."[178] He is admitting that billionaires are taxed at *half* the rate of the rest of us. And Republican Mark Rubio and half of FOX News moaned and screamed that Buffet was inciting "class warfare."

The Myth of Shared Sacrifice

In 2011, as he argued for slightly higher taxes on the top 10%, President Obama began to talk a great deal about "shared sacrifice." Even this is misleading: sacrifice implies pain and deprivation. Taxation that only decreases the size of a rich person's offshore bank account does not actually impose any kind of diminished lifestyle—not one whit of pain or deprivation. No sacrifice. Instead of looking at how much one pays in taxes, look at how much money a person has left *after* taxes and after paying out the basic "nut" for living expenses. The average middle class family owes more than they possess in assets. They are working like slaves just to have a mortgaged roof over their head. When they pay taxes, it is a literal sacrifice: they will eat less steak and more hamburger, to use a trivial but real example. For the lower middle class and poverty-stricken, paying taxes on groceries and gasoline causes them to ponder, "How can I feed my family the rest of the week, or have enough gas to drive to work?" Meanwhile, people with three homes, six cars, and a nest egg wish to complain about their tax rate.

Alpha Magazine reported take of the top earning hedge fund managers for the year before the crash began: the top earner for 2006 received $1.7 billion, the second highest received $1.4 billion, and the third made $1.3 billion. Incredibly, the tax code only taxed them at the much lower rate of capital gains (rather than the higher personal income tax). Capital gains, including stock dividends, are taxed at 15%... that's after losses, only on profit. But when a working mother buys diapers, every penny is taxed at 10% in my state, after her income was first taxed 14% for social security, and then more for state and federal income taxes.

The additional weakness to the "taxes are too high" whine of the rich is that many of them actually don't pay anywhere near the high rates that are claimed. We previously quoted a *USA Today* report that 7,389 tax returns showing $200,000 and more in gross income paid *zero* Federal taxes. When you see statistics showing that the rich bear all the tax burden, don't believe it. When you read or hear about the high rates applied to the rich, don't trust those theoretical numbers.

What do I mean by "theoretical"? The article or pundit-quote of numbers is usually based on basic IRS tax tables: "The upper class are taxed at 35%," omitting the fact that **no one *actually* pays that rate** in the end. Even if you were single with no dependents and took no deductions whatsoever, you would never pay 35% because of the way the formulas work—the "35% bracket" only applies to a small portion of income that crosses a threshold.[179] And a huge part of a millionaire's income can be sheltered in such a way that they will never even *partially* trigger the 35% bracket! The *USA Today* article proves as much, and Buffet confirmed it.

Perquisites

The picture is even more blurred by the fact that so much of the income of the top 20% is hidden, never a part of the mythical "progressive tax system." Most executives receive a portion of their income in tax-free categories, not reported as "salary" at all: fat expense accounts for travel, expensive restaurants, personal assistants and bodyguards, free educational opportunities, other perqs and amenities that the rest of us have to pay for out of pocket, out of *taxed* salaries. The wealthy often receive a portion of income as lower-taxed capital gains or enjoy tax-deferred income sheltered as pensions, trusts and annuities. They also enjoy a more significant tax break via the home mortgage interest deduction on their mansions. And the rich can afford creative accountants and tax shelters to maximize all of these possibilities, in effect making a portion of their wealth taxed at a rate of zero percent! Multi-millionaire Mitt Romney reported an effective tax rate of just 15%, thanks to breaks in the tax code for the richest. *Seventh Generation* CEO and founder Jeffrey Hollender confessed, "Why should I be able to deduct my second mortgage? If you have two houses, do you need a deduction on your second house? There are so many benefits the wealthy have."

We Already Have a Flat Tax

While the wealthy are skirting taxes, the slave who is mopping their floors has taxes withheld, sometimes with no idea how to take advantage of tax deductions, or even how to get a tax refund back when they overpay. **Graduated, progressive income tax represents far less than half of Federal revenues.** The lower and middle class pay a host of other, regressive, **flat taxes** (sales taxes, payroll/FICA taxes, utility taxes, excise taxes, property taxes, and more). When the poor man gases his truck to head to work, he pays the same rate of gasoline tax as the rich man fueling his yacht, as well as the same rate for Social Security and Medicare taxes. In many locales, the poor pay a huge sales tax on groceries and clothing (9.5% in my town). All of these are flat taxes! Federal, state and local taxes of all sorts, in the end, represents a huge burden on the poor and middle class and leave the rich unfazed. Yet, millionaires like Steve Forbes and Dick Armey are not satisfied, they even want to flatten the income tax. Greed has no bounds.

Indeed, to get the whole picture, **state and local taxes** must be factored in. The Institute on Taxation and Economic Policy, a non-profit, non-partisan research organization, shows that as a percentage of income, those taxes are actually a *reverse*-progressive tax. That's right, they extract a higher percentage of taxes vs. income from the poor and middle class than from the upper class! The bottom 60% of the population is taxed at the state/local level at about 10% of income; the richest, top 20% of population, are only taxed at 7%![180] This is when all taxes are factored in, unlike the cherry-picked stats you may see quoted in mainstream media. Greg LeRoy, founder of Good Jobs First, writes, "When large corporations control the tax system, ...working families and small businesses pay more, because states and cities… sustain public services… with regressive taxes."[181]

The Big Lie: Cutting Taxes Boosts the Economy

Republicans and Libertarians claim, *Cutting taxes on the rich boosts employment. Tax increases on the rich hurt small businesses, and thus cuts jobs.* Not true. The reasons our economy grew after

Reagan's tax cuts had more to do with the increase of women in the marketplace, the boon of computer technology, and increased defense spending. Studies have shown there is no direct correlation between tax rates and business boom cycles when viewed over long time periods.[182] Studies that show otherwise either: fail to look at a longterm window; fail to factor in deficit spending during the Reagan and Bush eras; fail to credit stronger factors, such as increased productivity, women entering the workforce, computer and technological advances, and global forces.[183] Economics in our new millennium is far more complicated than simple single-phrase fads imply. *Keynesian, Supply-side, Chicago School...* these exist because economics professors need something to put in the textbooks. How can I so arrogantly dismiss an entire "science"? Because I'm writing in 2011, and can look back at the train wreck of 2007-2008. Few economists predicted it, and none of the fad theories prevented it. Global economics is a wild horse that cannot be contained or controlled by "models."

    The Supply-side model, in particular, deserves our ridicule because it is merely a cynical ploy to enrich the Fourth Reich. Economist Paul Krugman stated, "The specific set of foolish ideas that has laid claim to the name 'supply side economics' is a crank doctrine that would have had little influence if it did not appeal to the prejudices of editors and wealthy men."[184]

    When you reduce taxes on the wealthy via Reagan-style tax cuts, studies have shown that the rich rarely put that bonanza into job-creation. Some of it will end up in an off-shore bank account, or spent on an overpriced Picasso, which creates zero jobs. And not all taxes going to the government is squandered; some of it does indeed create jobs through government spending on infrastructure, defense industry manufacturing and soldiers' payrolls, and civil service jobs. One thing is sure: cutting taxes on the rich worsens the Federal debt.

    The "big lie" behind justifying upper-class tax cuts is really a double-lie: 1. the false claim that "rich people" and "small business" are synonymous and 2. money in their hands creates jobs. Roberton Williams, a senior fellow with the Tax Policy Center sponsored by the mainstream Brookings Institute, states: "Only 3 percent of small-business owners are in the top bracket. They are not all what we think of as job-creating small businesses. A lot of them are hedge-fund managers and law-firm partners." And in the era of 2009-2012, taxes on the rich were low, corporations and the rich had mountains of cash, yet unemployment soared. Bruce Bartlett wrote in *The Fiscal Times* (August 19, 201): "It's axiomatic among Republicans that taxes on the rich are the single most important factor determining economic growth. If that were true, then the period from 1988 to 1990, when the top rate was just 28 percent, should have been the most prosperous in recent American history. During that time we had the lowest top rate since 1931 [but] the GDP growth rate fell to... just 1.9 percent in 1990. [Their] dogmatic belief that low taxes on the rich are the key to growth is transparent nonsense."

The Death of the Death Tax

One of the best arguments in favor of free enterprise and capitalism is that wealth is the reward for an individual's hard work. But in another hypocritical inconsistency, the greedy wail loud and long about the horrors of and estate or inheritance tax, the so-called "Death Tax." There is not an ounce of sweat involved in receiving a fortune via inheritance. But the Estate Tax has even been called "The American Dream Tax," claiming it destroys the American Dream. Hogwash. More accurate are those who call it "The Silver Spoon Tax" or the "Baby Trust Fund Tax," pointing out the true American Dream is not to establish dynasties, a new royalty that pass on wealth and privilege by birthright. When did America decide it wanted to return to the British royalty we sought independence from? From day one, the American Dream has always been that *anyone*, regardless of birth/class, can have the economic opportunity to be successful and prosperous by their own efforts, not from a largesse handed down by the dynasty before them! As Thomas Paine wrote in *Common Sense*: "For all men being originally equals, no one by birth [should] have the right to set up his own family in perpetual preference to all others forever... [since] his descendants might be far too unworthy to inherit... the advantage."

Clearly, the issue of inheritance tax is fraught with emotion and misinformation. Let's methodically and calmly straighten this out:

•Emotionally, I want to give my daughters a better life than I had, and I want them to inherit my sentimental bric-a-brac as well as a portion of my property. That common emotional desire is one reason I would never argue for a 100% inheritance tax, and one reason Western society would never tolerate it. But emotion aside, from a truly capitalistic view there is no logical justification for giving a multi-million-dollar estate to some lazy, spoiled brat who never worked a day in his life. It bestows no benefit upon society. It rewards indolence rather than industry. And thus, it is hypocritical for capitalists to support the abolition of inheritance tax: silver spoons are not consistent with bootstrap entrepreneurialism.

•But the wailers and whiners about a "death tax" have no legitimate beef: there is not, nor has there ever been in America, a tax that takes away a person's entire estate at death. In 2010, in fact, there was *zero* tax at death.

- At the end of 2010 and beginning of 2011, Congress debated what level of inheritance tax should be re-instituted. Not even the most liberal of Senators proposed anything near even one half of an estate. The "socialistic President" only supported a 35% rate—and even that is grossly misleading. In almost all serious proposals, the first $5 million of an estate would be exempt from ANY inheritance tax! Thus the rate for most millionaires would be 0%, not 35%. Even someone with a ten million dollar estate would be, overall, giving back to society only 17% of their largesse.
- And yet, even *that* is exaggerated. There are a number of other loopholes, exemptions and tax shelters that the rich routinely employ so as to avoid the estate tax. Cunning tycoons (Ken Lay of ENRON being a perfect example) invest in tax-free annuities, irrevocable trusts, pensions and life insurance plans that spread the payback to their families over time—in many cases tax exempt. The rich also "gift" thousands every year to their kin, tax-free, if they can anticipate a death or simply see the size of their estate growing beyond the five million dollar mark.
- According to a study by the Federal Reserve Bank of Cleveland, only 1.6% of Americans receive $100,000 or more in inheritance. Another 1.1% receive $50,000 to $100,000. On the other hand, 91.9% receive nothing (Kotlikoff & Gokhale, 2000). If estate taxes are not restored, we will increase the Federal debt $1 trillion over the next two decades all for the benefit of a mere 0.6% of the wealthiest Americans.[185] And Republican candidates actually brag about their opposition to the death tax.
- The lone social benefit of no estate tax is the preservation of small family businesses and family farms, especially those that involve large land holdings (necessary for large-scale farming) or where the capital is mostly invested in machinery/inventory necessary for the business to thrive. Of course, politicians trot out anecdotal stories or a teary-eyed, grief-stricken child of rich Big-Daddy. "We will lose the family business!" These anecdotes get reported to the media with little to no research or factual follow-up. Media rarely ask the harder questions of the grieving: "Have you actually looked at the tax laws? Can you set up an LLC or ILIT or other form of annuity or trust to shield taxation and diversify the holdings? How much of the financial trouble you are facing has to do with bad management or a changing marketplace?" For example, the loss of small family farms has almost nothing to do with the death tax, but rather, with government policies that favor large corporate agribusiness, such as Archer-Daniels, Cargill, Tyson, etc.
- Consider the case of Walmart. Sam Walton died in 1992, when there was a partial "death tax" in place. Surprise! The giant of all retail chains, with single stores grossing millions, did not go belly

up. Instead, we learn that the Walton inheritors continue to be on the list of the world's richest people.
   • According to Mike Lapham of the Responsible Wealth Program, "only about a quarter of 1 percent of estates will owe any tax, and each year only about a dozen estates with significant business or farm assets have trouble finding liquid assets to pay the tax."[186]

The Benefits of Taxing the Dead

We've heard again and again the exaggerated lore about the "burden" of a "death tax" on the wealthy tycoon's heirs. But what is the *benefit* of an estate tax? First, if we are all to enjoy the benefits of government, from transportation infrastructure to national security to government research, we need tax revenue. Even a modest estate tax on millionaires could raise a trillion dollars over a decade.

Second, at the end of every lifetime, trimming the top off excessive accumulations of wealth makes for a more fair and equitable economy. I've already chronicled how excessive wealth is product of luck, manipulation of markets, and tilted government policies. Sometimes that wealth is the result of outright criminal behavior—crimes which are difficult to catch. A once-in-a-lifetime inheritance tax offers a chance for society to retrieve a small portion of that largesse... a final chance at some economic justice. Just as the IRS was more effective at getting mafia gangsters behind bars than police were, a high-threshold death tax (exempting mom 'n pop businesses) offers somes justice, some balancing karma.

A so-called Death Tax is, actually, the only painless tax. When I am dead, I doubt I'll have much concern about the government taking back a bit of my wealth. The gnashing of teeth over this tax is inexplicable other than pure greed and desire to inherit wealth that one has not worked for. For some, it is not enough to inherit five million dollars for doing nothing other than winning the DNA lottery (being born into wealth), or to have the tax code, politicians, CPA's, the tax attorneys all working overtime to reduce their fair share of taxes. No, they want the cash loaded up in a hearse to go with them! They want death to the death tax... and resurrection to their fortune.

The Death of the Death Tax: The Canary in the Coal Mine

Why devote so much space and energy to this issue? The death of the death tax is the proverbial canary in the coal mine, showing us who really controls our politics. It's also a litmus test for candidates: those who oppose the death tax will not receive my vote because they obviously care more about protecting the dead than the living.

5% of Americans own 62 percent of the wealth in the U.S.,

according to *The Nation* magazine.[187] With the abolition of the inheritance tax, and the other systemic tilting of the playing field in favor of the already-rich, we are seeing the death of upward mobility, the death of the middle class. Without a bit of adjustment via an estate tax, neo-feudalism is complete. The king passes his property on to the royal-blooded, and the peasants nothing.

Summary

When someone spends all their time surrounded by affluence, being catered to, insulated from the daily struggles of the poor, their view of the world of finance can become biased. Isaac Asimov, in his *Foundation Trilogy*, writes of how it is unwise to keep one's foreign diplomat assigned to an embassy in an enemy land for more than a few years, because they begin to absorb the culture and mindset of that foreign environment and become soft towards the opposition. Spend every night on silk sheets, ride to work on heated leather seats in your Lexus or limo, and spend every day having your coffee brought to you, and your subconscious begins to find rationalizations as to why the lap of luxury is not such a bad thing. Power corrupts. Excessive luxury does the same.

Just as Gollum, a villain in *The Lord of the Rings*, became defensive and irrational when the ring of power was taken from him, likewise the oligarchs react to any hint of economic justice with grasping and squealing. "Class war!" Equating the bloody, mass-destructive horrors of war with a slight adjustment to the tax code—an adjustment that could only be implemented by the rich and powerful themselves—is absurdly irrational, and yet over two dozen pundits and politicians mouthed the phrase in the months (October 2010-January 2011) surrounding the congressional debate over upper class tax breaks... and no surprise, the tax breaks were extended. Screaming "class warfare" they indignantly whine, "How dare you take away a portion of my opulence!" Such deceptive hysteria should give us all pause.

~~~

Chapter 11: Getting There First—a Game of Monopoly
eBay, Facebook, Microsoft and the New Frontier

We must not tolerate oppressive government or industrial oligarchy in the form of monopolies and cartels.
                    -Vice-President (1941-1945) Henry A. Wallace

Ricky Bobby's America

In case you missed the movie *Talladega Nights*: Will Ferrell's satirical character, Ricky Bobby, is a NASCAR driver who lives by a creed of win-at-all-cost: "I'm just a big hairy American winning machine," and "Winners get to do what they want." We reward winners. We Americans are so steeped in sports competition, in "winning," that we fail to see **what a terrible metaphor that is for larger society, for economics and commerce**. Being there first in commerce does not even mean that person was the fastest runner, the superior athlete, or superior *anything*... nowadays being there first is mostly a function of luck, serendipity. Remember the short story in High School English Lit, "The Lottery"? It depicted the callous stupidity of singling out one person to be a loser. How much worse it is to do the opposite: to single out one person from a million to be a big winner, and leaving *everyone* else to be losers! We have a "lottery" economy, where one or two people win the big pot and the rest walk away with nothing. Ricky Bobby's race-car-driving father said, "If you ain't first, you're last." His statement is a parody of an American illness.

"Getting there first is everything." That's a serious quote from another movie, *The Social Network*, a film about the origins of the internet phenom, Facebook. The movie is inaccurate with details, but tells great truths about how millions are made in the new millennium. Watch it closely. Listen. The secret is not that Facebook founder Mark Zuckerburg is a genius. He is. But that's not what made him the youngest billionaire in the world.

He happened to be at the right place at the right time. He struck gold—gold that was already in the ground waiting for someone to discover it. Nowadays, being **first** at applying and integrating emerging technologies is more important than being the **best** or the most **innovative** at any specific idea. Zuckerburg's concept was not particularly original. When I say he "got there first," that just means he was first to reach the level of a *de facto* monopoly.

The Inevitability of Facebook

As Mark Zuckerberg began his enterprise, friend-linking internet sites already existed: MySpace, Friendster, and others—already utilizing most of the features that Zuckerburg pulled together into his version of social networking. Many key parts to Facebook were either already being done, or obvious, or suggested by other people (and in fact, he was sued by those who felt plundered of their ideas). Even the term "Face Book" was plagiarized. Zuckerburg had the smarts to write the computer code, and deserves to be well-paid. But he is a *billionaire* not because of a billion-dollars-worth of talent, ideas, or hard work. He did not cure cancer, he does not manufacture products, nor even risk his own money. He is insanely rich because he happened to be the one working the pick-axe when gold was struck. He didn't put the gold there; the internet put the gold there, and neither he nor Al Gore invented the net. Mark Zuckerburg stumbled onto riches. His biography, the book upon which *The Social Network* movie is based, acknowledges this truth in its very title: *The Accidental Billionaire*.

To put it another way: it was inevitable that one interactive site that allows a person to post autobiographical pictures, facts and comments would become **the "go-to" site**. When we were kids, a physical analogue to this social spot was called "the hangout," the place where all the teens knew they could drive to meet and chat with other friends. It is as if Zuckerburg hung a chalk board and a cork board up at the Dairy-Burger, for the kids to post their pictures, write each other notes, and leave phone numbers for new friend possibilities. Nice. Handy. But for that, we paid him billions? He didn't even own the Dairy-Burger where he put up the boards.

The way in which Facebook helps a person find and connect with friends is clever, but something hundreds of other folks could have invented—and did! Three Harvard seniors sued Zuckerberg for stealing their idea for a social network website called HarvardConnection (the suit was settled out of court). Another Harvard student, Aaron Greenspan, developed a web site called *houseSYSTEM* using a "Universal Face Book" that pre-dated "thefacebook.com" site. Author Scott Westerfeld had independently conceived, in a sci-fi book, a computer-based social media that included such things as "feeds and kickers" and "face rank."

Facebook R Us

And it's the *people* on Facebook, not the website itself, that attracts customers and gives value. It boggles the mind that Zuckerberg's product (which just exists in cyberspace) was valued at over $50 billion dollars in 2011! Goldman-Sachs, after benefitting from a government bailout, after ripping off investors, spent $450 million to invest in Zuckerberg's electrons-and-air real estate in early 2011.[188] Few products owe so much to so many people involved in the product as does Facebook; without you and me, Facebook would be worthless. Facebook's value is in *people* more than in technology. The content of Facebook (mostly chats and photos) is created by you and me, not by Zuckerberg. But all the money flows up.

Getting There First

During the California gold rush, it was often a case of who got there first, and who was lucky enough to have purchased land with gold on it. The American frontier held both great risk and great reward. One could argue that the prospector who had the courage and stamina to race across the plains to arrive at California deserved some reward. I agree. But would we think it fair to allow the first person there to own *all* the gold in California? That is, in effect, what we are doing with modern billionaires. To the victor go the spoils... but is winner-take-all a fair way for society to operate?

Today's frontier is the internet, where the rewards have been outlandish and the risks almost non-existent. Gold-rushers first put all their belongings in a covered wagon, to risk everything crossing the prairie. Many lost their lives and their fortunes. Today you might risk carpal tunnel syndrome; you can start an internet company for the price of a few latte's. And the rewards have little to do with the quality of the product, originality, hard work, or great investment, but mostly to do with who put together a working site, with a catchy name, *first*.

Casino Royale: Luck Trumps Skill

Lottery or casino, either metaphor fits our marketplace, where luck is more critical than the virtues that capitalism claims to enshrine. Luck trumps hard work, honesty, originality or excellence. **Being lucky is better than being the best**. Getting their first means "first to exploit." Microsoft's Bill Gates, like Mark of Facebook, did little that had not already been done by others... he just landed on Monopoly's *Boardwalk* before others. He was not the first to develop operating software, just the first to corner the market on the PC OS with a serendipitous affiliation with IBM.

Bill Gates and Zuckerberg both worked very, very hard. But so do several billion people every day on this planet, most paid less than $10 a day. And while Gates is a smart programmer who deserved success, even Bill himself admits that *chance* had a lot to do with his current status as billionaire. He got there first not because he had the "fastest covered wagon to California," but mostly because of sheer luck. His early access to a computer, before 99% of the population had even seen one, came from a combination of having wealthy parents who placed him in an upscale private school and the fact that someone at that school had the vision to install a teletype terminal that connected to one of the few mainframes in Washington state in 1968. Of this serendipity, Gates confessed, "I was very lucky."[189]

Author Malcom Gladwell, in *Outliers*, makes a strong case that luck had more to do with the fortunes made in the computer field than anything else... beginning with the luck of which *year* you were born in! He points out that about 80% of software profits went to pioneers-now-tycoons who were born in 1953, 1954 or 1955, including: Steve Jobs (Mac), Paul Allen (MS), Bill Joy (Sun), Steve Ballmer (MS), Scott McNealy (Sun), and Bill Gates. Yes, every one of those tech giants was born in that tiny window, 28 months apart! *Outliers* gives scientific/sociological reasons for that anomaly.

"Nothing New Under the Sun"

When Cicero famously said, *Sub sole nihil novi est*. ("There's nothing new under the sun"), he was not thinking of Sun Microsystems... or of Facebook. And Cicero was wrong. New inventions come along everyday. It's just that those who profit the most are not the innovators as much as the exploiters. As just mentioned, Facebook-like internet sites *already* existed that gave people a way to connect with friends.

You may ask, *Aren't you contradicting the point about "getting there first." Doesn't this prove that the better product emerged as the market winner?* No, this isn't analogous to the invention of the automobile, where a variety of people helped invent it, and companies like Ford and Chevy emerged as early market leaders because they improved the product and the price. Gates and Zuckerberg's products were at times aesthetically ugly (compare their look to *Myst*, for example), with clunky interfaces—hard to decipher for a neophyte. Since the very nature of the internet creates a winner-take-all environment where the first to get to a **critical mass of public awareness**—Facebook left competitors in the dust. With fortunate funding from the Napster founder, Facebook was able to promote and became "the *it* place" to hang out, thus developing a monopolistic snowball that made the competition irrelevant.

Old Ideas on the New Frontier: eBay

The idea of an *auction* is so old it even predates Cicero! If the founders of online auction site *eBay* had never existed, it is inevitable that others would have developed a similar monopoly: uBid.com, auctionsRus.com, auction.com, or whatever. The idea was not unique, nor even uniquely implemented, by the founders of eBay, they just happened to be at the right time and right place, *and* they benefit greatly from government help (the artificial removal of sales tax from their industry, and the already-existing government-subsidized freight/package transportation system).

By Thomas Sowell's "market formula," eBay's CEO Meg

Whitman is "worth" millions. But does anyone doubt that other mediocre execs would have enjoyed the same, or higher, profits, given her catbird's seat on top of a monopoly? eBay also owns PayPal, another monopolistic and unoriginal idea—together, it's like owning every property on the Monopoly board!

When it comes to auction sites, eBay is the only game in town. So the company inevitably grew under Meg's leadership. With such an obvious winning-concept and functional monopoly, a Cocker Spaniel could have been CEO with similar results. Or a monkey.

But Whitman's early success was not matched later on. Considering all eBay had going for it, the big picture is not one of excellence in leadership. From 2005 until her departure, ebay had problems. During Whitman's last full years as CEO, eBay's stock price fell by half, losing $30 billion in market value, in large part due to a string of troubled acquisitions she initiated. But from the stock's high until the day Whitman retired in 2008, eBay shares lost 54 percent. Over that same span, the Nasdaq technology index finished *up* 4.6 percent—even overcoming the losses of eBay, since eBay was a part of that index.[190]

Whitman Candy or Bitter Pill

I did not need to see falling stock prices to know that Whitman was not worth her insanely-large salary. Anyone who, like myself, had a problem with a purchase or sale on eBay and tried to deal with their nearly-non-existent customer service in the period of 2000-2008 would seriously question the competency (and worth) of CEO Meg Whitman's leadership. Imagine a billion-dollar firm that would not even publish a customer service number. Unlisted! Thousands of eBay sellers and buyers were not just irritated, they were *enraged* whenever something went wrong with eBay's tools or with a bad transaction, and could call no one for help. Yet, what choice did we have? eBay was where the buyers were. Just as with Facebook, the millions of participants in eBay are what bring it value, not the genius of a single CEO. One of eBay's own execs, Jay Lee, agreed: "What really matters are the 96 million registered buyers we have worldwide."[191]

Let's look closer at Meg's ability and see if she is, as economist Thomas Sowell would contend, *worth it*. One of her "genius" decisions was to buy Skype for $4 billion—eBay lost over a billion when Skype was later sold at a loss.[192] In 2005, she invested 100 million buying an auction site in China, which failed miserably.[193] If you or I lost our company a tenth of that, we'd have been fired.

Voter's in California also established her "worth": after spending millions campaigning for governor, she was soundly defeated. Meg had what one writer called "a spectacular loss." In a climate that favored her party, after outspending winner Jerry Brown six-to-one, she lost by 13 points. Whitman's fiascos illustrate how incompetent these multi-million-dollar CEO wunderkind-idiots can be, proving by their failures that Sowell is also overpaid and under-correct!

My purpose here is not to vent my frustrations with eBay (I even enjoy shopping there at times), but rather this: if a company or a CEO makes crazy profits, their product ought to be crazy-good. Instead, we often see monopolies resting on their catbird seats rather than striving for excellence. In this sense, I am a strong capitalist: a true free market would drive companies like eBay and Microsoft and Apple to be more responsive to customers. Instead, they seem to be oblivious to consumer complaints, at points settling for mediocrity.

The Game of Monopoly

Price competition is one of the best things about capitalism, but in our modern economy, competition is often stifled. Anyone who has played the board game, *Monopoly*, knows that if you have the only motel in town, you can charge a heckuva lot more. When someone corners the market on a particular product or service, competition ceases. Society has long deemed it necessary to either break the monopoly up into smaller (competing) businesses or limit the price gouging. Unfortunately, anti-monopoly and anti-trust laws are routinely circumvented... gamed. The game of Monopoly.

Though my family was poor, we lived in a fine home (the church supplied my father a large parsonage). So I had no realization we were poor until elementary school. At age 5, my first "feeling" of poverty was playing the game of Monopoly with my family. It was fun at first. But with bad luck, I had no "monopoly" sets of property and my money quickly dwindled. My brother owned the set of Boardwalk and Park Place, so with a sick feeling, I rolled the dice and landed on Boardwalk. I was too young to count quickly, and I just remember my mother, in a rare case of impatience, taking my small pile of tens and twenties and, without counting, handing them to my brother. I was informed that I could no longer play the game; I had lost. That was my first experience of poverty. Monopoly is not much fun when you are losing.

Board Walk, Park Place... and Microsoft

Microsoft is a winner in the game of Monopoly. Bill Gates landed on a very good spot! Imagine if you had an exclusive sales right—no one else on the planet could compete with you—to the key software on every personal computer on the planet. And imagine you could sell a product for over $100 that costs less than $5 to manufacture.

Most American homes have a computer, many of us have a desktop *and* a laptop, plus computers at work, with Microsoft Windows and Microsoft Word on each one! Even on my Mac, I must keep a copy of Microsoft Word, though I hate it and only use it occasionally to open files that a wicked person has sent me in MS .docx format.[194] That's how complete Mr. Gate's monopoly is: even though I run a completely different operating system and prefer a competitor's word-processor, I still can't escape the reach of the Evil Empire—as Microsoft is called by Mac users.

The sheer sales volume of MS Office is phenomenal; the profit margins are huge; the multiplication of the two made Bill Gates and other Microsoft execs richer than Midas.

Anyone who has used *both* Mac products and Microsoft/PC computers over the last three decades will tell you how much better Steve Jobs' Apple products were. But Gates had the good fortune to get there first, lucky to piggyback on an already-established IBM. So Steve Jobs biography is entitled, *Accidental Millionaire*, instead of *The Accidental Billionaire*. Billionaire Gates built a clunky product —Windows 95—but made twenty times the money Jobs did with the Mac OS. Capitalism is not supposed to work that way: the invisible hand of the market is supposed to give *the most to the best*.

The Slow, Arthritic Invisible Hand

And after thirty years, people are catching on that Mac/Apple has great products; Apple stock has soared. Thirty years—the length of the average career—is a long time for capitalism's mythical "invisible hand" to be corrective, to embrace the better mouse trap (or mouse). For much of that time, MS Windows controlled over 95% of the market. Even 90% of a market *is* a Monopoly.

So you see the point: capitalism brags that "market forces" will reward the better mouse trap. But it just isn't true today. Because MS "got there first," they left little room for innovative competitors. Particularly in the business community, being shipped with the business-standard IBM computers, MS-DOS/Windows enjoyed a scenario where people settled for an inelegant product because they needed compatible software. If there had been true product/price competition, Gates would not have his billions today.

Despite a Justice Department lawsuit, Microsoft managed to hang on to its software monopoly. Justice did show how that many of Gates' practices were unethical and monopolistic and coercive (particularly regarding its internet browser). The penalties were a slap on the wrist and nothing really changed. In 2004, the European Union found Microsoft guilty, but through appeal and soft enforcement, Microsoft continues unabated in exploiting its monopolistic position worldwide.[195] One example: recently, Microsoft Word changed its default file format, which resulted in many people buying an upgrade they didn't otherwise need or want. Microsoft products are like heroin: you realize that they aren't good for you, but you still need a fix!

Pawns in the Monopoly Game

Chess is not the only game with pawns. The saddest part of monopolistic firms such as Microsoft, eBay and Walmart is that the wealth is never shared with the entry-level workers—mostly Asian and Indian outsourced employees. As Bill Gates and Steve Jobs took their millions to the bank, over 20 workers were jumping off roofs at Foxconn, the Chinese manufacturing plant building MS X-Boxes and iPhones.[196] After bad press, the company kindly installed a "suicide net" around it's employee dorm.[197] According to an article in *Forbes*, the plant paid so poorly, its workers "can't afford even the entry-level consumer electronics products they spend their days making."[198] Foxconn implemented this "cure": they made workers sign a pledge that they would not "blame their employer if they try to kill themselves." This absurdity would be humorous if we forgot that real human lives were being lost because of the low pay, bad working conditions, and failure of executives to give a damn about the employees who are making them rich. Foxconn executive Terry Gou has a net worth of $5.7 billion,[199] yet pays his workers $176 a month.
If his workers don't have enough money to cover luxuries like food, that's okay, because Gou explains in his autobiography that "hungry people have especially clear minds."[200] And he dismisses the suicides because the numbers involved aren't statistically worse than other places. Still, Foxconn has been called a "labor camp," and even after the wages were raised slightly, over 300 workers staged a protest on the roof of the factory, threatening mass suicide."[201]

Monopolies and the Public Good

We understand that it is in the public good to allow some industries to have a limited monopoly. A classic example is electric power generation: it would be absurd to have duplication of the huge expense of power plants, substations and power lines, so we allow a single company to solely "own" the power business for a particular area—with a government regulatory commission keeping the price reasonable. We understand the need for anti-trust laws in some areas, yet we stand by and watch a lack of enforcement in others.

Even the biggest capitalist tycoons support government regulation when it is in their best interest. When railroad monopolies began charging exorbitant rates, manufacturing tycoons found their own profit margins eroded by the soaring transportation costs. Suddenly there was a political will to break up the rail monopolies.

A true monopoly—complete and singular control of an industry—is hard to achieve. So some companies have worked together to form *group monopolies*, sometimes called an *oligopoly*, cartel or syndicate, which in turn can manipulate prices at will. In either case, a monopoly or a cartel that gouges on price violates the most basic rule of civilized human behavior: do unto others as you would have them do unto you. An oil cartel would cry foul if suddenly all the grain-growing countries in the world formed a cartel to charge the oil countries $500 for a loaf of bread. (Why not form "bread cartels"? Some product categories have too many independent operators to form a cartel.) If you cannot accept the Golden Rule, you have no place in human society, where the rule of "Do unto others as you would have them do to you" is what separates us from savages.

The media should be assisting us by exposing unethical cartels and unfair systems. Government's top job after providing for national defense should be limiting monopolies, cartels and abuses of the marketplace. We need to broaden our understanding of what constitutes an unfair advantage in the marketplace.

Neil Armstrong Owns the Moon

We should never allow market dominance just by "getting there first." Balboa came to the New World as a stowaway on a Spanish ship. With help from the natives of Central America, he was the first European to put his feet into the Pacific Ocean, in 1513. He did not "discover" it—the natives already knew where it was and had guided him to it. Nevertheless, he claimed not only to have discovered it, but to own it! Balboa waded in up to his hips, sword in hand, to take possession of the entire Pacific Ocean in the name of the King of Spain—he laid claim to all that was in it and all the lands that touched it. No one honored the absurd claim of one man ruling half of the land and water of the planet.

Neil Armstrong did not lay claim to the entire moon. Even though he was the first human to set foot on it, he knew NASA and the taxpayers had put him there. He also understood that the moon should not belong to any one nation, much less one person.

Taking Hostages

Corporations try to lay claim to entire product lines and industries. The first pharmaceutical company that invents a new and helpful drug should certainly reap a reward: enough to pay for research and development and a bonus to incentivize innovation. But we need to limit the excessive profit margins in that industry. Pharmaceutical tycoons live in mansions built by sick folks because they are allowed to corner the market—to own the entire ocean—of a particular medicine. We need to eliminate this "lottery" economy, where consumers are price-gouged and the winner takes all.

The core of the ethical problem with monopolies is *kidnapping*: a monopoly "holds us hostage." Once the power company has us all hooked up to their power grid, without regulation, they hold us hostage to the need for electricity. We saw the consequences of this when ENRON controlled the price of power in California. Retirees on limited income suddenly found themselves having to choose between paying the power bill or buying groceries. Kidnappers always offer you two choices; neither is good. Watch the movie, *ENRON: The Smartest Guys in the Room*, and you'll agree.

Too Big To Fail?

The financial industry went one step further than kidnapping: they used **terrorism**, the catastrophic threat of another Great Depression. A modern absurdity is the re-naming of a monopoly as "Too Big to Fail." Suddenly the illegal monopoly is re-labeled as "an institution so large that it is essential to society to not only protect its monopoly, but to use tax dollars to do so." One of the justifications for bailing out major banks and insurance companies like AIG was they were "Too Big To Fail." Supposedly their size would cripple the cash flow of too many other banks, corporations and institutions, creating a domino effect of failure. Their complexity and interconnectedness means their collapse could create a ripple effect that could lead to a society-wide depression.

Applying this principle to Wall Street, once we call a few financial firms "too big to fail," we suddenly have admitted they are holding us hostage. They extorted millions from taxpayers through the Federal bailouts of 2008-2010... but the biggest rip-off in human history had already happened. When an industry becomes too big to fail, anti-trust, anti-monopoly laws need to kick in.

McKee writes in *Chasing Goldman Sachs*: "By the late 1990's, Wall Street had become a business dominated by global behemoths formed through a series of mergers. Even [smaller] businesses... became critical to the financial system because the linkages between those firms and the rest of the system grew exponentially."[202] That's another way of saying that the financial industry began to function as a monopoly or rigged conspiracy. John Costa, former head of UBS, admitted, "We lost the checks and balances...."[203]

Most upper management in these firms screamed like babies

when the Feds suggested limiting CEO compensation. Jake DeSantis of AIG (one of many who expected the government to pay for their failed risk-taking) had the audacity to say he was "being unfairly persecuted by elected officials."[204] John Thain and Merrill-Lynch—another firm guilty of using investor's funds and the Fed bailout to excessively enrich themselves—wasted $1.2 million dollars just to redecorate the executive suites, including $1,400 for a single trash can. After "earning" over $84 million one year, then expecting a $10 million bonus *after* the impending downfall of his company, Thain whined, "I really think I'm worth that."[205] *I failed; reward me.*

The unique position of Wall Street firms in overseeing *our* money begs for more reform than the insider-rigged "Reform Act" of 2010. It is as if we've hired bankers to count our money this way: "One dollar for you, two dollars for me, one dollar for you, two dollars...."

Sea Monsters and Giant Squids

The very nature of the financial industry and the closely-related insurance industry calls for closer scrutiny and stricter regulatory-enforcement. It is not only the problem of *too big to fail* and monopoly/cartel dangers, but also the very nature of "money-handling." These firms are not risking much of their own money, and not gambling a penny of personal fortune. Nearly all the villains of the 2008 crash are still making millions in the financial industry. Second, they are not manufacturing anything, not inventing anything, not really doing a lot to improve the world, yet entrusted with the hard-earned labors of billions of people. They handle *our* wealth with suction-cup tentacles; our money gets "stuck" in the hands of people who did little to nothing to generate the wealth in the first place. In all future oversight, crafting of reform legislation and policing of financial firms, we need an independent commission that consists not just of former Wall Street tycoons, but that also includes a few grandmothers, a union leader, a preacher, a teacher, a Peace Corps volunteer—people whose lives are not addicted to money, who are not blinded by the sheer power of millions to corrupt.

We have allowed the squid to grow bigger than its cage and now the monster rages, its manifold tentacles sucking the life out of our democracy. The de-regulation and banking-law changes (masquerading as "reforms") Congress enacted in the last 20 years fed the squid, built the house of cards, lined up the dominoes, and created the entangled web of interconnectedness. Just as an English major should hate the mixed metaphors, likewise an economist should be concerned about a mixed-up, entangled system that is so complex no one can predict the ways it warps our economic health. There were reasons for the fences set-up between banks and investment firms and insurance companies. Congress once saw the need for fences—to contain the sea monster. The use of computers and quantum mathematics did not make the waters safe; derivative math did nothing lessen the threat of squid attack. The monster grows and rages, its tentacles reach everywhere: Wall Street, banks, insurance, and Washington.

The Erosion of Values

People are not stupid. They observe this breakdown in ethics and fairness, and the result is that some people begin to feel justified in getting a piece of the pie themselves by declaring bankruptcy, failing to pay their mortgages or credit cards, cheating on their taxes, and worse. One of the keys to American prosperity has been the overwhelming honesty and lack of criminality by most of the populace. Many foreign governments are crippled by a system of corruption and bribes and by widespread crime. Russia, Africa and Latin America are rich with natural resources. But the average citizen there leads a miserable lifestyle because of a widespread lack of ethics. Ethics begins at the top.

The virtues and values of our founders (even if exaggerated at times) inspired Americans to be honest, thrifty, industrious and generous. Outsiders believe our affluence is tied to our natural resources. But if that were the lone source of middle class affluence, we would see oil and mineral-rich countries with a similarly-large middle class. Greed and lack of ethics in the upper classes robbed those countries of the enriching presence of an educated, thriving middle class. Sadly, our American middle class is eroding too.

Summary

We've seen how much luck is involved in making billionaires, including even their birth year. Malcolm Gladwell documented how the Top 100 of All Time billionaires were all born in times and places that had extraordinarily low taxes on the upper brackets. Those low taxes had little to do with their success, but allowed them to hoard vast sums without any counterbalance from the rest of the citizens of the planet. In other words, their good fortune regarding low taxation made the rest of us losers in the game of monopoly. Historically, most billionaires came into the club during eras of low taxation and lax regulation of anti-trust laws and of monopolies. Like today.

Too-big-to-fail firms were able to manipulate Congress, first creating loopholes and favorable de-regulation, then fleecing taxpayers with bailouts, all the while continuing to pay huge salaries and bonuses either directly or indirectly funded by TARP. We simply can't have a fair or productive society that works backwards, rewarding incompetence and criminality, while punishing thrift and hard work! The ongoing systemic problems expose the lies about "free market capitalism." The fat-rats who defend free markets, who claim the "invisible hand" will correct inequities in the system, don't believe their own lies. Indeed, they have asked for protection from that very invisible hand. In a truly free market, the failures by executives would have them bankrupt and jobless. But in post-modern America, failure has no penalty, no negative consequence. On Wall Street, failure is re-defined as winning, and the taxpayer atones for the sins of the rich. Too-big-to-fail and monopolistic practices guarantee that this backward winner-take-all system will continue.

~~~

Chapter 12: The New Pharaohs and Their Pyramids
The geometry of wealth; Amway is not the American Way

If we define an American fascist as one who... puts money and power ahead of human beings, then there are undoubtedly several million fascists in the United States.
                    ~Vice-President (1941-1945) Henry A. Wallace

Why Pyramids are the Problem

The Amway salesman came into our home at a time when we could not afford to buy diapers for our child without using a credit card. We were two working parents, both college educated yet needing additional income, forced to work a third job. So we tried selling home products—soap, vitamins, shoe spray and more—from the network marketing system whose name is short for "The American Way." The Amway salesman set up a pyramid-legged easel with a white board and began to draw circles. Comforting, inclusive, warm, communal circles. Eventually, however, the circles stacked up to make an unframed triangle or implied pyramid that revealed the secret of "network marketing": **a lot of people at the bottom, sending money upward to a few people at the top**.

That simple "Amway" pyramid is the same shape as Ponzi schemes, drug cartels, and most corporations. The Amway system is a perfect model of how wealth flows up a pyramid to the capstone... millions of entry level "distributors" first make no profit (they pay a fee for the privilege of being on the bottom rung), and every product they sell pushes profit upward.

The reason Amway pitchmen began to draw circles instead of triangles is that people became wary of "pyramid schemes," even if we don't fully understand geometry. That night, the Amway salesman literally said, "This is *not* a pyramid scheme." Which was a lie. There are two kinds of pyramid schemes: one legal, one illegal, neither ethical. Courts have determined Amway's structure is legal, because it does sell actual products and is thus not an illegal Ponzi scheme in the strictest sense. Admittedly, Amway's pyramid is not much different than Walmart's, where millions at the bottom buy products so that profits flow up to a few Waltons at the top. But it is still a *form* of pyramid scheme, with huge profits moving upward to the lucky few—or to reverse the metaphor, like an upside-down funnel, pouring money from wide sources into the narrow mouth of a CEO.

A Pyramid is Not a Triangle

In the early days of Amway and other "network marketing plans," they did not shy away from drawing their profit-pyramids on a white board as a triangle, showing how you move "upline" by getting more distributors under you. Even this is deceptive. Such a flat sketch fails to show the **geometric nature** of most corporate structures: two-dimensional triangle vs. a 3-D pyramid. A pyramid looks like it is made of four faces—four triangles. But just looking at the outer faces doesn't count the internal blocks that build the pyramid. Compare the geometric increase in wealth flowing to the top of a *pyramid* vs. a *triangle* in just four levels, in which a $5 profit is sent up the pyramid from each "sales associate" or "direct distributor":

Triangle, one side: 14 people serving one capstone= **$70**
Pyramid, four sides, plus the internal components: 72 people serving one capstone =**$360**

We begin to see the effect of geometric expansion of a "pyramid cash flow." And when you add more levels to the pyramid, the spread grows geometrically (exponentially) larger.

Whether it's Amway, Walmart or another corporation, the cash flow is not a simple linear triangle with a mere $5 profit moving "upline." Walmart, for example, has over 8,000 stores, each store with scores of employees, each moving millions of products in a year. This helps my brain begin to grasp the geometric size of "pyramid profits." Wages are paid to the lowest level of employees at nominal or "flat" levels (usually an hourly wage), while the highest members of the pyramid are paid at geometric wages.

Now let's use the same pyramid metaphor to look at how much work is done by the various levels of an organization or corporation.

Pay is Geometric, Work is Linear

Make your brain hurt and contemplate this reality: while pay for executives is geometric—receiving the *multiplied* fruits of all the thousands of employees beneath them—the execs' workload and production is NOT geometric, but linear. Why? **Because all humans have the same (nominal or "linear") amount of hours in a day!** And all humans, whether they are brilliant or slow, have a limit to how many meaningful work relationships they can sustain at one time. Research shows that **no individual is capable of more than 150 meaningful, social (or work) relationships at a time**.[206]

The Rule of 150

Forget your 900 "Friends" on Facebook—half of them you barely know, and on any given day you chat with just a dozen or so. As a pastor, I know that churches plateau as they hit 150 members, unless/until another staff person is added; churches with 2,000 members have a large staff and associate pastors because it is physically impossible to be a true, loving pastor to more than 150 people in a week. A car salesman would be happy to have 150 serious car shoppers speak to him in a month.

The point? An executive may have a million employees under him in the company flowchart, but his meaningful face time will be limited to a few levels on the pyramid immediately below him—the vice-presidents and top managers and his assistant. So when we speak of the "vast responsibility" or "enormous workload" of the CEO on top, we have no empirical data showing he works any harder than a middle manager.

So applying our pyramid metaphor: the number and shape of the "blocks" that you interact with in the pyramid remains the same **wherever you are in the pyramid.** And because of the limit of meaningful relations possible in a given day, a mid-level manager relates, in real terms, to about the same number of people/workers as the CEO or CFO does. The person at the base of the company pyramid is not actually at the bottom, but sits atop their own pyramid of relationships to *customers* (whether a retail salesperson in Walmart, or bottom-level distributor in Amway who is recruiting his friends and neighbors to be clients). Even employees who are manufacturing the product in a factory are relating to a finite-but-large number of consumers—via the products.

Therefore, mathematically-speaking and work-flow-wise, a minimum wage employee is usually connected to the same number of co-workers (or customers) as the one at the top. Probably more. In fact, forget 150: a corporate President has a secretary-gatekeeper who guards his time and access, so most CEOs tend to only relate in a meaningful way to twenty "under him" and another dozen alongside him on the Board of Directors. According to the Corporate Library's study, the *average* board size is less than 10 members.[207]

In sum, this geometry lesson raises questions:
•By what justification should money flow to the top?
•Why can't profits be shared in circular or lateral ways, instead of defying gravity and benefitting only the ones at top?
•Why do corporations and institutions even need to be shaped as a pyramid? Don't pyramids tend to insulate execs from the frontline?
•Why not have circular and communal models?

Peter's Problem with Pyramids

Theoretically, a person would rise "upline" in the pyramid due to longevity, loyalty, hard work, talent and effectiveness. Or as another metaphor puts it, to climb the corporate ladder by work and achievement. If only that were true. Too often placement on the pyramid is random. Some corporations leapfrog the young and beautiful over the long-dedicated gray heads.

In 1969, a maxim was coined for another problem with pyramids: "The Peter Principle." Dr. Laurence J. Peter and Raymond Hull, in their book of the same title, posited the *Peter Principle* as the key flaw of pyramidal hierarchies: "In a hierarchy, every employee tends to rise to his level of incompetence." They observed that as long as employees performed competently at their position, they tend to be promoted until they reach a position at which they *cannot* work competently. Yet the structure of the pyramid implies "superiority" simply because a person has risen above others in the hierarchy. So even though they may be incompetent, they remain, being unable to earn further promotions but also unlikely to be demoted. This confirms my own observation that executives tend to be viewed as super-human when, in fact, they are often more flawed than their "underlings." And while the top execs are treated to god-like-Pharaoh status and pay, according to Dr. Peter it is the still-competently-positioned underlings who accomplish most of the actual work. They even compensate for the CEO's incompetence by "managing upward," finding ways to help and even subtly manage superiors.

Solving the problems inherent in pyramids and bureaucracies is beyond the scope of this book. Humans are imperfect and no amount of re-organization can remedy that. We can, however, assert three general principles that would improve the fairness and efficiency of businesses, institutions and governments. In the alliterative spirit of Peter's Principle, let's call them *Moore's Maxims* (not to be confused with Moore's Law of computers... no kin to this author):

Moore's Maxims:
1. "Excessive upper-level executive pay does not increase a company's profits. It only leaves less money with which to pay other employees."
2. "The less a corporate or institutional structure is shaped like a pyramid, the better. Pyramids are for mummies and dummies."
3. "The best institutional structure is a circle with connecting spokes. The more lateral-accountability in a system, the more errors will be caught, the more justice will be administered, the better cross-pollination of ideas, and thus the better the morale."

A Classic American Pyramid/Pharaoh: Amway's Dexter Yager

Look more closely at a model of pyramid wealth-grabbing: *Amway* (and its *Quixtar* internet branch). Amway is aptly named because the American Way now means, sadly, enriching the people at the top. Amway started as a home distribution network for some good household products, but over time, the prices of their products inflated (even while production efficiencies were bringing down the cost of soaps, cosmetics, lotions, etc.), enabling huge bonuses to the people at the top. People like Dexter Yager, called "the crown prince of Amway," realized the best way to make money was not so much in selling the *product* as in selling the *pyramid*. Yager did not start Amway nor design its products; he freeloaded on its structure like a giant leech. Steve Butterfield, in his book *Amway: The Cult of Free Enterprise*, explained how Yager, a Pharaoh on top of the Amway pyramid, profited twice from distributors: first via the actual Amway products, second by selling underlings his own tapes and books..

"He sells the business as the American Dream… but for the average distributor, it's more like a nightmare," says Butterfield, a one-time distributor for Yager. Butterfield and other critics have pointed out what they call "questionable sales tactics."

I've seen these tactics first hand. They rarely exaggerate about the products. The products work. The stretch comes in convincing people with no sales experience that they can become rich via sales. My distributor drove a Cadillac and lived in a mansion, so as to create an illusion of great Amway success; I learned that these were purchased with loans and money from his separate career.

Selling the Prosperity Religion

Yager, a friend to Jim and Tammy Bakker of *PTL Club* fame, also preached a "prosperity theology," claiming that God *wants* you to be filthy rich and materialistic. Instead of printing Scripture, they published and widely-circulated a picture book of rich Amway distributors, showing them smiling inside their mansions, beside their pools, riding in their boats, polishing their fancy cars. That idolatry-based gospel worked for Dexter, helping him suck money up from the masses at the pyramid's base. At one point, he wore a 10-carat diamond ring on each hand, a diamond-studded Rolex on one wrist, the other sporting a matching bracelet with "DEX" spelled in diamonds. His fleet of cars, once numbering fifty, included three Rolls-Royces and four Mercedes. Plus four boats, a jet, and a huge homes on Lake Wylie and in Florida. His victims rarely bother to think: "Gee, his millions came out of the pockets of people just like me." Very little of Amway's or Yager's revenues come from retail sales to people outside the sales pyramid.

Perhaps early in Yager's career, he saw how it became increasingly difficult to sell Amway products at their inflated retail, thanks to the low prices in Walmart and dollar stores, so instead, Yager began to sell something less tangible: *the allure of wealth*. He sold a dream. He had found that getting hundreds of people under him as "distributors" (who became wholesale customers themselves) was easier than selling people retail products at retail prices. Yes, the distributors could buy the products at wholesale, but they were still spending hundreds of dollars monthly, having been persuaded that the more Amway products in their home, the better salespeople they would become, and the closer their dream. Yager shifted the emphasis away from the high-quality of the products, toward the dream of wealth. Most sales pitches to recruit new distributors spent two minutes talking about the products and two hours talking about the joy of sexy dollars and the economic potential in building pyramids, er, networks.

A Rose by Any Name Still has Thorns

Fighting the "slander" of being called a pyramid scheme, they searched for rosier names, and called it MLM: multi-level marketing. As more people learned of the pyramid-like nature of MLM, they then began to call it "networking," using circles, not triangles, on their charts. But Amway wealth did not come from circular flow of money. Success was only possible by rising higher in the pyramid. How do you rise higher? By putting lots of folks *underneath* you. They actually used the phrase, "underneath you" as they drew the circles, knowing you climb upward by stepping on shoulders. Yager hoped you'd forget that **it is mathematically impossible for the majority to win at pyramids.**

Indeed, less than 1% of Amway's salespeople make above poverty wages from the scheme.[208] The masses at the base level of Amway *lose* money, as the fees, the costs of motivational tapes/books, and product-mark-up-dollars funnel upwards to those nearer the top of the pyramid. According to Amway's own data, 99% of all Amway sales representatives in 2001 earned on average of less than $14 per week—and that's before deducting overhead.[209]

More Pharaohs

The Amway corporation was founded by Richard DeVos and Jay Van Andel, whose worth at one time was estimated by *Forbes* at **$4.5 billion each!** You'd be rich, too, if you could convince a million people to work for you for below minimum wage *and* to buy all their household products from you in the process.[210] As bad as Walmart is, at least they don't make you pay for your own shipping.

Speaking of Walmart, these two pyramids do have another thing in common: the hypocrisy of trumpeting "The American Way," while selling products that now are mostly made overseas. And of course, the Asians doing the actual work of making the products are paid pennies, while people who were good at drawing circles and pressuring people with propaganda make millions.

A Personal Side-Story about Dex

As a young man desperate to find extra income for my family, I once went to an Amway seminar in Nashville and heard Dexter Yager speak. I quit the cult-like environment of Amway when I heard "Dex," in person, report how he had just shared a conversation with a "black lady" who seemed content in her job as the hotel elevator operator. He praised her because she "knew her place." A few rows in front of me, I saw a young black couple get up and exit. I exited with them in my heart, but in body regretfully stayed to hear the rest of Yager's presentation because I was captive as a guest of my upline distributor. Yager's two-hour-long speech was filled with his arrogant ramblings, boastings of his wealth, and insults for anyone who questioned his pyramid plan. I will say he honestly *believes* it is not a pyramid scheme, since it is not an outright Ponzi scheme. But Yager and most fat-cats fail to understand the ethical problem with systems that funnel money geometrically upward from a wide base to a tiny elite. The elites don't see an ethical problem in making tons of money by exploiting the efforts of thousands of people "beneath them"—the "small people," as BP Chairman Svanberg calls us, the low-paid schmucks who "know their place."

One More Example of an Elite Pharaoh: Reverend Pat

The elitism of Pyramid Pharaohs, the ethical failure of politicians, the false prosperity gospel of television evangelists—all came to a single nexus in the person of "the Reverend" Pat Robertson. Robertson—who ran for President in the eighties, sided with nefarious African politicians, claimed to have magical power over hurricanes, embraced the false prosperity gospel without shame—he loved the Amway "get rich" pyramid plan. Unfortunately for Pat, he found out you can't buy your way to the top, and he did not want to bother with the long climb up Amway's pyramid. So Pat invented his own private version of Amway, a vitamin business called *Kalo Vita*. According to Rob Boston in, *The Most Dangerous Man in America: Pat Robertson and the Rise of the Christian Coalition*, "Robertson lives on the top of a Virginia mountain, in a huge mansion with a private airstrip. He owns the Ice Capades, a small hotel, diamond mines, a vitamin company (Kalo Vita) involved in a multi-level marketing scheme..., the Family Channel... all estimated to be worth between $150-200 million."

How does a televangelist, who is supposedly involved in non-profit work, manage to create such a towering fortune for himself? **Pyramids, power politics and twisted ethics.** Robertson's numerous private business hierarchies pushed expenses onto the tax-exempt, religious interests of his Christian Broadcasting Network. Robertson was allegedly caught using CBN money and equipment to aid his diamond mining operation —a double good deal for Pat, seeing as he exploited miners in Zaire for ridiculously low wages, and managed to use CBN's infrastructure to cut costs even more. His counterfeit Amway didn't last. How much did he extract from the pyramid's base before it crumbled?

Pyramids and Politics

Why devote so much space to this topic? Two reasons. First, the unethical pattern of pyramid-money-funneling is not only found in MLM soap-sales but also in *most* corporate profit-reaping. We need to understand how it creates an exponentially-large mountain of cash that comes not from building a better mousetrap, but by the multiplied work and dollars of the masses at the pyramid's base.

Second, we need to beware of how the purveyors of the various pyramid and MLM schemes are **distorting the political process**. Companies and individuals involved in MLM give millions to conservative, pro-business politicians to continue a hands-off policy toward pyramids. According to the watchdog group, *Common Cause*, one of the single largest donations to any political party was $2.5 million from the Amway Corporation to the Republican Party in 1994. They've continued to donate more since. In 2004, Amway founders Richard DeVos and Jay Van Andel gave $2 million to the right-wing group "Progress for America."[211] MLM's are also allied with the U.S. Chamber of Commerce to protect their shady industry with yet more lobbying efforts. Pat Robertson was instrumental in founding and funding the so-called "Christian Coalition," which in my own state of Alabama once opposed tax relief for the poor in favor of rich landowners and insurance companies. This only scratches the surface of donations across the years by the unholy marriage of rightwing "Christians" and Amway/MLM fat-cats working for political protection from regulation. Only the tobacco industry has as much "survival instinct" in its political lobbying and its public marketing campaign.

Many of us feel that the claims and business practices of the multi-level marketing industry are already in violation of FTC policies and federal court rulings. But the existing laws need to be strengthened, as does enforcement. This topic goes beyond the space and scope of this book, but to learn more, simply google "Amway scam" or "MLM pyramid fraud" or "Pat Robertson exposed." Or look into the archives of *Mother Jones* magazine, or view the NBC Dateline (May 7, 2004) hidden camera look into Amway recruitment meetings that document their deceptive claims and false promises.

Summary

The only good lesson we can draw from this sad history is the obverse hope: if we **build a network of truth and hope, we can turn the pyramid upside-down**. If we can persuade a few people in leadership (in media, politics, and religion) to grow a heart and gain an understanding of how greed is the number-one human evil, and they in turn "network" and persuade a few, and so on in a "pyramid of truth-telling," we can make widespread societal improvements. We can create co-ops and profit-sharing circular corporations. We can change government back to one "of the people, by the people, for the people."

The wealthy are far more dependent upon the poor than the other way around. The base of the pyramid is feeding the top, which means they *need* us. All excess money moves upward, but most work is done at the base... and greater political power could be exercised at the base. Pyramids have always been the way of this world, but now the base of the pyramid consists of BILLIONS of people, and the top still consists of a handful of elite. We outnumber the Pharaohs.

The unbridled greed, arrogance and extravagance of the Pharaohs is now one of the great evils of our world, at the root of much starvation, disease and war. Yet, sadly, many conservative, well-intended Christians have blindly accepted Yager and Robertson's twisted view of religion, and bought into their flawed "prosperity gospel" and twisted notions of "The American Way."

I can think of nothing more "American and apple pie" than **Jimmy Stewart** and the movie "It's a Wonderful Life." The speech against the villainous, monopolistic banker, Mr. Potter, in which George Bailey (played by Stewart) passionately defends the average workingman, should be shown at the business schools of every college in America. George Bailey understood that the "little people" at the bottom are the source of a community's wealth. Here's an excerpt: "Just remember this, Mr. Potter, that this 'rabble' you're talking about, they do most of the working and paying and living and dying in this community! People were human beings to my father, but to you, a warped, frustrated old man, they're cattle. Well, in my book he died a much richer man than you'll ever be." *Et tu*, Mr. Yager.

~~~

Chapter 13: Oil and Energy—A Case Study on Greed

I hear comments sometimes that large oil companies are greedy companies or don't care, but that is not the case with BP. We care about the small people.
    ~BP Chairman Carl-Henric Svanberg, after the Gulf Oil Spill

Children of Peasants, Slaves of Nobles

People—little people and big people—are literally dying because of the actions of the mega-rich, on BP oil rigs and particularly in the sweat shops and famine-plagued locations of the Third World. The International Labour Organization estimates that up to 72 million African children work in harsh agricultural conditions.[212] Millions more work in factories. Worldwide, it is estimated that 218 million child laborers endure working long hours under harsh, dangerous conditions.[213] Most of these children will never have the opportunity to attend school, but they will have the opportunity to work like slaves to enrich Western profiteers... er, noblemen. Every year, 22,000 children die in work-related accidents.[214]

Case Study: Oil

We could tug on your heart strings with story after story of starving and dying children in Africa... but for U.S. readers, the great pain of the Third World remains abstract. Geographically distance becomes emotional distance. So we turn closer to home for a case study on the consequences of greed, to a topic near and dear to some of the people nearest me: **the Gulf Coast oil spill.**

In the summer of 2010, a few miles from my home, a sea captain killed himself. For his lifetime and his father's before him, Captain Allen Kruse ran a family fishing and shrimping business in the Gulf of Mexico. Running a boat for shrimping or fishing is a hard, hot, risky business. I've known several shrimpers and fishermen across the years. Shrimpers follow a variety of Federal regulations to protect the marine environment, and they provide Americans with affordable seafood from an ecologically-sustainable natural system. Commercial fishermen risk their lives on the unpredictable waters, but they make a decent living. All of that came to an abrupt end in my hometown when the Deepwater Horizon, a drilling rig operated by BP and Halliburton, exploded into our Gulf of Mexico and began the greatest oil spill in human history. Decisions were made before and after the spill that were motivated by greed and expediency rather than concern for human life or the environment. Captain Allen Kruse, along with 11 drill workers, paid the ultimate price, and millions of us along the coast were impacted in multiple ways. My own daughter lost her job thanks to BP. So yes, BP may accuse me of bias and sue, but the facts will stand.

BP: Portrait of Corporate Ineptitude, Painted in Black

CEOs are paid millions for their excellent work, right? Work that is complicated, requires brilliance and sophistication, right? A big part of their job is to maintain the corporate image, to present the company as competent and caring. One acting lesson should be enough: just stand in front of the camera, speak articulately with a sincere tone while wearing a smile. And don't say anything stupid. A fifth grader could do it!

But not **Tony Hayward**. The public relations handiwork of BP CEO Tony Hayward was so inept that he took a horrible PR disaster—a giant black oily mess ruining the most beautiful waters and beaches—and found a way to put even *worse* smudge marks on BP's image. This is a model of greed, and also proves my earlier point that CEOs are vastly overpaid and overrated.

Just weeks into the crisis, with eleven families grieving the loss of their fathers, Hayward had the audacity to complain, "I want my life back." This betrayed his greedy self-centeredness *and* his stupidity, in one swift statement! *Self-centered* in that he whined of slight personal discomfort from a crisis *he* was responsible for; *stupid* in that he said it in front of a microphone. He complained of losing some of his precious recreational time, when eleven men literally had lost their lives. In the worst of the crisis, he got his life back: he was seen out yachting in a separate (clean) ocean with his gas-guzzling, million-dollar yacht, while Tracy Kruse was burying her husband, and we on the coast were trying to keep our fragile economy afloat.

I Want Allen's Life Back

Five minutes from the spot I'm typing these words, Allen Kruse kissed his wife Tracy goodbye for the last time on June 23rd, 2010. Just after sunrise, he headed off again to captain his charter boat—but this time as a BP sub-contractor to spot oil, deploy boom and eventually skim oil. His fishing business had died after the April 20th, 2010 oil spill. Allen was 55, the father of pre-teen boys, Cory and Ryan, and daughter Kelli.

After another frustrating BP training meeting, Allen climbed into the wheelhouse, full of anger and depression over the sea life killed by the millions of oil dumped by BP into "his" gulf. Frustrated over the ineptitude of BP's follow-up, he put a gun to his head.

His young wife, Tracy, explained, "Nothing was easy working with BP. Everything was hard, and it consumed him. He wasn't crazy. He'd been a charter boat captain for 25 years, and all of the sudden he had people barking orders at him who didn't know how to tie up a boat to a pier." According to a local paper, "The spill left Allen Kruse emotionally devastated. It robbed him of his passion for taking customers out to the Gulf to fish for red snapper and grouper." Traci quoted her late husband as having said, "Our whole lives [are] surround[ed by] this, this oil... everything is oil."

From the beginning, Allen was unhappy with the glacially slow process of BP's so-called "clean-up." "He couldn't believe they were sitting there at Zeke's Marina doing nothing," Tracy said. "He wanted to get out there and work and help clean up the oil." BP has tried to bury everything in paperwork: one BP invoice alone required 52 pages to fill out, according to Tracy.[215]

The Kruse's experience is not an isolated aberration. I had friends working in the BP clean-up, as well as friends and family frustrated with BP's arbitrary claims process. All of us who dealt with BP were struck with how slowly they did *everything*. If I had to used one word to describe BP—besides greedy—it would be: incompetent.

BP is one of **the most profitable companies in the world**, proving again a major theme of this book: the greatest wealth does not go the smartest company nor to the hardest-working entrepreneur, but to the lucky and to the conniving. The oil/gas industry exploits a God-given free resource, avoids taxation, gleans subsidies, all while charging exorbitant prices for energy. With impunity. Since 1998, the industry has put more than a billion bucks into politics.[216] No surprise that these most profitable companies receive hundreds of millions in IRS refunds and Federal subsidies.

The Proof in the Pudding: BP Oil

Back to the oil spill by our "poster child for failed capitalism": I saw with my own eyes a substance resembling chocolate pudding washed up on the pristine white beaches. I grew up as a child near the beaches of South Alabama, and now live there again. Oil "pudding" and tar balls still can be found on our beaches and waters of the Gulf of Mexico, but the worst of it is probably at the bottom of the sea beyond our eyes. A year later, dead fish are washing up on the beach where I live. Dead fish and chocolate-oil-pudding is a macabre feast, served up as a visual reminder of the old saying, "the proof is in the pudding." BP is a visible case study in greed and incompetence.

Other books, articles and news reports have chronicled it. Early in the Deepwater Horizon explosion/oil disaster, in May of 2010, a *Wall Street Journal* investigation showed that BP's rush to complete the behind-schedule project led to several poor decisions to cut corners. The conservative, pro-business *Journal* confessed they found it hard to get at the full truth, because BP supervisors were "already hiding behind lawyers." But the *Journal* showed how BP short-cuts—some violating MMS rules and standard practice—and pressure from BP execs to speed-up the process were clearly responsible for the disaster. The *Journal* reported that "a top BP official" wanted to move prematurely to replace the protective drilling mud with lighter seawater. That, coupled with a failure of the blowout preventer, were only part of a variety of mistakes that led to the explosion and oil gusher. "The haste [saved] BP about a million dollars a day, but at the [later cost] of a dozen human lives and the largest ecological disaster in history." And even before they dug an inch into the gulf sands, the BP plan was a lie: BP's environmental response plan included protecting walruses. The only walrus within a thousand miles of the Gulf is in the New Orleans Zoo! In an effort to pinch pennies, BP had simply used boilerplate from an arctic plan rather than actually making an intelligent contingency plan for possible disasters.

Before and After and In-Between: Greed Throughout
BP's greed continued in the year *after* the disaster. They were slow and arbitrary in the way they paid claims, according to Alabama's (conservative) political leaders. Governor Bob Riley accused BP, and its affiliate claims director Ken Feinberg, of "extortion" (Riley's word, not mine). The Republican Governor pointed out that the clumsy process pushed businesses unfairly toward a final settlement that included signing away the right to sue BP. The Governor said, "If you have the capacity to turn them down with no explanation and make them sign away their right to sue, that's extortion." Alabama Attorney General Troy King wrote in a separate statement: "BP and their multimillion dollar shill, Ken Feinberg, have intended from day one to deceive and exploit Alabamians who have been victimized in order to protect BP and their partners from accountability." Again: these damning epithets were not coming from leftwing anti-corporation radicals, but from conservative, Southern Republicans and pro-business newspapers.[217] A year and a half after the spill, after an extensive Federal investigation, the *Pensacola New Journal* headline read: "IT'S BP'S FAULT." The article stated, "BP violated federal regulations, ignored crucial warnings, was inattentive to safety and made bad decisions..." resulting in the death of "eleven rig workers" and the spill of "some 200 million gallons of crude...."[218]

Who Pays?
In addition to those who paid with their very lives (the oil workers, the boat captain, the baby dolphins that washed up on our beaches the following year), **taxpayers** inevitably end up picking up part of the tab for corporate irresponsibility.
To be fair to BP, they are not the only energy company to suck on

the government nipple. The petroleum/energy industry not only gets a free gift from God via the naturally-existing oil reservoirs *underground*, but *underhand* they get a second giant gift: from government. *The New York Times* reported in 2010 that the U.S. government subsidizes the oil industry **billions** of dollars annually. The article, published while the Deepwater Horizon was still gushing oil into the Gulf, reported that "an examination of the U.S. tax code indicates that oil production is among the most heavily subsidized businesses, with tax breaks available at virtually every stage of the exploration and extraction process."[219] According to the CBO, the oil industry's "welfare benefits" are $5 billion annually—year after year. With tax breaks for oil-field leases and drilling equipment, and the Foreign Tax Credit, some petroleum companies are taxed at an effective rate of only 9% while other businesses face rates of over 25%. The Foreign Tax Credit supposedly gives companies a credit for any taxes they pay to other countries. It costs Federal coffers about $850 million a year. Here's how: foreign governments collect money from oil companies through royalties—payment for the oil taken from the foreign country. Foreign governments, informed of the U.S. tax code, agreed to rename the royalties as income taxes, allowing oil companies to deduct 100% of what not a tax, but merely a product cost. Creative arrangements like that are why oil companies escape fair taxation.[220]

In the same year as the oil spill, BP reaped U.S. tax credits (including ethanol incentives) worth about half a billion dollars. MSN.com further reported: "Before the Deepwater Horizon debacle, BP was writing off 70% of the cost of leasing the rig from its owner, Transocean, for a daily savings of $225,000. In turn, Transocean avoids U.S. taxes by registering its offshore drilling rigs in the Marshall Islands, one of the world's five biggest shipping registries, accounting for about 1,500 vessels."[221]

It was widely reported that Transocean Ltd., the sub-contractor who shares guilt with BP over the Gulf spill and the death of 11 drill workers, awarded its top executives "big bonuses for making 2010 the best year ever for safety..." —the same year of eleven fatalities and of thousands of marine animals and humans poisoned by the toxic oil![222] If that was their best safety year, what was their worst? A few of the executives later donated their bonuses to the grieving families, reminding me that not everyone at the executive level is a greedy, heartless son-of-a....

Salt on My Wounds

The summer I began writing this book, I could not enjoy a swim in my nearby gulf waters, thanks to BP's pollution. But that's okay: seeing my lack of saltwater, U.S. Representative Joe Barton was kind enough to throw salt on my wounds! The Republican from Texas had the unmitigated gall to **apologize** for U.S. government attempts to hold BP responsible for their oil spill damage. Barton said to BP President Tony Hayward, "I'm ashamed of what happened in the White House yesterday. I think it is a tragedy of the first proportion that a private corporation can be subjected to what I would characterize as a shakedown.… I apologize."[223]

President Obama (who had himself accepted campaign contributions from Big Oil) had politely discussed with BP what options were available for BP to compensate the millions of victims of their incompetence. If anything, many critics believe Obama became an "enabler" for BP's attempts to mitigate potential lawsuits. To apologize and call this mild attempt at accountability a "shakedown" is not quite in the category of apologizing to Hitler for Jews clogging up his concentration camps... but it's close.

I tremble to think that a corporation can receive billions from taxpayers in subsidies, then completely contaminate one of our most important tourist and seafood ecologies, and a Congressman wants to apologize to the corporation! That may be the single most egregious example of a politician selling us out to corporations in my lifetime.

And yet, why be surprised? According to www.opensecrets.org, individuals or PACs associated with the oil and gas industry have donated billions to politicians of all stripes. Oil was Congressman Barton's biggest patron, donating more than $1,448,380 to Barton's campaigns since 1990—making him Public Enemy Number One among all House members for donations from the petroleum industry. Big contributors to Barton include BP, as well as Anadarko Petroleum (a 25 percent stakeholder in the Deepwater Horizon oil field). They clearly got their money's worth in Joe Barton, who speaks boldly for the oil companies on a variety of bills that benefit them at the expense of the taxpayer.

Oh Lord God, I apologize to you, on behalf of the human race, that we elected "a tragedy of the first proportion" like Joe Barton!

Antonia Juhasz, an activist shareholder from the Gulf Coast, read a letter written by the father of one of the men killed on the rig. She read the letter despite an attempt by BP Chairman Carl-Henric Svanberg to cut her off.[224] It reads in part: "This was no act of God—BP, Halliburton and Transocean could have prevented this," states the a letter from the father of Gordon Jones, an engineer on the rig. "But it would have taken more time, more money, and you were too greedy to wait. You rolled the dice with my son's life, and you lost." Jones left behind a pregnant wife and a two-year-old son.[225]

Apologies to Chevron, Exxon, et. al.

My personal affection for the Gulf beaches keeps BP in my focus, so I apologize to Chevron, Exxon and the other oil companies for not giving them attention. They all are guilty of raiding public oil reserves, and of environmental carelessness. Exxon has its own history with a reckless oil spill in Alaska, and Chevron has damaged Angola and Ecuador, among other places.

Chevron most recently bought a PR campaign (with ads seen on most major TV networks in April and May of 2011) of a pretty lady sincerely spreading an outright lie: that of Chevron's tremendous profits (about $20 billion in 2010), "every penny and more went into bringing energy to the world." That statement could only be made if a company showed no profit—the "and more" implies they had to borrow to make ends meet. Nonsense. And no mention of the fact that Chevron paid its recently-retired chief executive, Dave O'Reilly, over $40 million.[226] To even *use* the word "penny" in the context of a trillion-dollar conglomerate is disingenuous.

I'm not the only one to catch this lie. Rep. Ed Markey (D-Mass.) filed a complaint about the misleading Chevron TV ad to the Federal Trade Commission. Markey's statement: "Even as Chevron reported $6.2 billion in profits over the first three months of 2011, potentially questionable television advertisements by the company claim that it spent 'every penny and more' of the $19.1 billion in 2010 profits on 'bringing energy to the world.'" Markey even wrote Chevron to ask it to explain their claim in contrast to the fact that they spent $6.5 billion buying back its own stock in 2010 and only $1.1 billion on "exploration for energy." In a letter to Chevron Chairman John Watson, Markey said that he was concerned that the TV ad "deceives consumers." Markey calls attention to another obvious proof of the lie: the fact that the very television ad campaign cost millions! How can a PR campaign "bring energy to the world"? A second point in this: a CEO, paid millions, was dumb enough to authorize a PR campaign that is so blatantly deceitful, now millions of viewers view Chevron as untrustworthy! With a low bar set by bumbling BP exec Tony Hayward, petroleum execs can authorize spending millions on a backfiring PR campaign and still keep their jobs.

A Gooey Mess on the Monopoly Board

Like spilling chocolate pudding on the Monopoly board, cleaning up the mess that is the petroleum business isn't going to be easy. There are too few oil companies, too closely entangled, in ways that create a *de facto* monopoly. The mess is so obvious, even Fox News' conservative pundit Bill O'Reilly has stated that oil and gas business is "not a free market." He has more than once implied that the oil companies are guilty of price-fixing and windfall profiteering. O'Reilly points out that gasoline is such a necessity in modern society that it deserves the same kind of government price controls that electric utilities face.

But this won't happen. Politicians love the "chocolate pudding." The undue influence the energy business has upon elected officials, here and internationally, is daunting. They don't spend "every penny" on bringing us energy; they spend millions on bribes, campaigns and lobbying to keep the *status quo*.

ENRON: When Con Jobs Go South

Alex Gibney, Producer of the documentary film, *ENRON: The Smartest Guys* in the Room, stated, "The story of Enron exposes *the major flaw in capitalism, which is, the crude belief that raw self-interest left untethered will always result in the best possible social good*. It's not so."

The majority of Americans are extremely moral people when it comes to money. Consistently, polls, hidden-camera "real-life" tests, and psychological experiments have shown that most people will not steal from others. Nevertheless, that still leaves a significant number—millions—of people who will steal if they are given the opportunity to do so with impunity. It is hard to prove that wealthy people are any more prone to theft and greed, but obviously the inarguable fact that *some* people are always willing to steal or take advantage of others should prompt us to see the absurdity of the claims that "free market forces" and "invisible hands" will somehow, magically, self-police.

Nowhere is this more shockingly demonstrated than in the rise and fall of Texas-based energy-trading company, ENRON. We won't waste trees here retelling every detail of the long and complex tale, but instead refer the interested reader to the book, *The Smartest Guys in the Room*, by Bethany McLean and Peter Elkind. These are not two leftist whackos, but thoughtful reporters from *Fortune* magazine, generally a cheerleader for capitalism. They expose the scandal of three executives—Ken Lay, Jeff Skilling and Andy Fastow—who allowed greed to drive them to create a bubble or pyramid-scheme based not on the real creation of energy, but on the manipulation of stock and the artificial inflation of energy prices.

What ENRON Wrought

Lay, Skilling and the other insiders made over a billion dollars in easy profits, but in the end were responsible for the complete loss of jobs, pensions, and savings/stocks by thousands of innocent employees, such as a power lineman who lost $345,000 of life-long accumulated pensions almost overnight. Here's a lineman who, for over twenty years, went into the freezing cold or sweltering heat to fix powerlines so that children would sleep comfortably, rewarded for his years of toil and dedication with a complete loss of his retirement funds. He did not gamble those funds away; when his utility company was purchased by ENRON, his pension fund went with the purchase. By contrast, the men in suits were enjoying air-conditioned caviar, clubs and strippers, first-class jet-setting, and worked hard at not much of anything. Did ENRON produce one electron or one btu of natural gas? Yes, initially, but in the end, its profits came from computer manipulations... mouse clicks. They produced nothing but chaos, causing massive power blackouts in California, stranding babies in elevators and defrauding grandmothers. According to California Governor Gray Davis, after de-regulation, the cost of electricity in his state went from $7 billion to $27 billion in a year—a 400% increase. The ENRON traders, who were largely responsible for manipulating the price upward by a variety of unethical practices, were tape-recorded bragging and laughing aloud of how, in their own words, they were "stealing from Grandma Millie." Perhaps some of those grannies, who sat in the dark and struggled to pay their power bills, felt a sense of vengeance when CEO Ken Lay died of a heart attack. But his wife, after crying alligator tears on television over how much money *she* had lost, is still eligible to receive fat annuity payments for a continued life of ease.

Learning from ENRON

Lessons from the ENRON scandal are many. We learn of how large banks and "reputable" firms, like Arthur Anderson accounting and Merrill-Lynch, were eager to jump on board a profit train regardless of how crooked the tracks or dark the destination. ENRON's stock went up 90% in one year. That alone should have told people something artificial and bubble-like was happening. But rather than ask questions, Merrill-Lynch caved to pressure from ENRON and fired analyst John Olsen because he would not give ENRON a "BUY" rating. Olsen was one of the few who early on saw the emperor (Ken Lay and cohorts) had no clothes.

Fortune magazine ranked ENRON as "Most Innovative" company five years in a row. Lesson: don't expect the private sector/free market to self-police. To the contrary, we see that the most "reputable" firms are willing to throw away ethics in favor of profits—even to the level of criminality. Banks that made investments in ENRON's LJM and related shadowy investment divisions and fronts included G.E. Capital, J.P. Morgan, CS First Boston, Citigroup and Merrill-Lynch. If these names sound familiar, it is because many of them were also heavily involved in derivative trading and the tax-payer funded bailout[227] California power companies also colluded in inflating the price of energy.

Collusion

Ironically, it was a *Fortune* reporter who began to take the inflated wind out of ENRON's sails. Bethany McLean wrote an article that simply asked whether ENRON's stock price was inflated. For this, she incurred the wrath of Lay and Skilling. Skilling had the self-righteous nerve to accuse Bethany of being "unethical," and condescendingly insulted her intelligence. Lay mocked her. Lesson: wealth tends to make people arrogant, which in turn leads to a whole series of evils (greed and pride are two of the seven deadly sins, but in Chaucer's poem about the vices, it is *Pride* that leads the parade).

We also learned that Ken Lay had an extraordinary amount of access to the White House, through both George Bushes and also through Vice-President Cheney. That access certainly influenced energy policies. But even beyond Lay's connection, ENRON was the fruit of twenty years of fertilizer poured upon politicians by Wall Street and free-market tycoons to create a climate of de-regulation. Again, the disaster of the California utility crisis—so severe it brought about a voter recall of Governor Gray Davis—shows the fallacy of de-regulation. Lesson: great wealth uses great political influence to manipulate government.

The final lesson of ENRON is not final at all, but ongoing. It presaged the economic collapse of 2008 in that when regulators allowed ENRON and Anderson to begin the accounting practice of "marked to market," falsely claiming future profits as current profits, they were tilling the soil in which derivatives would thrive.

The Culture of Greed

Alex Gabney, in his ENRON DVD commentary, makes the point that economic evil is not spawned by any one individual, but arises in a *culture* of twisted ethics, an environment that says to people, "It's okay to steal from the middle class because we are all doing it." We will not reform the system by the passage of one or two laws. True change will happen only when we change the culture, the ethical milieu of our age. We must change the cultural belief that billionaires "earn" their money. It is simply impossible to "earn" a billion dollars by one's singlehanded efforts.

When I was a child, I enjoyed my Erector set, a toy that allowed you to assemble a crude model car with a small electric motor, four wheels and a chassis to hold two small batteries. "Look what I built," I bragged to my dad. I'm sure he smiled and patted me on the head. But had I really built that toy car? My dad had purchased the

Erector set with *his* money. The bolts, metal plates, motor and other parts had been manufactured in various places by various workers. I played with it on the sidewalk, never grateful that someone's tax dollars had funded the pavement. Nor did I give a nod to Edison, Farraday, or others for discovering the principles used in the motor and batteries. No, look what *I* had built! Most executives boast: look at "my" corporation, the businesses that "I erected." They show no more gesture of appreciation for the group effort than my six-year-old self.

Summary
This book is not primarily concerned with exposing government corruption. Other books do a better job of that. Our first task here is to show that executives do not deserve their outlandish pay. The same formula—greed, incompetence, shady ethics, and arrogance among executives—that brought disaster to BP, ENRON, AIG, Merrill-Lynch, Tyco, and Worldcom can be found in many other companies' board rooms. In the failure of each of these firms, the people responsible were not the blue-collar or middle-class hard-working employees, but the fat-cats at the top. Yet, Thomas Sowell says we have neither the right nor the qualifications to question the pay of these executives! Even a monkey can recognize stupidity. If a monkey had run all of these firms, they may still have failed, but they would have at least done so ethically and for a lot lower salary! We have not seen monkeys conspire to steal from, lie to, or exploit workers.

ENRON, BP and the Wall Street Crash of 2008 were the ripened fruit of Reaganesque de-regulation... poisoned apples that, if they had all ripened at exactly the same time, could have been fatal for America. Only fate separated these calamities in time, which gave breathing room between each fiasco long enough for taxpayer money to avert another Great Depression. Trillions of dollars of hard earned pensions, along with Federal dollars and precious natural resources, were destroyed by the greed, theft and incompetence of ENRON, BP and Wall Street. The seed that grew this poison fruit was planted in the minds of Americans by the Great Communicator, Ronald Reagan: "Government is the problem," and "Free markets and de-regulation are the solution." The Fourth Reich had found the perfect mouthpiece for their propaganda: a trained actor who looked like your kind old grandfather! Who can really blame the American people? The media did nothing to shatter the illusion.

Government is a problem, but of all the things that it does poorly, regulation is one thing it alone can do. No one else has the muscle to stand up to the playground bully—because this bully has hundreds of well-paid lawyers and lobbyists on its side. Ken Lay and Tony Hayward and Bernie Madoff proved conclusively what happens without regulation: greedy executives will throw caution aside and gamble anything—our environment, our children's economic future—to make a fast big buck. And rather than being afraid of Federal regulators, they know that the Feds will pick up the tab when they lose at the "casino." BP never fully reimbursed local, state and federal governments for their costs associated with the spill/clean-up. Nor would Californians have had electricity if government had not stepped in to rewire the short-circuit left by ENRON. Nor would Wall Street still exist without TARP and the trillions of bailout dollars from the Federal government. Those who repeat Reaganomics' mantra against "big government" are the very ones who depend upon big government to fix the destruction they leave behind as they take their billions to the (Swiss) bank. The government fails us not because it gets in the way of the "free market." It fails because the Fourth Reich has bribed government, tilting the rules in its own favor. Bad, corrupt government *is* a problem, Mr. Reagan.

The final chapter of this book offers some solutions, some ways to move forward to a better world. (Do read the Epilogue, as well!)

~~~

Chapter 14: Hope and Solutions
Individual, Government and Private Sector Solutions

Hope is like a narrow path in the country: when many people walk on it, a wide road comes to be.

~Lin Yutang, paraphrased

We are at war, a world war, a war for the future of our planet. Almost every indicator shows that we are moving to a two-class society: the rich vs. everyone else. Even the self-interested rich ought to see that the death of the middle class means the loss of a buffer, the draining of the castle moat, clearing the way for the mobs to storm the castle. That we don't have a literal, bloody class war amazes me, but the peace probably owes something to the existence of a moral middle class which, so far, has bought into the myth that hard work can insure their children prosperity and a high quality of life. As I write this, riots in Britain and throughout Europe are becoming commonplace, driven by the rage of unemployed youth and class disillusionment.

But as more and more lose hope, if we begin to see the future only as a bleak contrast between the have-lots and the have-nots, who can predict how the war will end? There is still time for a truce. There is still time for voluntary change by the wealthy and the powerful. An idealistic dream? Maybe. Yet dreams can come true.

Three Eyes Blind?

Some will dismiss this treatise as the whining of an envious underclass. Even if that were true, my envy would not exonerate your greed. As my mother often said, "Two wrongs don't make a right."

I don't wish harm for Bill Gates or Warren Buffet—we appreciate their philanthropy. Taxing the rich in a punitive manner is not politically feasible nor would it create a utopia. Solutions have to be win/win. So in this final chapter on "Solutions," we do well to heed the warning about "lose/lose" found in an old Greek fable:

Zeus sent his son, Apollo, to earth to answer two mortals who were petitioning the gods to fulfill their wishes. Both mortals were flawed: one was greedy, the other filled with envy. Mighty Apollo considered their separate requests and decided to connect the two: "I agree to grant your prayers in this way: the thing that one of you requests will be given you, but the same thing also will be given to the other man, twofold." The greedy man's insatiable, limitless desire prompted him to defer the choice to the other man—in this way he would receive twice as much of whatever blessing the first man asked!

But his greed backfired: since the jealous man could not bear the thought of the greedy man getting twice his own reward, he spitefully announced his wish for a curse, not a blessing: "Blind me in one eye." He was willing to suffer through life one-eyed in order to enjoy the sick pleasure of having condemned the greedy man to a double fate: *two eyes blind, a life of total darkness*. The wise Apollo reported back to Zeus about human wickedness, about *schadenfreude*, spawned by jealousy and greed. The gods laughed at such human folly that rejoices when bad things happen to others.

Everyone Loses in Class Warfare

A violent class war would be just as much a lose/lose fool's errand as three eyes blind. I want all eyes to see... to envision win/win solutions across class lines, harming no one. We say "fire the rich" jokingly, rhetorically. The middle class does not want to shoot the rich or storm the Bastille or start anarchic riots in the streets. We all want solutions that lift up the whole society.

Jesus offered a radical solution for greed: "Sell all that you own and give it to the poor." There is another way. Bill Gates and Warren Buffet suggest **giving away half your fortune**. A good start, if they will do it. I suggest giving away 100% of your *excess*, and what you keep for your own comfort and security can be shared.

Solution Number One: Sharing is Winning

Sharing is the first item on our list of solutions, because it is achievable, a painless win/win. Even Jesus' disciples reacted with skepticism at his suggestion to give away all that a person owns, calling such sacrifice "impossible." But **sharing does not require sacrifice**. Sharing does not mean deprivation. In fact, sharing brings joy. Possessing a few luxuries motivates a person to continue working hard, thus a vow of poverty would be counter-productive for most of us. Rewards do boost productivity, and productive work can be personally fulfilling even as it benefits the whole society. Do your best to improve the quality of life for children everywhere, then lay your head on the pillow at night guilt-free. Share yourself, your expertise. Successful in business? Volunteer to help a struggling young family's small business. Join SCORE, a nonprofit organization that connects experienced (often retired) business leaders as mentors for young entrepreneurs and business start-ups.

Sharing Justifies Your Luxuries

Sharing provides ethical "cover" for life's luxuries. Let me illustrate: I love water and boating. We could not afford nor justify the expense of a $30,000 ski boat. So my family and my cousin's family went in halves on a used boat. The $5,000 used boat thus only cost me $2,500. This arrangement also cut all maintenance and upkeep costs in half. The sharing of this luxury went further: we routinely invited "boatless" friends to accompany us. This made boating even more fun for us, and helped others resist the urge to buy a boat, knowing they could use ours. (Most boats spend 90% of their time moored, unused.) We also, several times a year, hosted boating parties for the youth groups of our two churches. We enjoyed sharing the thrill of teaching some kids how to waterski for the first time in their lives. Many of the youth had never even been on a boat.

I've also shared automobiles. For a variety of good reasons, I once had an "extra" car. I made it known that our old station-wagon was available for free use by those in need. One poor family used our car for an extended period to help them through a hard time when they could not immediately afford to get theirs repaired. I've had groups of friends share vans or pickup trucks rather than each buying a big truck. Sharing of vehicles makes environmental sense.

As long as there are children who have no clean drinking water, individuals who own excessive unused possessions should be absolutely ashamed of hoarding. And I'm not letting the rest of us off the hook. If you have an abundance of anything, why would you not want to share it? An empty vacation home? Rent it out and give the revenue away. Extra space in your own business facility or store? Be an incubator for someone' struggling new business start-up. Own a lot or acre of unused land? Offer a free lease to an eager family who needs a garden. Do you have a large yacht or sailboat? Offer a day of sailing to all the kids in the local high school who raise their grades a letter or who have straight A's in a semester. Do you spend thousands building and maintaining a backyard swimming pool that no one uses? Throw a party for the neighborhood kids once a month in the summer. Most of the amenities the fortunate take for granted would be an exciting, once-in-a-life-time experience if shared with the less privileged children in your area.

A secondary benefit of sharing is the connection it offers with your community and with people of lower social station. Becoming involved in their lives, you begin to understand their needs. Empathy grows through sharing. The rich sequester themselves in gated communities and hideaway in the First Class plane cabin. Interaction with the rest of the world is key to finding solutions.

Solution: Give

Sharing is a painless form of charity, of love for neighbor, and as I said, the joy of sharing is an easy place to start. But sharing is not enough. It must lead to the next two levels charity: 1. **giving from**

abundance, and 2. **sacrificial giving**. Most of us, if we give at all, give out of our abundance, a "tip" from our excess. Painless. The second form of giving is to sacrifice something—to feel a bit of deprivation because of our generosity. To give even when it hurts requires a spiritual motivation. Most Americans don't even begin to approach that level.

Bill Gates is an example of "giving from abundance." He and wife Melinda are applauded as great philanthropists. But frankly, they do so only at the first level: they give painlessly out of their vast riches. Have you seen the Gates mansion? Not home to deprivation.

Much of the philanthropy of mega-rich individuals and corporations is suspect. It doubles as good PR. Philanthropists give to their own pet causes, usually to artsy or intellectual pursuits that tend, in turn, to benefit their own class. Their giving is not a sacrifice as it does not cause any strain or reduction in their standard of living. For a billionaire to give a million is far, far easier than the tithing of middle class church-members I've known. Dedicated Christians, Jews and Moslems generally give a "tithe" (10% of their income). If you are a working class person who can't make ends meet, giving 10% requires real, actual physical suffering: it may mean living in a smaller house, eating less tasty food, driving a used car that needs maintenance and doing that work yourself. Nevertheless, there are millions of generous, working-class people who tithe. When they put money in an offering plate, it humbles me and encourages me to be more generous. I think of my former church-member and friend, Bev, who raised thousands for our church but drove an ancient automobile with no air conditioning in 100 degree heat!

A wealthy man once told me that tithing hurt him more than it did me because, he said, "I make a lot of money, thus my 10% check is a *big* check that hurts to write!" When I wrote a 10% tithe check each month, it may have been smaller than his but it required me to make hard choices about things my family would go without. True sacrifice is simply not experienced by those who continue to live in lavish luxury. If giving away money that otherwise was going to sit unused in a bank account hurts you, perhaps you are sick with greed and the sacrifice would be a healing act. It hurts to get healed! Before antibiotics, cauterizing a wound was excruciating pain, but it saved an arm from amputation. Greed is an addiction. Freedom from addiction always requires pain and deprivation. When a wealthy person writes a big check, the pain they are feeling is not truly a loss of comfort, it is the pain of withdrawal from greed-addiction.

Government could lessen the pain if it extended tax breaks to *everyone* who gives. The "charitable deduction" is an efficient way to encourage wealth to move into churches, colleges and other care agencies. Tax laws should be changed so that all taxpayers, regardless of their filing status, get a direct deduction for generosity. Capitalists and conservatives should support this, since they point out (correctly) how non-profits are more efficient with our dollars. Share. Enjoy. Then learn the joy of giving. Finally, give til it hurts.

Solution: Reform Government, Don't Destroy It

Government is a necessary evil. Government is the only beast big enough to take on the Fourth Reich monster. But it is not very efficient at using tax money. A lazy, bloated government bureaucracy is no better than a corporate one. Higher taxation is not a quick solution. Anti-tax, anti-big-government sentiment is so high, and the government debt so large, solutions must be more complex and nuanced than "tax and spend." Conversely, the solutions must be more intelligent than a "slash and burn" gutting of worthwhile government programs. Conservatives focus on cutting so-called "discretionary spending," which is at once the area of smallest government spending *and* some of the most socially beneficial.

All major religions and systems of ethics demand that we protect the vulnerable of society—children, the aged and infirmed, the poor and even the unlucky. But churches, synagogues and other faith organizations just do not have the muscle—or the calling—to police and control the worst elements of our society, both individual and corporate/commercial (as in consumer protection). That is a job for government. Government needs to be smarter and more involved in making sure the kids on the playground play fair and honest. As long as millions of children are starving in the world, as long as millions more have no quality of life, no art or leisure or play, as long as all our little ones know is subsistence living, then I'm willing to have the flaws that come with an activist government. A little inefficiency is a price we pay for justice. The power of government is a necessary counterbalance to the power of monopolistic wealth.

Growth in government is not a panacea. Bureaucrats spend money that isn't theirs with more profligacy than they spend their own. Nevertheless, the choice is stark between government rule versus chaos and corporate banditry. Libertarians live in a dream world where human nature and market forces create a productive utopia and control profiteering. The 2008 Wall Street fiasco proved that is more nightmare than dreamworld; human nature moves toward greed, not efficiency. Without government, the worst elements of society take over. This has been demonstrated historically each time a government has collapsed via war or coup. As bad as government can be, it is usually scrutinized more closely, and held more accountable, than corporations. The private sector can be even more wasteful, even more evil. The occasional failure of regulations and regulators does not make a case to abolish them.

Related Solution: Peace (and reduced military spending)

Another purpose of government that is a "necessary evil" is to wage war. Libertarians are extraordinarily naive to think the world would be fine if we cut our military budget to the bone and became isolationists. And yet, how can any thinking person complain about the tiny bit of Federal waste in discretionary spending while ignoring military spending, when a thousand times more waste is squandered within defense-related budgets? The fat in the defense budget is greater than any other aspect of our bloated government. All totalled, the U.S. spends well over **One Trillion Dollars per year** on military! Remember, this includes more than just the Army or Pentagon, but also Homeland Security, the FBI, the CIA/secret budget, veterans benefits, plus debt payments owed on previous wars. We could have purchased the entire country of Afghanistan more cheaply than we waged war in it! We spend more just on F-35 jets than the entire GDP of Australia.[228] Trillions go into the pockets of defense contractors each decade, and some experts believe as much as a third of that is wasted. Why, then, have I relegated war to a small and late section?

First, I'm not an expert in the field. Second, the topic of military waste deserves an entire and separate book... and such books have already been written. Third, when we call for defense reforms, we get accused of being communists. If I were to crusade against military spending, I'd be branded "unpatriotic," "soft on defense" or "anti-military." I am none of those. I greatly respect our soldiers. Some of my friends and relatives are veterans, and they report that the military does many humanitarian actions. "We don't just blow stuff up," one soldier reminded me. And we live in a wicked world with real threats, large (China) and small (individual terrorists). We should always have a military smart enough and strong enough to be a deterrent on paper and a solid shield in real life.

But defense spending is THE largest category in the Federal budget, and for that reason alone, one of the places most in need of fat-trimming. This fatty animal is a "sacred cow," not only because of the "patriotic vote," but mostly because of defense-industry lobbyists; politicians of both parties are unwilling to kill the cow or to put their own fat in the fryer. A huge chunk of the electorate grew up with WWII or Cold War mentality (fear), believing passionately that our very survival depends on giving *carte blanche* to the military budget. However, public opinion can be changed if we enlighten folks to the facts: we are being ripped off by the military-industrial complex, and it is not making us safer. This is the conclusion of Republican Dwight Eisenhower and of Robert Gates, Secretary of Defense under George W. Bush—not exactly doves.

Even Military Men Agree

Some military officials may be reticent to blow the whistle on the scam of out-of-control defense spending, because many of them look forward to lucrative post-military careers working for defense contractors. But thankfully, many high-ranking military officers speak the truth. "Ike" Eisenhower, a WWII hero and Army general before he became President, famously sounded the warning with these words in 1961: "There is a recurring temptation to [choose] spectacular and costly action [as] the miraculous solution to all current difficulties. A huge increase in defense... must be weighed in the light of a broader consideration: the need to maintain balance between cost and hoped for advantage...." This stalwart Army General went on, as President, to boldly warn of a "conjunction of an immense military establishment and a large arms industry... [whose] influence... is felt in every city, every State house, every office of the Federal government... [W]e must not fail to comprehend its grave implications... and guard against the acquisition of unwarranted influence [of] the military-industrial complex. The potential for the disastrous rise of misplaced power exists and will persist." Not the words of a pacifist liberal, but of a hardened World War II soldier and conservative politician.[229]

Since this is a chapter on "Solutions," here's an example of a cost-cutting solution: energy efficiency in the military. Our military is the world's largest single consumer of fuel and energy! The amount the U.S. military spent annually on air conditioning in Iraq and Afghanistan: $20.2 billion. Annually! That's bigger than NASA's entire budget. Of course we want our troops as comfortable as possible. But the widespread use of inefficient diesel-powered generators running air conditioning for *uninsulated* tents is absurd. A simple $20 reflective solar blanket thrown over the tents would have, alone, drastically reduced the cost, and thus saved lives by requiring fewer risky fuel convoys.[230] NPR reports that over a thousand soliders have been killed while transporting fuel for camps. Cheap, low-tech efficiencies could have easily saved lives and money. On the other end of the spectrum, expensive hi-tech hardware is purchased in excess and redundancy. The military has over a hundred different *types* of planes and helicopters with a price tag ranging from half-a-million to two billion apiece, each needing millions worth of spare parts warehoused. Additionally, aircraft require a huge investment in pilot training. Unmanned drones and cruise missiles are the most efficient, accurate part of our inefficient military system. Consolidation and streamlining of models across the many branches of the military, and reduction of total numbers of planes/helicopters, with increased use of pilotless drones, would save billions. And aircraft are not even the biggest waste in our military. The money spent on *wheeled* vehicles (trucks, tanks, armored vehicles) is so huge no one is really sure of the total.

None of this compares to the trillions wasted on nuclear weaponry. We had over 32,000 nuclear warheads/bomb at the peak of the Cold War.[231] A "mere" 2,000 would destroy every major city and military base in Russia *and* China. Why did we build another 30,000 at a cost of trillions? The only reasonable explanation: the defense industry pushed for it. The mind-boggling waste in the nuclear program goes beyond the bombs themselves... trillions more were wasted on unnecessary and unused infrastructure and delivery systems. For example, from 1946-1961, we spent $7 billion on the Aircraft Nuclear Propulsion program to produce nuclear powered aircraft. Number of planes built for our billions: zero. Knowing that just two small nuclear explosions brought the mighty nation of Japan to its knees, I cannot believe it was necessary to have more than 1,000 nuclear warheads, even for deterrence. There is evidence that if we reduced our spending on the military, other nations would in turn reduce theirs. **We spend too much, we waste too much, we bomb too much.** In an interconnected world, is China going to bomb the U.S. when we are its best customer? The bigger threat to our national security is a shaky economy.

Solution: VOTE! Contact Congress and Give 'Em Hell

There are things that government alone must do, but that does not mean we give *carte blanche* to fraud and waste. Of course, to get reform in government, *we* have to take action: vote, campaign, lobby, educate and change public opinion. So we begin with the standard, "Contact your Representatives." Most politicians are ego-driven: ambitious, desirous of leading a purposeful life, relishing the feeling of being a VIP with power. The need for public approval and "status" is part of their psychological profile, but so is their lust for corporate bucks. Make them choose. Confront them at "town hall meetings" and civic club speeches. Make them uncomfortable. Bring some facts from this book and challenge them publicly with questions, such as: "Congressman, real wages for working Americans have shrunk over the last 20 years, while wages for CEOs have soared. What are you going to do to bring sanity back to our system?" Or: "Why are corporations given tax loopholes and subsidies instead of small businesses?" That question cannot be easily dismissed as one from a "whacko liberal." At these events, about half the crowd will *be* small businesspersons. Be brave enough to follow-up the politician's rote answer with a second, probing question. Hold them accountable.

Less effective but still important are letters, calls and emails. Do they make a difference? Only when vast numbers protest. Politicians admit that they are influenced by communication from constituents. They reason correspondents are likely to be voters. That's what moves them most: votes. Even one vote is valuable to them. Public opinion means little; only voters—those who *actually* vote—truly count. Signing an email-circulated petition is a waste of time, as they have no way to ensure that the list of names is genuine. Most such emailed chain letters have no mechanism to forward the completed email to Congress. Political emails are usually just tools to spread partisan lies. Ignore them. Write your Congressperson directly, using the government website, "Thomas":
www.thomas.loc.gov/home/contactingcongress.html

Peaceful protest gatherings, like "Occupy Wall Street," and like the civil rights marches of the past, do make a difference. If for no other reason, they capture media attention. But in the end, all that really counts is to Vote! Vote! Vote!

Everyone Must Be a Solution

Solving poverty and economic injustice must involve everything and everyone: non-profit charities, the for-profit private sector, faith organizations, educational institutions, and world governments.

Perhaps it is cliché, **but change has to start with "the man in the mirror,"** as Michael Jackson once sang. Individuals must make a better effort to share resources. What are we saving for, and what are we spending for? More stuff to fill our closets? No hearse has ever pulled a U-haul. Or as the famous philosopher Anonymous put it, "When the chess game is over, the kings and the pawns are swept into the same box." And most of your trinkets will be swept into a dumpster. If we are not, individually, being generous, we cannot blame the rich for all the evils of the world. *Everyone* must be a part of the solution, everyone should be helping the poor, everyone should bolster the middle class, everyone should reduce waste, fraud and inefficient use of resources. Small changes by the middle class can make a huge difference because of our sheer numbers.

The middle class can make an easy commitment to two areas of positive change—**health** and **energy waste**:

Solution: Healthcare Cost Control

If we confiscated all of Bill Gates' billions, it would not save Medicare or solve the healthcare cost crisis. The problem is *huge*, excuse the pun: Americans are an overweight, sedentary bunch. Overeating and under-exercising are creating massive costs for Medicare and Medicaid and private health insurance—which in turn, we all pay for through taxes and higher premiums. Health-related costs weigh heavy (ha) on small businesses, limiting their hires.

Being forty or more pounds overweight will almost *guarantee* that later in life, you will need either diabetes care, knee surgery or back pain treatment, which can incur costs of $100,000 or more. Diabetes can entail lifelong costs to society of a million dollars per patient.

Often disease is no one's fault. Stuff happens. But in many cases, these costs be avoided by the simple choice to eat less and exercise more. Obesity raises the risk of developing several diseases, including Type 2 diabetes, heart disease, hypertension, sleep apnea, some cancers, osteoarthritis and back injury. Diabetes and hypertension rates in the USA have risen markedly over the last twenty years. Dr. Jeff Levi, executive director of Trust for America's Health, states: "Since 1995, obesity rates have risen by 90% in ten states and have doubled in another seven. Today, the state with the lowest obesity rate would have had the highest rate in 1995... we can't afford to ignore the impact obesity has on our health and... health care spending."[232]

Along with obesity and substance abuse, smoking is part of the "trilogy of bad habits," avoidable bad habits that guarantee increased, but unnecessary, health costs for society. We have "sin taxes" on tobacco and alcohol because of the inherent costs these place on our healthcare system; to be fair, we should consider taxes on unhealthy snacks and drinks, with the revenues enhancing healthcare. Everyone has a personal responsibility to stay healthy. It's a win/win.

Solution: Energy Efficiency and Reduced Waste

When tourists visit the United States, they are often struck by how wasteful Americans are with energy use. Our cars, trucks, recreational vehicles and spacious homes all seem outlandishly oversized to Japanese and Europeans. Americans don't think twice about jumping into a 4-door, 4,000-pound SUV to drive solo across town—even if an economy car sits beside it in the driveway. And if all Americans would simply turn off lights and appliances they are not using, the monetary savings and the boon to our environment would be phenomenal. Obvious, even condescending —but apparently we need the reminder! New and eco-friendly energy sources are needed and commendable, yet we have a **cheaper, faster and ecologically smarter** solution at a our fingertips: the "off" switch. **Conservation**. People laughed at Jimmy Carter's edict to be stingy with thermostats in restaurants and businesses, but the collective savings would be immense. These are easy solutions, painless efficiencies that save money and resources without any real deprivation... all in the category of no-brainers. Some of our "righteous indignation" at the lavish waste of jet-setting tycoons needs to be directed at ourselves. Compared to the impoverished child without a crayon, I am a fat-cat tycoon, too.

Solution: Embrace, Promote, Distribute Technology

We can bring relief to the Third World by quickly spreading and employing known technologies. Some small examples: •Efficient LED lighting driven by inexpensive tech (older solar cells and batteries) could save on pollution from kerosene and paraffin lamps/candles, reducing respiratory problems and improving oxygen levels in homes and huts. A very small amount of money could be transformative in this manner. In places where power grids are not practical, having a cheap, on-site, low-voltage power-source could provide a way to operate simple computers/cellphones. Electronics gadgets that are outdated in our culture (meaning, a year old) could be donated to remote areas for inexpensive internet access and communication. Such information and communication access would in turn improve commercial markets as well as the flow of ideas about democracy, health, and social progress. •In Third World cities, immediate replacement of out-dated and inefficient heating and cooling systems with high-efficiency heat pumps, combined with weatherization/ insulation, can cut energy consumption in half. •In villages, clean water and proper sewage can transform the health and happiness for all—from a small investment in improved water wells and sewage handling. Civic organizations have proven this, investing small sums and simple technologies for big results, like $10 foot-powered pumps and water filtration eradicating water-borne disease in remote places. •Establishing shared ownership, common property and village-owned tools and technologies is another cost-effective transformation of life quality. Anyone who has ever used a public library or rented a truck instead of buying one sees the value of this model. We can put machinery, tools and computers in place for shared common use by those with limited individual resources.

Solution: Develop Sustainable Models for the Third World

A good thing about Third World challenges: *small* amounts of money and technical advances can make *huge* improvements. The phrase "Third World" is no longer in favor, but I still prefer it to the clunky "undeveloped regions" or euphemistic "emerging world." Large parts of the Third World have spotty development, not yet "emerging" into prosperity or technology. If a nation is emerging, I'd call them "Second World" and reserve the phrase Third World for conditions that are so poverty-stricken and low-tech that visiting them is truly like stepping onto another planet. Not long ago, we frowned upon a patriarchal Western imperialism that imposed our WASP values and models onto remote, primitive societies, robbing them of their culture. But the horse is out of the barn now: even Amazonian tribes know about, well, *Amazon.com*! They yearn for the same modern miracles of technology that we enjoy in food production, medicine, electronics and communication. When it comes to Western aid, we can be humble and work with the indigenous populations, using technologies that fit the geography and culture of indigenous peoples. We can partner, as equals, with less-privileged nations to offer the best of Western models for boosting productivity, ameliorating hunger, disease and violence. The U.S. Global Health Initiative is one example of the principles of partnership for deployment of appropriate technologies. Secular think-tanks, foundations, philanthropists and UN/governmental organizations should partner with faith-based missionaries, who are knowledgeable of grass-roots needs *and* of Western resources. Another good model for this was the malaria-nets program of the United Methodist Church, in which that Christian denomination partnered with the deep pockets and promotional abilities of Hollywood to fight malaria.

Yet another proven model is **micro-finance**. Micro-loans by non-profit organizations entrust a small amount of money, $50-$100, to poverty-stricken, Third-World potential entrepreneurs. With low interest, these have proven to be highly successful in helping people start home businesses. They soon pay back the loan. It can be as simple as a villager purchasing four goats and within a year, having a goat farm that produces milk and meat and baby goats. Muhammmad Yunus won the 2006 Nobel Peace Prize for his work in expanding micro-lending around the globe. Billions have been loaned in this fashion in India, creating jobs and opportunities for more than a million people. The microfinance concept still works as long as it is kept as a non-profit endeavor.

Appropriate models. If you look at houses in much of middle America, they do not vary much from sixty years ago. Most of our infrastructure and lifestyle is modeled after the architecture, transportation and residential developments of the post-war boom. The suburban American model (big cars, big houses, big distances between home and work) cannot be sustained going into the future for over six billion people. Why emulate American models in housing, transportation and industry in places limited resources? That mimicking can appear silly. One humorous photo that circulated via email was of a poor farmer using a broken-down, chopped-up heavy automobile as an ox-wagon—when a native-built lightweight wooden cart is far more efficient than the metal hulk.

Ha-Joon Chang writes about this and other mistakes of Western imposition onto the Third World, in his books *Bad Samaritans* and *23 Things They Don't Tell You about Capitalism*. Chang made these good points: "The real cause of African stagnation in the last three decades is free-market policies that the continent has been compelled to implement.... What makes the poor countries poor is not the absence of entrepreneurial energy at the personal level, but the absence of productive technologies and developed social organizations," and, I add, technologies which fit their *sitz in leben*, their lifestyle and situation.[233]

We need a non-profit, coordinating clearinghouse to develop, test, and distribute the best simple technologies—that don't depend on 120 volts AC power or require frequent parts-replacement. Many of these inventions already exist. Nothing would be more universally-beneficial to humanity than cheap, clean energy, benefiting children in an African village and manufacturing plants in Silicon Valley. Which brings up our next point.

Solution: Invest in Renewable Energy

The problem with our energy strategy is that the *total* cost of coal, oil, gas and nuclear usage is rarely reported or considered. For coal and oil, the one-time nature of the resource (mine it, burn it, lose it) is downplayed, and government subsidies (tax breaks, low royalty rates for land use/mineral extraction) are not factored in. Nor are the environmental damages. Post-Chernobyl, Post-Three Mile Island construction of new and safer nuclear plants became prohibitive even before adding in the costly and dangerous disposal of spent nuclear rods that take 10,000 years to de-compose. After the tsunami at Fukushima, one would think we'd be told the true cost of "safe" nuclear energy. Not so. GE was a major partner in the design/build of the Fukushima reactors that melted down in Japan. GE is well-connected with politicians who foist high-priced and unwanted nuclear plants on the public. Virtually every nuclear construction project of the last 40 years has cost more than originally projected. So why should we trust current projections about price-per-kilowatt? Over seven billion bucks were squandered on the Yucca mountain disposal site, all for naught as the project was scrapped as unsafe. Tens of thousands of tons of radioactive waste sit around nuclear reactors in the U.S. alone. A 2003 study estimated an *additional* $7 billion will be needed to move these materials into safer containers even *before* building a safer, longterm storage facility.

One would think that Big Coal and Big Oil would protest the subsidy-situation for nuclear, but they are all part of the interdependent club of multinationals also receiving subsidies — pups of the same litter sucking at the same teats on the government hound.

We need a massive public investment to R&D clean, renewable energy sources. Why don't we do this? Because people scream "Socialism! Let the free market develop energy!" Yet the energy industries and utility companies receive billions in government help. These long-standing companies have entrenched connections with our political system, and the last thing they want is *true* free-market competition. Politicians shout against Big Government even as they take campaign contributions from industries milking that very same Big Government. When you hear a politician criticize solar power, I'll bet a tank of gas they have received donations from coal, petro or utility companies—or from all three!

Let's team up with someone who has already constructed a huge fusion reactor in outer space, offering free megawatts to us every day: God! Solar energy is God's plan for our energy needs. Free and clean. One example of a promising solar technology: a silicon "leaf" that mimics photosynthesis, designed to float in a pool of dirty water (even in sewage), using sunlight to split H2O into hydrogen and oxygen which can then be converted into electric current. Daniel Nocera and MIT believe a single such leaf in a gallon of water could produce a day's worth of electricity for a Third World household.[234]

Solar energy has so many advantages: waste by-products are off-planet, the source reactor (the sun) requires no start-up cost, no fuel or maintenance cost, and its energy is distributed sans wires or pipes all around the globe. This last factor is exactly why capitalist powers do not want it developed: it is hard to re-package, sell or meter the sun. The biggest consumer bills—and biggest eco-damages —come because of centralized power/energy/oil/mineral consortiums. So solar energy is exactly where we should demand *our* government invest. Solar power is democratic. Solar power benefits everyone... except Big Coal and Big Oil. BP and Exxon invest in solar only to hedge their bets, furiously trying to figure a way they can profit from it while currying public favor with feel-good ads like BP's "Beyond Petroleum" or Chevron's "We Agree" propaganda.

Global warming and energy-related pollution will be the over-riding economic issue for the next 20 years. Warning against too-extreme measures, Bjørn Lomborg offers doable solutions in his book, *Cool It: The Skeptical Environmentalist's Guide to Global Warming*. He suggests funding research for smart, cost-effective de-centralized technologies, such as new building materials, grass parking lots instead of asphalt, solar heating, etc. Eco-pragmatism.

Solution: Help Children and Parents

The people with the greatest burden to carry in our society are working parents—young single moms in particular.[235] The top of the economic pyramid benefitted from the increased productivity of working mothers, but it did so by expecting the new slaves to push the stones up the inclines of the pyramid's base *while carrying a baby*! Entering low-paying jobs, parents are forced to pay for daycare as a near-zero-sum game. Most studies show that children who start daycare as infants are less healthy in every measure—physically, emotionally, intellectually—versus those who had an attentive mother who kept them at home for the formative years. This is another area where churches, government and businesses must work together for the common good: establish quality job-site daycare so that during breaks, moms (and dads) can interact with their children. Anyone who has the illusion that the poor are comfortable with their lot in life should also have to experience the heart-rending feeling of leaving your toddler in daycare for eight hours a day, five days a week. And it applies on the other end of childhood: it pains us to not be able to provide the best things for our children. My daughters had to settle for a state college, as we could not afford an ivy-league opportunity. I don't expect a utopian world where every child goes to Harvard... but for my children and many others, funding even a state college tuition is extremely difficult. Yet in the 2011 "debt-ceiling debate," politicians cut college scholarships —while leaving oil company subsidies intact.

Solution: Reform Banks, Loan to Small Businesses

Defenders of the ultra-rich call them "job-creators." But it doesn't take a billionaire to create jobs. A relatively small amount of capital—$10,000 to $50,000—can help launch small businesses, the true job creators. The U.S. model for economic growth over the last 30 years has been to get easy credit available to *consumers*. Consumer-based debt-driven growth is foolish, leaving Americans with housefuls of frivolous trinkets and a burden of interest and anxiety. A bit of guided, business-minded credit, aimed at entrepreneurs with a stated purpose of developing jobs, is a much, much better plan. In the U.S., if there is any government program that needs more money and more streamlining, it is the Small Business Administration.

I tried to get an SBA loan at three different times in my life. The paperwork involved for a small loan was on par with my doctoral dissertation. After investing many hours filling out the forms, my application were rejected: three times. In contrast, credit card companies are willing to loan me $20,000, without collateral, in about three minutes with just my signature. Why, then, does the government require a circus act of hoop-jumping, plus proving I have up-front start-up cash and collateral, for an even-smaller SBA loan? Why hasn't the SBA been involved in its own version of microfinance, making make small loans available with a streamlined application process for small entrepreneurs? Take a little risk with a little money to help the little guy. We risked billions in mega-loans to AIG and GM. This is an area where the pro-entrepreneurship philosophy of Republicans and the "looking out for the little guy" approach of Democrats could come together in a bipartisan reform.

Solution: Link CEO Salaries to Reality

If we can't convince corporations to roll back excessive CEO salaries, at the very least, we should challenge the Fortune 500 CEO's to voluntarily *freeze* their salaries for a period of five years. And ultimately, salaries should be limited: linked to both longterm profits and to the wages of the lower-paid workers of their companies. I won't rehash the iron-clad arguments made earlier, that no one needs or deserves to make a billion dollars, but I will address concerns about salary limits:

-**Objection**: *Limits seem arbitrary... how do we determine amounts?* **Answer**: Life is arbitrary. But a logical way to set limits is in relation to the lowest hourly wage in the company or institution in which the CEO or celebrity or athlete is employed. One hundred times the bottom hourly wage would be a generous limit.

-**Objection:** *Limits de-incentivize*. **Answer**: There is no evidence of that. Once a salary exceeds a million annually, the "incentive" becomes abstract. When a person has all the necessities of life, plus ample luxuries, money no longer motivates them significantly. *Status* does. Personal achievement and fulfillment matter more. Why does Hollywood need a different awards program (*Oscar, Emmy, Golden Globe*, etc. etc.) every month? They work hard not for the extra million but for the extra acclaim. Corporations would compete for talent by offering the most exciting and satisfying work environment and the most career fulfillment.

-**Objection:** *Government should not tell us what to do*. **Answer:** It is high time media and pundits answer these demagogues who talk about how "government has no right to tell us what to do." Government is *us*. The voice of the people. If you believe in democracy, then you believe the PEOPLE, not the plutocrats, can and should determine which policies are helpful for the whole society.

-**Objection**: *You are trying to limit my freedom*. **Answer:** Freedom *always* has limits. The Fourth Reich limits our economic freedom by exploiting the working class. Our lost wages pay for their jet-setting, yacht-running, mansion-building greed. So maybe we have a right to limit *their* freedom to some degree, too.

Solution: Accountability in Salary and Profits

Pay should be based on real performance (isn't that what capitalists want!?), not on bubbles and windfalls. If a manager or CEO does inept work, they should not be rewarded. Capitalists like Tommy Newberry tout the divine (or natural) law of reaping and sowing, sometimes called *karma*, but they only want half the equation—the bountiful harvest. They walk away from the drought years. They want the reward, not the risk. Any salary beyond a comfortable cost of living should be in the form of commissions or bonuses that are **tied to the long-term health of a corporation**. This would be a win/win/win, fostering long-term stability in a company, increased profits to share-holders, and better sleep for executives.

Suzanne McGee reported that a few Wall Street firms "began to tweak their compensation packages in late 2008 in response to the public outrage, introducing the concept of the clawback to... pay packages."[236] *Clawback* means that a firm or its shareholders could pull back part of top managers' bonuses for a period of five years. Performance bonuses would not be a lucky windfall based on a brief "bubble." Equity manager Tom McNamara and Columbia University professor Joseph Stiglitz propose that commissions and bonuses be tied to the long term profit of the client. If a firm recommends a stock or derivative that tanks, and the client loses money, that loss should apply retroactively to the broker who pushed the flawed product.

Solution: Proactive Consumer Protection and Regulation

Governments around the world must be far more aggressive in consumer protection. This *begins* with **policing false advertising**. When a marketer tells a lie about a product or service, that lie constitutes a *theft* (aiming to take your money without fulfilling the promise of the product's advertisement). Marketing deception should be treated as theft, with fines or imprisonment. *Caveat emptor* is horrible, evil, public policy; it is Latin for "Screw the consumer."

Consumer protection would not require pages of new regulation. It simply requires a clear, firm law, with definite enforcement. The Federal Trade Commission (FTC), the Federal Communications Commission (FCC) and the Justice Department need to ask the question, "What can we do to help average Americans?"

The deception in advertising and product marketing is so widespread and common, I'd waste space giving examples... but the lies begin with the word, *Free!* You've heard the joke about "the three big lies." There are *four*: advertising a "Free" product is the fourth big fat lie. We are assaulted daily with "free offers." Every time in my life I have succumbed to something "free," it has cost me time and money. Trial offers, money back guarantees, free-just-for-calling... there is always a catch or fine print, beginning with a pricey "Shipping and handling fee." My "free" phone from T-Mobile cost me $26 and a two-year pricey contract renewal. The frequent, lying misuse of the word *free* is one example of hundreds of marketing deceptions—illustrating the need for more aggressive consumer protection. The brainwashers have convinced people that all regulation is evil. *Stupid paperwork*, they call it. Some regulation *is* stupid. But having *no* regulation is truly moronic, as the Chinese discovered when children were poisoned by toxic metals in unregulated paint on toys. Thousands of regulations are already in place, but the **enforcement**, the policing, is weak.

Solution: De-Centralize Everything

Size matters. And it turns out, *small is better*. Public policy should be aimed at de-centralization, localization and preferential incubation of small businesses. This is where we find the greatest efficiencies and the best hope for equitable opportunity. Malcolm Gladwell makes a good case for this in his book, *Tipping Point*, which shows both anecdotal and statistical evidence for what he calls "the rule of 150": that *small* **organizations are more effective** in many ways, beginning with the fact that the maximum number of individuals in a working group that can have real, meaningful, social relationships is about 150.[237] This principle was tested and proven by the high-tech firm, W. L. Gore and Associates, that made Gore-Tex. Gore Associates and other models have shown that when human organizations get too large, they become inefficient, even corrupt. In big, cold bureaucracies, there is a "pass the buck" mentality, a lack of commitment, relationship, and accountability. "The rule of 150" should be extrapolated to both government and small business.

Large corporations have their place. Economies of scale, national advertising and name recognition, greater access to markets, and other advantages of big business can bring less expensive goods to consumers. But small community-based businesses have their own set of advantages—especially for local towns and employees. Because of the profit advantages in "super-sizing" or "Walmart-ization," laws and regulations should be engineered to favor the small businessperson as a way to level the playing field.

Current laws and corporate practices are biased in the opposite direction. Big government and big business hold sway. How do we change that? The solution is political. Stop evaluating our politics and choosing our politicians based on party labels or one-issue focus. Every law, every bill passed, should endure the scrutiny of,

"Will this make the Big bigger or will it help the average citizen and the small businessperson?" No more bulldozing mom 'n pop.

When I was a child, there was a bully on the playground, a giant compared to us younger kids. I organized a "league of superheroes," consisting of the weaker nerds and misfits like myself, to outnumber him, and he never bothered us again. Small businesses should do the same: organize together and lobby for change.

Solution: A Tobin Tax and an Internet Tax

The middle class simply cannot bear higher income taxes. And some economists are skeptical about diminishing returns via higher income taxes on the rich, because the rich move their companies, assets or selves to an island tax haven. But two huge areas of our economy skate along tax-free: **tax internet sales and financial/stock transactions**. These easy-to-impose taxes would have minimal impact on the poor and middle class. Even Ronald Reagan's former finance guru, David Stockman, supports the concept of a tax on financial transactions and stock sales/transfers. Nobel Prize-winning economist James Tobin proposes a tiny percentage of tax be levied on financial transactions—tax those speculators who make profit but not product. A **Tobin Tax**, (also called a "Robin Hood tax") would apply real-time minuscule deductions on each trade—money that would hardly be missed, yet could raise billions to pay down the federal debt. Stockman states: "We have a massive casino [Wall Street, Chicago Mercantile, etc.] that is doing nothing [productive] but churning transactions," and it's making billions—free of taxation. Stockman adds, "There's no productive value for Main Street or the real U.S. economy" on Wall Street.

Politicians love to brag that they support "family businesses," and yak about how "the small businessman [sic] provides most of the new jobs in America." They use family businesses as an object lesson in why we should eliminate inheritance tax. But the proof of politicians' hypocritical favoring of large corporations is the **free ride given to internet corporations via no sales tax**.

My friends David and Brandy own a small mom-n-pop music store. When they sell a guitar, they compete with the volume-buying power of internet music stores, AND they have to charge 10% less gross to be competitive because of a 10% sales tax, while eBay and MusiciansFriend.com pay none! Republicans are often the loudest to mouth support for small business—yet they still refuse to place fair taxation on the biggest threat to the small town merchant: online sales. And Democrats, beginning with Al Gore, are just as supportive of this anti-small business tax exemption. An online sales tax may sound regressive, but since the poor are not buying big-ticket items, and usually buy locally, the taxes collected from them would be tiny. But huge revenues from taxing big-spenders online could pay down the national debt—an investment in our future.

Other Tax Reforms

Even as I argue for more aggressive taxation of the rich, the middle class and the working poor need tax simplification and tax relief. The TEA Party is right in this regard: the amount and variety of taxes we pay is astounding. In many states, even the poorest still pay state income tax, city income tax, regressive sales tax on every item purchased (9.5% on groceries in my town), cell phone tax, land phone tax, electricity and home-heating-fuel tax, property tax, and eight taxes related to owning/operating an automobile, excise taxes, toll road (a tax via a fee), and on and on. Add to that business taxes for those who try to be self-employed. In 1914, the median family's *total* tax rate (as a percentage of salary) was .1%; today it is approaching 30% (while Mitt and Warren pays half that).

There are over 10,000 pages to the tax code/law, and 4,000 pages of IRS forms. The amount of money we spend on tax calculation, filing and collection at all levels is itself a drag on the economy. Most of us, even tycoons and corporations, would be willing to pay a bit more taxes by losing a tax deduction-loophole or two if, in trade, we received a reduction in the complexity of accounting/tax filing. Tax reform that *simplifies* should easily receive bipartisan support.

Proposing tax reform makes me nervous. When the topic of tax reform arises, conservatives quickly mention a flat tax. A flat tax has popular appeal because the populace has such a visceral distaste for the current IRS system and its complexities. When Steve Forbes, Herman Cain or Libertarians like Rand Paul propose abolishing the IRS and instituting a flat tax, the public cheers because of a disdain for the IRS and its maddeningly-complex forms. Unfortunately, they forget that a flat tax is just one more scheme to enrich the rich.

Solution: Election Reform; Term Limits; Third Party

Here the Tea Party and the Republican "Contract with America" once had the right idea (in word if not in deed): **term limits**. The reason limits are needed is simple: power corrupts. Absolutely. The longer a politician wears the ring of power, the more it ruins him. No counter-argument about the value of veteran politicians outweighs that. Nevertheless, let's address a few concerns about term limits.

Argument: "The public can vote-out their veteran Congressman any time they want to." Theoretically they *could*, but they *don't*, and so this begs the question. The point is, the power and money

advantages that come with incumbency make it almost impossible for the average citizen-candidate to unseat an entrenched Congressperson. Indeed, over the last fifty years, Congressional incumbents have been re-elected over 90% of the time. Term limits would give a counter-balance to the incumbent advantage.
Argument: "Experienced politicians are to be valued. It takes years for a Congressperson to learn the skills of the office; long, repeat terms build competency in our leaders." That small truth is outweighed by two facts:1. Skilled, experienced staffpersons are easily hired to bring competency to Congressional rookies, and, 2. Competency is a *negative* trait if it is in the skill-set of a corrupt official. Career politicians who become skilled at graft and manipulation are not a boon to our republic! And rare as hen's teeth is a politician not warped by the affectations of power; the career politician develops an egocentric sense of entitlement. When everyone around you treats you as special, over the years it becomes inevitable that the subconscious mind begins to internalize the praise and deference, and the ego inflates. Decision-making becomes arrogant, as in "I'm smarter than the electorate." Yet most of our career politicians are of mediocre intellect. Staggered, limited terms would regularly bring in fresh energies, fresh ideas.

    The need for political reform goes beyond just the need for term limits. We need a **Third Party**, because the current two-party system is electing idiots and criminals. Examples of political stupidity abound, but the 2012 Presidential campaign had some of the more humorous gaffes. Governor Rick Perry stated in one debate, "We're going to see Iran, in my opinion, move back in [to Iraq] at literally the speed of light." Perhaps Perry knows of some secret weaponry that allows Iranian aircraft to break Einstein's laws… or perhaps he doesn't know the meaning of the word "literally."[238] Or take Candidate Herman Cain, who said he feared China might be "trying to develop nuclear capability," though it was widely known that China has had an A-bomb since the sixties.[239] Under the current system, *money* is far more important than *brains*! But worst of all, look at the outright financial corruption. In 2010, over forty Congresspersons had been convicted of felonies.[240] What more evidence do we need that the current system of electing politicians is in need of massive reform? We are held captive by two political parties who no longer represent their constituencies. In 2012, according to a CNN poll, only 11% of the population approved of how Congress is handling its duties! Both parties serve their masters in the Fourth Reich of the Rich. The Obama administration is riddled with Wall Street insiders, and Obama is "owned" by the rich elite, beginning with bankers and lawyers. George Bush and Mitt Romney *are* part of the rich elite, and we all know of the influence of corporations like Halliburton, BP, ENRON, etc. A strong Third Party would not be a panacea but could increase accountability in our political system and break our political malaise. For more ideas and discussion of what such a movement might look like, go to **www.skypolitics.org** and read about "Transcendent Politics," which seeks "synergies for the common good" at the nexus of wide political opposites. Dr. Paul Ray has studied these ideas and writes: "A new political constituency is emerging, whom I call the New Progressives.... [T]hey are at right angles to Liberal left and Social Conservative right, and they are directly opposed to Big Business Conservatism."[241] Ray sees hope in the rising segment of the population called "Cultural Creatives." These voters will expect politicians to deal "with the big, difficult, emerging issues of our time, such as global warming, globalization, health care, education, the information society, control of biotechnology, giant corporations out of control, violence around the world, and new fears about the future of their children."[242]

While Ray is optimistic that progressives are rising, he fears the monied power of plutocracy is rising faster. We must reform campaign laws, including a constitutional amendment to overturn the "Citizens United" court ruling, to drastically limit the size of corporate PACs. We must also limit total dollars spent, and eliminate the 30-second TV political spot. Voters cannot make an intelligent, informed decision based on slick, deceptive 30-second ads.

We no longer have a citizen Congress "of the people, by the people, for the people." It is impossible for the average person to be elected to high office with such astronomical campaign costs—half a million for a small Congressional seat. Shouldn't that bother us?

Solution: Reduce Government Debt and Secure Social Security

Republican President Dwight D. Eisenhower said in 1954: "Should any political party attempt to abolish social security, unemployment insurance, and eliminate labor laws and farm programs, you would not hear of that party again in our political history. There is a tiny splinter group... that believes you can do these things. Among them are a few other Texas oil millionaires, and an occasional politician or business man from other areas. Their number is negligible and they are stupid." [243] But flash forward to 2011, and we find Ike's own Party attempting the very things the wise General warned against! We cannot sustain the continued acceleration of the size of our national debt. Not only is the debt growing ($15 trillion, a mind-numbing number), the *rate* of that growth is swelling too. Paying out over 25% of income tax revenues for mere **interest on the national debt is unsustainable**. The problem emerged because of bad decisions on both sides of the aisle: Democrats spending too much, and Republicans bloating the military budget even while cutting taxes on the rich and on corporations.

Solution: Welfare Reform, End Entitlement Thinking

Most critics on the Left or the Right applauded Bill Clintons' Welfare Reform Act. Too many able-bodied persons received government monies for doing nothing—a waste of government money and human productivity, but also de-humanizing to the recipients. People benefit by having meaningful work to do. All world religions clearly support justice for the poor, but those same sages state those who are able to work, *should* work. Scripture teaches that work can be a curse *or* a source of joy, meaning, satisfaction and purpose. An ethical economy would provide meaningful work for all people. Malcolm Gladwell states, in his book *Outliers: The Story of Success*, that "three things—autonomy, complexity, and a connection between effort and reward—are [what] work has to have if it is to be satisfying."[244]

More welfare reform is needed, but it should cut both ways. Not only should we continue to hold recipients accountable, we need to streamline the various agencies in charge, reduce bureaucracy and duplication, making it simpler to apply for aid in all its forms *and* better protect against fraud, to ensure that recipients are not triple-dipping with multiple milkings of local, state and Federal coffers.

But the bigger savings for taxpayers will be in eliminating welfare for corporations (see Chapter 10). And the best kind of "welfare" is for government to invest in small business start-ups that create jobs.

The Problem is a Solution

In referring to economic problems, Ronald Reagan famously said that government *was* the problem... a guise to remove government regulation and increase corporate profits. In a way, he is right: faulty government is a huge problem. Good government is also part of the solution. The worst crashes/recessions of the past 120 years were not because of over-regulation or by some failure on the part of the American worker, but rather, because of a failure of government oversight of Wall Street and monopolists. The simplistic answer is to throw away our broken government; **the better solution is to fix our broken government**. Reform.

If anything, regulation doesn't go *far enough*. **Break up banks and insurance agencies that are "too big to fail."** The book, *13 Bankers*, makes an ironclad case for this, which I will not re-trace here except to quote one sentence: "Despite the widespread assumption in both New York and Washington that big banks provide societal benefits... there is no proof these benefits exist...."[245]

Even establishment Republican Alan Greenspan now agrees that overly-large institutions are dangerous lions: "If they're too big to fail, they're too big.... you've got [to eliminate] the competitive advantage they have, because of the implicit subsidy, which makes them competitively capable of beating out their smaller competitors, who don't get the subsidy."[246] Limiting the size of financial institutions and mega-corporations is essential to preserving democracy and protecting small businesses—whether it be American firms like Goldman Sachs, AIG, Microsoft, Apple, or Blue Cross, or multinational conglomerates. And this is one solution that *only* governments can achieve. No "market force" will do that because the very nature of monopolistic power makes beasts who are too big to control with just a wispy invisible whip. Do not be seduced by the simplistic-sounding utopian dream of Libertarianism; history has never shown a society thriving without strong government. With a Libertarian Lax-rule, the biggest banks and corporations would become the *de facto* kings of our jungle!

Solution: Aggressive, Intelligent, Balanced Media
The media is bogged down in partisan agendas, parroting sound-bite press releases from those in power. Mainstream media lives on the corporate dole—advertising revenue. Corporations have no desire to see reform and have been known to pull ad revenue in order to influence reporting. Bernard Goldberg dedicated an entire book (*Bias*) to exposing how personal bias among liberal reporters slanted news coverage from 1970-2000. But in the last ten years, FOX news and conservative talk radio have shown their own right-wing bias. **Truth** is a victim as *both* sides lose objectivity and balance, swayed by personal bias and by corporate ad dollars. Investigative reporting is a dying art. Support independent, aggressive investigative magazines.

Solution: Buy My Book!
I'm serious. Books and the internet offer an antidote to poison media. The last solution I offer is this very book itself. Buy it, borrow it, but more importantly, pass it on to others. Changing laws is a secondary concern. First we must change **attitudes**... cliché or not, we must change hearts and minds. That is rarely achieved via television shows and pundits. Soundbites don't persuade, they just agitate or reinforce prejudices. **Only *books* can change core beliefs.** Support the bi-partisan, web-based grassroots movement,

www.FireTheRich.org — part of their work includes assisting in distributing this very book. If you read this book from cover to cover with an honest and open mind, I think you'll find it worthy of sharing— deserving of your word-of-mouth promotion. Even if my book infuriates you, at least agree: **this is a debate that deserves attention in the public square.** To counterbalance the enormous influence that wealth has on the political system we must educate enormous numbers of voters about the growing evil. Distribute these books to your state and local politicos, to your wealthy friends... and enemies. Words have power.

We run out of space here, but there are many other fine books that offer solutions... one of the best is *The Price of Civilization: Reawakening American Virtue and Prosperity*, by Jeffrey Sachs and Richard McGonagle. Books have the answers if politicians and citizens would just read them. Books teach solutions.

In their book, *13 Bankers*, Johnson and Kwak confirm my notion that changing hearts and minds about greed is possible. And they prove it by showing the opposite: their chapter sarcastically entitled "Greed is Good," chronicles the influence of books and movies of the eighties and nineties upon Ivy League students who confess they never considered careers in high finance until Hollywood made it "sexy." From Gordon Gecko and Sherman McCoy (of the movies *Wall Street* and *Bonfire of the Vanities*) to the real-life junk-bond king, Michael Milken, their ethical lapses were overshadowed by their glamorous, lavish lifestyles. When Wall Street recruiters came to raid the top schools of its top students, the fans of cinema were receptive. For good and bad, books and movies do make a difference in attitudes. In the fifties and sixties, Christian ministers visibly took the high road on civil rights, preaching about the need to have compassion for the underclass. It seemed impossible, but they succeeded. A major metamorphosis of law and public opinion transpired regarding race. Change is possible.

It is not too late for America, **not too late for the world to forge new systems of ethics and economics. But a monkey can't do it.** Solutions won't happen accidentally or automatically. The work of reform will be hard and will require legions of smart, dedicated human agents of change.

But our modern challenge is a cakewalk compared to other movements across the centuries: the leap from barbarism to civilization; the emergence of faith, morality and religion in the face of tyranny and nihilism; the end of legal slavery; women's suffrage; the defeat of communist and fascist dictatorships; civil rights and the end of apartheid. Out of gratitude to those martyrs who kept the human story alive with hope, let us arise from complacency, let us speak out, let us strive for "happily ever after." We can do it.

~~~

Epilogue

Never give in. Never, never, never, never.... Never yield to the apparently overwhelming might of the enemy.... These are not dark days; these are great days—and we must all thank God that we have been allowed... to play a part in making these days memorable in the history of [the human] race.
~Prime Minister Winston Churchill

The Unsustainable Course
Mikhail Gorbachev gave a warning which we rarely hear in the mainstream media, but which is representative of how most of the world is beginning to feel: "It is time for America's electorate to be told the blunt truth: that the present situation of the United States, by which a part of its population is able to enjoy a life of extraordinary comfort and privilege, is not tenable over the long run [while] the world lives in abject poverty, degradation and backwardness."[247] And the growing gap between rich and poor is so wide, the human mind cannot grasp the sheer size of the chasm. Ted Turner could give away seven new Cadillacs every day of his life and he would still die a multi-millionaire. One man, Warren Buffet, could buy every privately-owned home in the entire state of Wyoming.

The problem is international. Protection of the mega-wealthy is the one principle that unites tyrants and leaders around the globe, from mafia chiefs in Moscow, to royals in Britain, to tribal leaders in Africa, to drug lords in Chile. Think about it: if the government suspects that you might be doing something illegal in your home, they can knock down your door and search your underwear drawer. But many international banks provide shelter for the rich, a secrecy which cannot be penetrated even when known criminals have money stashed there. The leaders of this world do indeed conspire to protect each other's wealth. Hitler's "reich" or "rule" failed, but has been replaced with a quieter tyranny: the Fourth Reich of the Rich.

There are only two things that can stop the Fourth Reich: **truth** and **hope**. Principles of fairness, honesty, and democracy, the ideas expressed in our Declaration of Independence—the right to an equal pursuit of life, liberty and happiness—can prevail.

Truth and Hope
I am, at heart, a minister. So I pray for divine assistance in this holy task of bringing justice to the underdog. With that said, allow me to echo the words President Abraham Lincoln, who likewise believed in a divine hand of God, stronger than the invisible hand of the market:
- "As I would not be a slave, so I would not be a master. This

expresses my idea of democracy."
- "Any people anywhere, being inclined and having the power, have the right to rise up, and shake off the existing government, and form a new one that suits them better. This is a most valuable—a most sacred right—a right which we hope and believe [could] liberate the world."
- "Let us strive to deserve... the continued care of Divine Providence, trusting that in future national emergencies, He will not fail to provide us the instruments of safety and security."[248]

The "instruments" Lincoln was referring to are *us*. May God give us the inspirational wind to trumpet the coming of a new and better day. And by trumpet, I do not mean a musical instrument, but again, the weapon of *words*.

The Power of Words, Redux

Can words change the world? Jesus used words not swords, and over time, the violent Roman Empire became Christianized. Thomas Paine's *Common Sense* was read by nearly every literate colonist, thus creating the popular support necessary to win American independence. Indeed, John Adams said, "Without the pen of the author of *Common Sense*, the sword of Washington would have been raised in vain."[249] Harriet Beecher Stowe's novel, *Uncle Tom's Cabin*, turned the tide of public opinion against slavery. Rachel Carson's book, *Silent Spring*, is widely credited with launching the environmental movement. Now the internet is proving to be a powerful agent of change. *Moveon.org* may have tilted the 2008 Presidential election. The TEA Party would not have come to be without the internet. And the internet sites for both movements consist mostly of **words**.

A war fought with words requires patience. The most dramatic example in my lifetime is the civil rights movement. It was born of words, starting in the pulpits of black churches, eventually gaining enough strength to overflow into the streets. And yes, a few times violence entered the equation. Some would point to the martyrdom of Martin Luther King as crucial in swaying the hearts and minds of white Americans. But without the soaring rhetoric of King's oratory ringing in our ears, King's death would have been for nought. The dramatic social changes and legal reforms wrought by the civil rights movement were not won by mob violence or gunfire, but by words—words that took decades to weave their way through ears and eyes into hearts. Words like Dr. King's famous "I Have a Dream" speech: "[O]ne day this nation will rise up and live out the true meaning of its creed: *we hold these truths to be self-evident, that all men are created equal*." Legislation was important, but the laws were the fruit, not the root, of social reform. The seeds of justice are **words**.

Debate Need Not Bring Division

In response to Warren Buffet's proposal for billionaires to pay more in taxes, Congressman Paul Ryan cried "class warfare" and claimed progressives are "sowing social unrest and class resentment." "You are practicing the politics of division!" is the accusation made by wealthy ultra-conservatives against those of us who call for economic justice. My reply is: *I am not the one who built my house in a gated, elite enclave!* It is the rich who choose to disassociate themselves from the broader society, who sequester themselves in First Class airplane seats and guarded skyboxes far above the madding crowd. Whatever cultural divisions that exist between classes, I certainly did not create nor encourage. We focus too much on our *differences* as reasons to hate and separate, instead of embracing variety, instead of working cooperatively for a better society, instead of teaching our children to celebrate and learn from our rich cultural differences.

At our worst, we all tend to generalize, even demonize, those we don't understand, or those with a different religion or skin color, focusing on negative racial or nationalistic associations rather than looking for the positive. We react with fear and suspicion to new ideas. There was a hit record some conservatives sing: "You've got to stand for something, or you'll fall for anything." We wonder if they might still sing it if they knew the phrase originated with Black Muslim leader Malcolm X. Let's rise to the challenge of not painting every Muslim as a terrorist, or every Hispanic as a drug-running illegal alien, and I will try not to look at every white man who drives a Rolls Royce as my enemy!

Hope for More than One

The last word I offer is the word hope. Hope—belief that we can make a difference. For me it started with the audacious hope that my lone voice might be heard via this book. I was inspired, in part, by the touching but well-worn story about the day hundreds of starfish washed up on a Florida beach, stranded by the receding tide. A lady noticed a young man on the shore as he picked up stranded starfish one at a time and gently tossed them back into the ocean. She chided, "Young man, don't you realize that there are miles of beach and hundreds of starfish all along it. You can't possibly make a difference!" The young man listened politely, then bent down, picked up another starfish and threw it into the sea, past the breaking surf and said, "Well, I made a difference for *that* one."

The story encourages us to believe that each one of us can make a positive difference in the world, no matter how small, even if we only help one person. But **the truth is, we need a bigger effort.** There are not a hundred stranded starfish, there are *billions*.

There are stranded "starfish" all over Asia and Africa—children dying of famine and drought. There are stranded starfish in the orphanage I visited in Mexico, and in the hills I've climbed in Appalachia. There are stranded starfish in the backwoods and ghettoes and barrios of the U.S. In the Emerging World, where both of my own children have done mission work, the needs are so great as to be overwhelming. But *some* improvement is better than none. I optimistically believe we can make giant improvements in the quality of life for children everywhere. We will need a sweeping systemic approach. Education. Ethical change. A populist movement.

Without the courage to challenge conservatives and libertarians to re-examine their *laissez-faire* attitude toward economic inequities, the problem will grow to such proportions that all hope may be lost. Cynicism already reigns: the majority of citizens do not vote.

Two years before taken by an assassin's bullet, Robert Kennedy spoke to a divided Cape Town, South Africa: "The imperfections of human justice, the inadequacy of human compassion, the defectiveness of our sensibility toward the sufferings of our fellows; they mark the limit of our ability to use knowledge for the well-being of our fellow human beings throughout the world. And therefore they call upon common qualities of conscience and indignation, a shared determination to wipe away the unnecessary sufferings.... It is from numberless diverse acts of courage and belief that human history is shaped. Each time a man stands up for an ideal, or acts to improve the lot of others, or strikes out against injustice, he sends forth a tiny ripple of hope, and crossing each other form a million different centers of energy and daring, those ripples build a current which can sweep down the mightiest walls of oppression and resistance." That hope did not die with RFK.

The Window

A narrow window of opportunity remains open. Actual votes are still more powerful than dollars. I believe this window will slam shut unless change begins soon. The money machine driving politics is gargantuan and growing. For the year 2000 political campaigns, the Democrats and Republicans amassed over $830 million in combined hard and soft contributions, mostly from corporations, wealthy individuals, and narrow-interest PACS, including ones representing the selfish interests of sectors of the economy that reap windfall profits, such as pharmaceutical companies and trial lawyers.[250]

A Tip of the Hat Can Change the World

I spoke earlier of having witnessed progressive economic

legislation shot down in my own state, despite Governor Riley's good efforts. He gave me hope that Republicans are open to change, as he invited me to speak to his entire Cabinet. They nodded in approval as I told them this story of how the end of Apartheid in South Africa began with a gesture as small as the tip of a hat:

"A little boy was walking down the sidewalk with his mother when they came face to face with a man who tipped his hat to the lady. The stranger then stepped off the sidewalk in deference to her and her son. The little boy was amazed by that small act of kindness. You see, this was 60 years ago in South Africa, where the practice of Apartheid meant that black people were to step off of the sidewalk and give way to white people. Yes, even a woman and child were expected to step off the sidewalk in deference to a white male. But this had been the reverse. So the little boy later asked his mother, 'Who was that white man? Why did he break the law and tip his hat to you?' She explained that the man had done so because he was a Christian, an Anglican priest. This made such an impression on the little boy that then and there he decided to become a minister himself. And in time, he did. That little boy, Desmond Tutu, grew up to become the bishop instrumental in freeing South Africa from Apartheid. So you see, a gesture as small as the tip of a hat can, and did, change the world!"

A Tip of the Hat and a Broken Crayon

Small acts of kindness by enough of us can make a difference. If you skipped over the second chapter, go back and read the story of the broken crayon. Please. As long as millions of children never have the simple joy of a coloring book and crayons, or sleep fitfully and shivering without bed or blanket, or don't have access to a clean cup of water, how can you own a second Ferrari, a third home, or a first yacht? A smidgen of luxury may be justifiable if it motivates you to work harder and more productively. There is nothing inherently evil in enjoying the fruits of your labor. But no matter how successful or smart you are, you can drive only one car at a time, live in just one mansion at a time.

Excessive consumption and wealth hoarding spawns all kinds of evil. Some of the pain is physical and palpable; some of it is mental and emotional, such as the growing sense of despair among the dwindling middle class. Award-winning journalist Chris Hedges writes: "I struggle with despair all the time.... [But] if we remain fearful, then we will be further stripped of power as we barrel towards this neo-feudalistic state... a world of masters and serfs.... But I'm not going to let despair win."

Goodness and love are shown in the simple acts of hope and sharing. In my dream world, we would "compete" in generosity, in finding ways to make our communities and world a better place. I dream of a world where education, art, music, laughter and spiritual transcendence are no longer subservient to commerce and materialistic greed. Quite simply, I long for a world where love triumphs over greed, where people come before profits. In pragmatic terms, a ***populist capitalism***.

Populist Capitalism must include the words "Give" and "Share," as a command for all of us, not just for the rich. Inculcating a widespread spirit of giving is my first goal. But if we cannot persuade the wealthy to be more generous voluntarily, then we have a moral duty to petition governments to place limits on exorbitant wealth accumulation. Policies that reduce wealth pyramids and bubbles can be shaped that preserve the best of capitalism while still being reasonable and fair. We, the majority, the hard-working and moral citizens of this planet, must speak up.

This book is my effort to do just that. Share it.

~~~

Proverbs 31:8-9:
"Speak up for those who cannot speak for themselves,
for the rights of all who are destitute.
Speak up and judge fairly;
defend the rights of the poor and needy."

~~~

I see in the near future a crisis approaching that unnerves me and causes me to tremble for the safety of my country. As a result of the war, corporations have been enthroned and... the money power of the country will... prolong its reign by working upon the prejudice of the people until all wealth is aggregated in a few hands....

~attributed to Abraham Lincoln in an 1887 journal, but never verified

~~~~

About the Author

Dr. Lance Moore lives on the Gulf Coast, where he is a musician, minister and author of fiction and non-fiction. His other books can be found in online bookstores or ordered below.

Books by Lance Moore

A Monkey Could Do It:
How Wall Street Robs Main Street
The Value of Work and the Values of Class Warfare

Majestic Twelve Minus One
She's Dying to Know the Truth... They May Grant Her Wish

The Neurotic's Guide to God and Love
Seven Mistakes that Make Us Crazy, and Eight Ways to Change

Outdoors with God
Finding God in the Beauty and Adventure of the Great Outdoors

Order online at www.Sky-Fy.com

Or email: sky@sky-fy.com

Promotion via:
Sky-Fy Publishing and Third Coast Media

~~~

ENDNOTES:

[1] www.robinsonlibrary.com
[2] *A Short Treatise on Political Power*, pamphlet by John Ponet, 1556
[3] *Common Sense*, pamphlet by Thomas Paine, 1776
[4] ibid
[5] see *Retirement Heist: How Companies Plunder and Profit from the Nest Eggs of American Workers*, by Ellen E. Schultz (Penguin Books, NY, 2011)
[6] *Mother Jones* magazine, p. 29, March/April 2011
[7] www.theatlanticwire.com/opinions/view/opinion/Just-How-Rich-Is-Hosni-Mubarak-6918
[8] John Nance Garner, quoted by Otto Friedrich in *F.D.R.'s Disputed Legacy*, Feb. 1, 1982
[9] see www.learnnc.org/lp/editions/nchist-worldwar/5835
[10] *Mother Jones* magazine, June 2010
[11] www.ppionline.org
[12] *Mother Jones* magazine, p. 28, March/April, 2011
[13] World Institute for Development Economics Research—using statistics from 2000
[14] CNN, April 14, 2011
[15] reported on *Fox News* TV, September 18, 2011
[16] Tommy Newberry, *The War on Success*, (Regnery Publishing, 2010), page 127
[17] www.moneyfactory.gov/uscurrency/annualproductionfigures.html
[18] www.zimbio.com/member/hwboomer/articles/1856697/Billion+Dollars+Mean
[19] *Forbes* magazine, March 2010
[20] www.fox.presidencia.gob.mx/buenasnoti
[21] Zack Smith is a pseudonym for an actual bank robber/addict... the numbers used here are rounded, assuming Zack only "worked" at his hold-ups on weekdays.
[22] www.reddit.com/r/Economics/comments/e8b0r/citigroup_attempts_to_disappear_its_plutonomy
[23] Citigroup finally woke up and realized this paper might be bad PR, so the geniuses have been trying to remove it from the net. Hopefully it can still be found it at: www.reddit.com/r/Economics/comments/e8b0r/citigroup_attempts_to_disappear_its_plutonomy
[24] *The Week*, p. 12, August 5, 2011
[25] *The Week*, p. 4, July 29, 2011
[26] www.businessinsider.com/lloyd-blankfein-says-he-is-doing-gods-work-2009-11#ixzz1EYUgM5do
[27] Thomas Paine, *Agrarian Justice*, 1795
[28] *Reader's Digest*, August 2010
[29] *The Week*, p. 40, February 11, 2011
[30] www.money.cnn.com/2011/02/22/news/economy/income_inequality/index.html
[31] *CNN*, Febuary 27, 2011
[32] David Roeder, *Chicago Sun-Times* columnist and YourMoneyWatch website, both from 2007; confirmed by the accounting firm Howard, Fine & Howard
[33] *The Chronicle of Higher Education*, April, 2011
[34] *Chasing Goldman Sachs*, p. 170
[35] Thomas Sowell, *Economic Facts and Fallacies*, Basic Books: NY, 2008
[36] ibid, p. 142, 151...plus his op-ed pieces
[37] ibid, p. 143
[38] pp. 150-151, and this idea runs throughout Sowell's books and op-eds
[39] ibid, pp. 149-152
[40] ibid
[41] op-ed in *Mobile Press-Register*, 2009]
[42] www.businesspundit.com/the-worlds-most-controversial-ceos
[43] www.seattletimes.nwsource.com/html/opinion/2008936833_opinb29jacoby.html
[44] www.thetruthaboutcars.com/2008/11/toyota-to-cut-executives-salary, by R. Farago

45 www.fool.com/investing/dividends-income/2008/03/06/washington-mutuals-shady-compensation-plan.aspx
46 *CNN Money*, February 12, 2005
47 Ann Killon, *Sports Illustrated*, December 2009
48 *Mobile-Press Register*, July 11, 2010
49 *The Washington Times*, February 17, 2009
50 www.foxnews.com/politics/2009/02/18/postmaster-general-gets-pay-bonus-agency-falters
51 *The Washington Spectator*; also see www.alternet.org/story/145705/the_richest_1_have_captured_america's_wealth_--_what's_it_going_to_take_to_get_it_back
52 http://money.cnn.com/2012/01/16/news/economy/Romney_Bain_taxes
53 *Chasing Goldman Sachs*, p. 202
54 http://www.globallabourrights.org/reports?id=0034
55 *The War on Success*, p. 121
56 www.abcnews.go.com/WN/glenn-beck-social-justice-christians-rage-back-nazism/story?id=10085008
57 Newberry, p. 92
58 ibid, p. 93
59 See *The Virtue of Selfishness*, Ayn Rand, 1964, Signet Books: Chicago
60 Widely reported; see *The New Republic* at www.tnr.com/blog/jonathan-chait/80552/paul-ryan-and-ayn-rand
61 *Mobile-Press Register*, Saturday, July 24, 2010
62 *The Interpreter's Bible, Kittel's Theological Dictionary of the New Testament*, etc. Also www.theberean.org/index.cfm/fuseaction/Home.showBerean/BereanID/5996/bblver/DAR
63 from the New International Version
64 www.moorethink.com/2011/08/06/a-prayer-for-ricky-meany/
65 *San Antonio Express-News*, Sunday, June 12, 2011, "Governor's Modest Religious Donations." The minimum standard for Christians is 10%, the *tithe*. Perhaps he gave more in secret not listed on his taxes... doubtful, since he needed the tax-deduction.
66 CBS News "Face the Nation," June, 2011, and widely reported in print media.
67 Luke 6:20-24, excerpted.
68 Luke 12:48b
69 "Sakyamuni's spirit: dialogue with a journalist", by Han Yongun, Vol. 2, 1973
70 *The Shambhala Dictionary of Buddhism*, ©1991, Shambhala Publications
71 from "Book II," in *The Buddha & His Dhamma*, by Dr. Babasaheb Ambedkar: (Bombay: Education Department, Government of Maharashtra, 1992)]
72 *Buddhist Scriptures*, ed. Donald Lopez, ©2004 Penguin Classics
73 James R. Ware, trans., *The Sayings of Confucius*, NY: New American Library 1955.
74 Sources: *Towards Understanding Islam*, by Abul A'la Mawdudi, translated by Khurshid Ahmad, published by The Islamic Foundation, UK (pages 17, 86-93, 115-116); *The Oxford History of Islam*, ed. John Esposito, Oxford University Press, 1999: *Understanding Islam and the Muslims*, The Islamic Affairs Department, The Embassy of Saudi Arabia, D.C.
75 Peter Smith, *An Intro. to the Baha'i Faith*, Cambridge Univ. Press 2008, pp. 143-144
76 *The Interpreter's Bible*, previously cited
77 www.salon.glenrose.net/default.asp?view=plink&id=13989
78 *Mobile-Press Register*, Saturday, July 24, 2010
79 Newberry, p. 116
80 *The Mobile Press-Register*, October 31, 2010
81 www.centralparknyc.org/visit/general-info/faq/
82 wiki.answers.com, "How Rich is Ambani?";www.business.blogs.cnn.com/2011/03/07/cost-of-slaves-falls-to-historic-low/
83 www.unhcr.org/refworld/docid/3ae6ad3914.html
84 www.en.wikipedia.org/wiki/Household_income_in_the_United_States
85 *Forbes* magazine, www.forbes.com/lists/2006/10/Worth_1.html
86 *TIME* magazine; www.alarise.org; Alabama Tax Code

87 *Retirement Heist: How Companies Plunder and Profit from the Nest Eggs of American Workers*, by Ellen E. Schultz (Penguin Books, NY, 2011)
88 *The New York Times Digest*, p. 4, August 31, 2011
89 "America's Richest Tax Breaks" www.money.cnn.com, 4/26/2011
90 March 9, 2011, *Forbes* Magazine
91 Congressional Budget Office, 2007
92 Edward Wolff, Bard College, and Federal Reserve data
93 Thomas Sowell, *Economic Facts and Fallacies*, Basic Books: NY, 2008, p. 125]
94 Source: AFL-CIO
95 *The Nation*, p. 36, April 15, 2011
96 *Mother Jones*, p. 24, March/April 2011
97 Malcolm Gladwell, *Outliers: The Story of Success*, (Little, Brown: NY, 2008) p. 127
98 *The Week* magazine, July 1-8, 2011, quoting Fareed Zakaria
99 see charts by Professor Emmanuel Saez of University of California, Berkeley, or www.money.cnn.com/2011/02/22/news/economy/income_inequality/index.htm?iid=HLM
100 Sowell, p. 129
101 ibid
102 www.satyagraha.wordpress.com/2009/07/14/college-tuition-hyperinflation and www.campusgrotto.com/top-100-colleges-by-highest-tuition.html (total tuition, fees, room, board, books, etc)
103 Sowell, p. 129
104 ibid
105 Gary Scharrer, *San Antonio Express-News,* Monday, June 13, 2011
106 *TIME* magazine, April 25, 2011, p. 14
107 AP report, "Sweatshop Labor," by Madison Grey, *New York Times*, October 28, 2010
108 www.huffingtonpost.com/al-norman/a-10-minimum-wage-at-walm_b_75815.html
109 www.abcnews.go.com/Business/walmart-ceo-pay-hour-workers-year/story?id=11067470
110 The highest child poverty rate in 20 years: www.cnn.com/2010/HEALTH/06/08/children.wellbeing/index.html?hpt=T3
111 ABCNews.com, ibid: 2009 study by the Institute for Policy Studies found that CEOs in the country's S&P 500 companies make, on average, 319 times more than the average American worker... also see www.inteldaily.com/2010/07/middle-class/
112 elliscountypress.com/inspirational/10401-the-butterfly-effect-how-your-life-matters.html
113 *Iowa Farmer Today*, March 16, 2005
114 Henry A. Wallace, *Democracy Reborn* (New York, 1944), edited by Russell Lord, p. 259
115 Bill Moyer, *the Howard Zinn Lecture Series at Boston University,* October 29, 2010
116 Des Griffin, *Fourth Reich of the Rich*, (Emissary Publications: 1976) p. 119; and Carroll Quigley, *Tragedy and Hope: A History of the World in Our Time*, (NY: Macmillan, 1966), pp. 323-324
117 *The Chronicle of Higher Education* reported in November 16, 2010, that over 30 private colleges pay their college president over one million dollars per year; the *average* teacher's salary is about $50,000, and entry pay is under $30,000.
118 www.gregpalast.com
119 *The Nation*, p. 11, November 29, 2010
120 *Mother Jones*, p. 29, March/April 2011
121 www.huffingtonpost.com/2010/10/27/senate-millionaires-club-getting-richer-bigger_n_775022.html
122 www.dailymail.co.uk/news/article-1359491/US-Presidents-rich-list-White-House-leads-fortune-3-quarters-end-millionaires
123 Center for Responsive Politics; Edward Wolff, Bard College; *Mother Jones* magazine, March/April 2011
124 cited in the documentary movie, *Maxed Out*
125 *The Progressive*, February 2011, p. 38

126 *The Progressive* magazine, October 2010, p. 33
127 www.huffingtonpost.com/2011/06/16/scott-beason-aborigines-comment_n_878703.html
128 Howard Zinn, *A People's History of the United States*, (HarperCollins, NY 2003), Ch.1
129 a word employed even by conservative historian Samuel Eliot Morison in 1955
130 http://www.msnbc.msn.com/id/44084236/ns/health-behavior/#.TkLlQHNvV-A
131 quoted in *Chasing Goldman Sachs*
132 *Greed, negligence behind BP oil spill*, CNN, May 03, 2010, Donna Brazile
133 www.news.yahoo.com/s/nm/20110228/us_nm/us_massey_security_0]
134 www.aflcio.org/corporatewatch/paywatch/ceou/database.cfm?tkr=MEE&pg=1
135 www.thirdworldtraveler.com/Asia/Bhopal_20yearslater.html
136 www.news.com.au/world/chernobyl-hero-iouli-andreev-accuses-japan-of-putting-profits-before-nuclear-safety/story-e6frfkyi-1226022324462
137 *Mother Jones* magazine, December 1999
138 from Swanson's essay, 2002, at www.democraticunderground.com
139 Excerpted from *A Christmas Carol*, ©1843, Charles Dickens
140 *Wall Street and the Financial Crisis*, Senate report of April 14, 2011, April 14, 2011, found here: www.nytimes.com/interactive/2011/04/14/business/14crisis-docviewer.html
141 *Good Housekeeping*, February 2010, p. 107
142 All calculations here are rounded approximations for simplicity; credit cards vary in exactly how they calculate interest and fees
143 *Rolling Stone* magazine, August 19, 2010
144 *The Week*, June 3, 2011, "Bank CEOs keep failing upward"
145 *Chasing Goldman Sachs*, p. 177, 180
146 *Inside Job*, directed by Charles Ferguson, Sony Pictures
147 ibid
148 *13 Bankers*, p. 106
149 widely reported in *Inside Job*; *13 Bankers*, *Rolling Stone* and other media
150 *Rolling Stone*, November 25, 2010
151 article "Home Wreckers," in *Mother Jones* magazine, November/December 2010
152 *Wall Street and the Financial Crisis* Senate report (see above); and
    Rolling Stone, May 26, 2011, "The People vs. Goldman Sachs"
153 Senate report
154 Senate report, p. 165
155 Senate report, p. 166
156 Allan Sloane in *Fortune 500*, October 26, 2010
157 http://www.halliburtonwatch.org/about_hal/chronology.html
158 Source: U.S. Department of Health and Human Services
159 www.goodjobsfirst.org/states/alabama lists multiple sources for all the numbers used in this section
160 www.goodjobsfirst.org/states/alabama; "Incentives to Steelmaker Break State Record," *Mobile Press-Register*, May 12, 2007
161 A section in the state tax code allows Alabama-based insurance companies meeting specific criteria to have lower taxes on premiums. According to the Legislative Fiscal Office, this benefit saves ALFA insurance about $1.5 million per year.
162 *Birmingham Post-Herald*, and "VOICES for Alabama's Children," a non-profit agency... www.alavoices.org
163 *The Week*, p. 40, February 11, 2011
164 *The Price of Civilization: Reawakening American Virtue and Prosperity*, by Jeffrey Sachs and Richard McGonagle (Random House, NY: 2011)
165 *The New York Times*, March 26, 2011, "G.E.'s Strategies Let It Avoid Taxes Altogether"
166 *The Week*, p. 40, February 11, 2011
167 *The New York Times*, March 26, 2011
168 ibid
169 Farm Subsidy Database at farm.ewg.org; Wikipedia, CNN

170 *Mobile Press-Register*; Alabama Citizens for Constitutional Reform Foundation
171 *The Economist* magazine, August 7, 2003
172 *Alabama Arise* at www.arisecitizens.org/index.php?option=com_content&view=article&id=88&Itemid=51
173 As of early 2011, according to article entitled *Corporate Tax Reform: Talk Grows Louder*, January 15, 2011
174 www.walmartsubsidywatch.org
175 David Cay Johnston, *Free Lunch*, (Penguin Books, NY: 2007), p. 82-83
176 ibid, p. 80
177 In addition to Johnston's book, read: *Job Scam*, by Greg LeRoy; *The Best Democracy Money Can Buy*, by Greg Palast; Arianna Huffington's *Pigs at the Trough*. Also read more about corporate subsidies at: www.goodjobsfirst.org
178 http://www.nytimes.com/2011/08/15/opinion/stop-coddling-the-super-rich.html
179 www.moneychimp.com/features/tax_brackets.htm
180 www.itepnet.org/whopays3.pdf Data from 2007; see page 118 of their report
181 Greg LeRoy, *The Great American Jobs Scam: Corporate Tax Dodging and the Myth of Job Creation*, (Berrett-Koehler Publishers, 2005), p. 176
182 Jonathan Chait, *The Big Con: How Washington Got Hoodwinked and Hijacked by Crackpot Economics*, (Boston: Houghton Mifflin, 2007)
183 Economic Policy Institute, Washington, DC
184 Paul Krugman, *The Return Of Depression Economics And The Crisis Of 2008* (W.W. Norton, 2009)
185 Citizens for Tax Justice, 2010
186 *The Nation*, December 20, 2010, p. 5
187 *The Nation*, December 13, 2010, p. 4
188 *This Week* magazine, January 14, 2011, p. 38
189 Malcolm Gladwell, *Outliers*, p. 54-55.
190 Russ Mitchell, www.baycitizen.org/meg-whitman/story/ebays-lost-years/
191 www.vccircle.com/500/news/ebay-tries-new-tack-to-woo-china
192 www.en.wikipedia.org/wiki/Meg_Whitman#eBay
193 www.vccircle.com/500/news/ebay-tries-new-tack-to-woo-china
194 www.itskeptic.org/microsoft-evil-genius-docx-format
195 www.foxnews.com/story/0,2933,115047,00.html
196 www.en.wikipedia.org/wiki/Foxconn#Employee_suicides_and_deaths
197 *Mother Jones* magazine, p. 29, March/April 2011
198 as cited in *This Week*, June 11, 2010
199 www.forbes.com/profile/terry-gou
200 www.businessweek.com/magazine/content/10_38/b4195058423479.htm
201 www.bigthink.com, Newsletter of Jan. 22, 2012
202 *Chasing Goldman-Sachs*, p. 183
203 ibid
204 *Chasing*, p. 180
205 *Chasing*, p. 182
206 Malcolm Gladwell: *The Tipping Point: How Little Things Can Make a Big Difference*, (Little Brown: NY, 2000)
207 www.investopedia.com/articles/analyst/03/111903.asp#ixzz1T8pRJSjd
208 *The Charlotte Observer*, Sunday, March 19, 1995
209 *The Amway Industry*, by Robert L. FitzPatrick and Susanna Perkins, found at www.transgallaxys.com/~emerald/files/theamwayindustry.doc.pdf
210 Sources: personal experience and conversations with Amway distributors; article in *The Charlotte Observer*, Sunday, March 19, 1995, by Jim Morrill and Nancy Stancil; *NBC Dateline*, May 7, 2004
211 *Newsweek*, "The Secret Money War," September 20, 2004.
212 cnn.com/2011/04/06, article entitled "The Dark Side of Chocolate"
213 International Labour Organization, "The end of child labour: Within reach," 2006
214 www.freethechildren.com

215 Brian Kelly, *Pensacola News Journal*, June 27th, 2010
216 *The Progressive* magazine, January 2011, p. 60
217 *Mobile-Press Register*, November 9, 2010
218 *Pensacola New Journal*, September 15, 2011
219 *The New York Times*, July 3, 2010
220 www.money.cnn.com/2011/04/26
221 www.articles.moneycentral.msn.com/Investing/Extra/10-big-industries-on-the-federal-dole
222 *The Nation*, p. 36, April 15, 2011
223 *Washington Post*, June 18, 2010
224 www.money.cnn.com/2011/04/14/news/companies/bp_meeting
225 CNN, April 14, 2011
226 www,forbes.com, June 2011
227 C-SPAN, particularly comments from Senator Carl Levin, who stated that Merrill-Lynch "knowingly participated" in illegal activities, like hiding ENRON's debt-size.
228 *The Atlantic* magazine, quoted in *The Week* magazine, August 19, 2011, p. 19
229 *Public Papers of the Presidents*, Dwight D. Eisenhower, 1960, p. 1035- 1040
230 www.npr.org/2011/06/25/137414737/among-the-costs-of-war-20b-in-air-conditioning
231 http://www.brookings.edu/projects/archive/nucweapons/50.aspx
232 www.medicalnewstoday.com/articles/230780.php
233 *The Progressive*, April 2011, p. 44
234 *The Week* magazine, April 15, 2011
235 This is not a sexist statement, just a fact: generally, women make lower wages than men, and many single women lose income during maternity, and are more likely to be the primary caretaker and thus bear disproportionate burdens with extra stress upon their time/finances.
236 *Chasing Goldman-Sachs*, p. 200
237 Malcolm Gladwell: *The Tipping Point: How Little Things Can Make a Big Difference*, (Little Brown, 2000)
238 www.texastribune.org/texas-politics/2012-presidential-election/liveblog-abcyahoowmur-gop-presidential-debate
239 http://www.cbsnews.com/8301-503544_162-20128920-503544/herman-cain-incorrectly-suggests-china-doesnt-have-nuclear-capability
240 http://politicsdownanddirty.blogspot.com/2010/02/how-many-us-senators-and-congressmen.html
241 The New Political Compass, a white paper by Paul H. Ray
242 ibid
243 www.snopes.com
244 *Outliers*, p. 149
245 *13 Bankers*, p. 213
246 Alan Greenspan, "The Global Financial Crisis: Causes and Consequences," lecture at Council on Foreign Relations, October 15, 2009
247 Special to the *Washington Post*, December 2000
248 from Lincoln's eulogy for Henry Clay
249 www.newyorker.com/archive/2006/10/16/061016crbo_books
250 *The American Prospect*, December 4, 2000

www.ingramcontent.com/pod-product-compliance
Lightning Source LLC
Chambersburg PA
CBHW081821280526
45789CB00007B/2295